EPHRAIM'S FOUNDING FATHER

The Story of Reverend A. M. Iverson

by Paul and Frances Burton

1996
STONEHILL PUBLISHING
Ephraim • Door County • Wisconsin

Printed in the United States of America

Stonehill Publishing
Paul and Frances Burton
Post Office Box 250
Ephraim, WI 54211

Library of Congress Cataloging In Publication Data
Authors: Burton, Paul R., and Burton, Frances M.
Title: Ephraim's Founding Father
1. History 2. Biography 3. Wisconsin 4. Moravian

ISBN 0-9650769-0-3

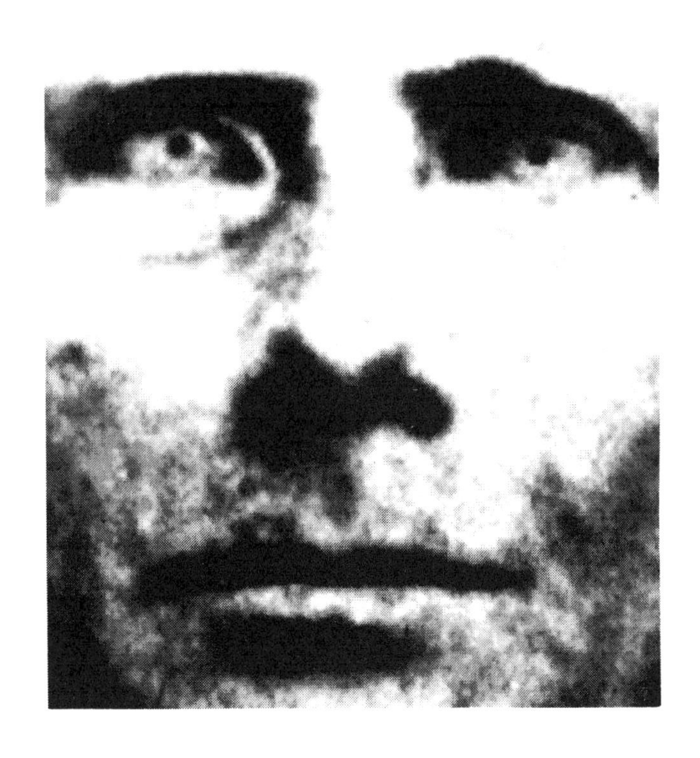

Andrew Michael Iverson
1823 – 1907

For Julie and Mike,
And Their Children

CONTENTS

ILLUSTRATIONS

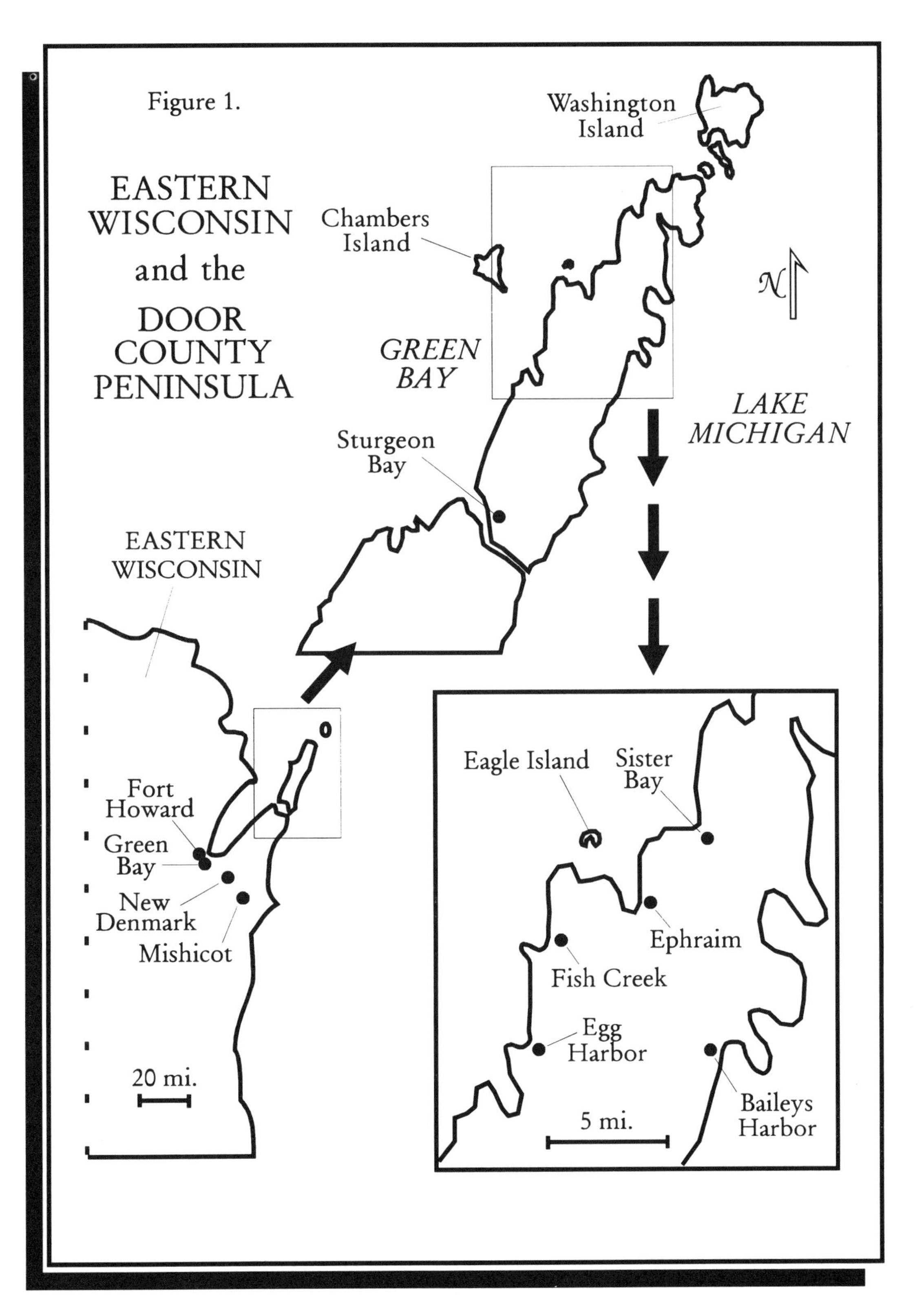
Figure 1.
EASTERN WISCONSIN and the DOOR COUNTY PENINSULA
Washington Island
Chambers Island
GREEN BAY
LAKE MICHIGAN
Sturgeon Bay
N
EASTERN WISCONSIN
Fort Howard
Green Bay
New Denmark
Mishicot
20 mi.
Eagle Island
Sister Bay
Ephraim
Fish Creek
Egg Harbor
Baileys Harbor
5 mi.

PREFACE

Of what relevance is the story of Reverend Andrew (Andreas) Iverson? Beyond the fact that Iverson was a fascinating and compelling personality, his story has a much broader significance. It chronicles the plight of immigrants in America, the struggle to carve communities in remote wilderness areas of the early midwest, the search by isolated settlers to find religious meaning, the competition among religious sects for converts among these rugged settlers, and the hardships and joys of pioneer life in Wisconsin in the middle to late 1800s. Iverson's story is one of tragedy and weakness, but it is also a story of his many contributions to the settlement of Wisconsin's Door County peninsula. Our purpose in writing this book is to document and describe the life of this extraordinary Moravian missionary to America.

Along the northeast edge of Wisconsin there is a rocky finger of land extending northward into Lake Michigan (see Fig. 1, p. ix). This is the Door peninsula. The small village of Ephraim is located along its western shoreline and its permanent population now stands at about 275 people. During the summer, the population of this scenic hamlet may swell to 2,000. Until the early 1900s Ephraim was accessible, in any practical sense, only by water, and in the early and middle 1800s the area was a wilderness, densely covered by great forests.

The story of Iverson and his evangelical mission in frontier Wisconsin, and his efforts from 1853 to 1864 to establish Ephraim, are tales worth telling, for he was an exceptional man. It was the force of Andrew Iverson's personality and spirit that sustained the establishment of Ephraim by Scandinavian immigrants determined to find a new and better life for themselves in America.

Our book would have been impossible without Iverson's own literary efforts, completed when he was 76 years old, in recalling and writing a chronicle of his life as an immigrant evangelist from Norway. His recollections, written in Norwegian, were carefully translated by John Boler, who finished the work in 1929. This is the document (21) that provides the framework around which our book is constructed.

The book is in two parts. The first part closely follows Iverson's written recollections as translated into English by Boler. The narrative describes events as set forth by Iverson, and we quote freely from Boler's translation (all the quotations in our narrative are Iverson's unless otherwise indicated). His words artfully capture events that occurred some 40 years earlier, and in telling his story he reveals a great deal about his life as a frontier evangelist and his efforts to bring the word of God to immigrant settlers. We took restrained liberties in underscoring feelings and views that were implied or glossed over in Iverson's writings. We also used information from some of his letters to the Moravian Church administration in Bethlehem, Pennsylvania, to fill out the narrative, and for the sake of completion we occasionally added facts about places, people, and circumstances from other sources. To keep the narrative moving we selected passages from his recollections that could be woven together to create an interesting story.

The second part of the book is comprised of the many notes included in the Appendix. These notes are as factual as we can make them and are meant to take the reader beyond the bias and omissions found in Iverson's recollections. This section provides a more comprehensive picture of the life and times of Iverson. We used many written sources, both published and unpublished, and we interviewed many people in search of specific, general, and background information about the circumstances relating to Iverson and his Moravian colony, which was founded only five years after Wisconsin became a state.

How accurate is Iverson's memory of events which occurred 40 years earlier? In his insightful review of Iverson's recollections, Scandinavian scholar Harald Naess attempts to answer the question of how well Iverson remembers (31). "The answer is that in this case he remembers remarkably well, as we can see from other sources such as Iverson's own contemporary reports, his letters to members of the Bethlehem Provincial Elders' Conference Board, and reports by other observers—all of which help fill in the gaps in the memoir and give us a closer picture of the man and his work." Naess also notes that the value of Iverson's manuscript is in its "composite picture [and] in its story" rather than its historical detail.

Iverson was a remarkable man who was dedicated to his followers and to God. He was charismatic, courageous, strong-minded, and mystical. And as with all mortals, he was flawed. With God's help he was the force that established an equally remarkable village that still reflects many of its founder's virtues.

Paul and Frances Burton
Ephraim, Wisconsin
Winter, 1996

Prologue

Three grueling days of traversing the frozen bay on foot had failed to dampen Andrew's enthusiasm. Shivering slightly in the biting February wind, he now stood on the shore of Eagle Island and stared intently across the snow-covered ice of Eagle Harbor. He had nearly reached his destination.

From his vantage point on the rocks, the Reverend Andrew Iverson looked east into the morning sun. He saw a timber-covered shoreline that formed a deep crescent around the harbor. Evergreens rimmed the edge of the ice, backed by a tall hardwood forest, now bare of leaves. On his right a towering limestone cliff appeared to rise directly out of the frozen lake. To his left, a series of bluffs became smaller and smaller as they stretched off toward the northern horizon. With his attention still focused on the distant shore, he buttoned up his dark wool coat and pulled on his heavy gloves. After signaling his four waiting companions that he was ready, he exchanged a few words with them in Norwegian and then set out on the two-mile trek across the ice, crunching toward the desolate, uninhabited land that would soon be known as Ephraim.

Ole Larsen was a member of the group of explorers on that cold morning in 1853. Walking as briskly as the frozen bay would allow, he soon caught up with Andrew. He was the owner of Eagle Island, where he had built a log house and dock. Because he made his living fishing and selling cordwood to passing ships, he was quite familiar with the area. He had invited Andrew to his island and was an enthusiastic host. After all, how many visitors did one receive in such a remote place in February? Andrew was an especially welcome guest, since he was an old friend and a fellow Norwegian.

Larsen was aware that his friend was searching for a new home for his flock of parishioners. His daughter, Pauline, was one of these parishioners and she had confided in her father that they were unhappy with their current location in Green Bay. He recommended the Eagle Harbor area to Andrew, telling him of the "excellent government land, as yet not taken, [including] hundreds of acres with the most beautiful hardwood timber on it." He encouraged Andrew and his followers to visit the land and invited them to be guests in his home. In addition to his hospitality, Larsen offered to be their guide.

The other members of the small expedition on that bright, wintry day were Gabriel Wathne and Abraham Oneson (formerly Aanesen) from Andrew's congregation in Green Bay, and Melchior Jacobs, who had joined them in Sturgeon Bay. Although they walked in companionable silence, each man was preoccupied with his own thoughts.

Gabriel Wathne could not help reflecting on the difficulties of their long, weary walk over the ice from Green Bay. Their first night had been spent with strangers in Bay Settlement, where they were housed and fed for a small charge.

The next day they covered about 30 miles over the snow-covered ice and were very tired when they reached the little shanty of A. Thompson near Sturgeon Bay. Thompson was also Moravian, and he extended a warm welcome to his cold and exhausted visitors. They stayed with Thompson an extra day, which gave them a close look at the poverty-stricken pioneer life. Although Wathne was filled with hope as he trudged toward the shore of Eagle Harbor, he did wonder about the fate of their congregation if they settled in this beautiful but isolated land.

Abraham Oneson also thought about the difficulties of their expedition as he walked toward the distant shore. He remembered particularly the anxiety he had experienced yesterday when they discovered a three and a half foot wide crack in the ice that exposed a dark band of clear, deep water. The rift "seemed to extend for miles westward from the shore without diminishing in width." After considerable discussion, the group decided that the best plan of action was to take a run and leap over the opening. Oneson was filled with dread at this prospect, since he had exceptionally short legs.

Andrew ran and jumped first, making it on the first attempt, followed by successful jumps by Wathne and Jacobs. Oneson shuddered as he remembered his terror when it was his turn. He had been "almost paralyzed with fear and in a sorrowful tone declared that he would not dare to attempt the jump." Andrew spoke words of encouragement in brisk Norwegian and assured his panic-stricken companion that they would stand ready to "grab him" on the other side. Finally Oneson found his courage. After rocking back and forth in preparation, he made a short run followed by a great jump. His foot barely reached the opposite edge, but the others grabbed his arms immediately, as promised, and pulled him forward onto firm ice. The profound sigh of relief Oneson uttered "caused them all to laugh at the whole ludicrous performance." He was relieved that they encountered no further difficulties, except fatigue, and arrived at Larsen's late that evening.

Melchior Jacobs appeared dejected as he plodded along, but his spirits began to rise as the group neared the distant shore. He had been despondent about losing his small piece of Sturgeon Bay land in a legal dispute, but when Andrew and the others shared their dreams with him, his hopes for a new start grew. As a devout Moravian with a reputation as a good judge of land, he had gladly accepted the invitation to join the expedition.

Although somewhat stiff after the long journey northward over the ice, Andrew was thankful that their expedition from Green Bay had been relatively uneventful, and that no blizzards or subzero drops in temperature had forced them to seek shelter to survive. He now moved eagerly, covering the two miles from Eagle Island very quickly, and his thoughts turned from the rigors of the trip to the hope that lay ahead. "I wonder if our dear little congregation will ever be located on this land by this bay in such romantic surroundings and with that high bluff in the opposite direction so grand in appearance?" That morning he had "prayed earnestly to the Lord that the investigation might be crowned with success and that we might find a good place for our little congregation."

Allowing himself to imagine that the site of his new community lay only a few hundred yards ahead, his excitement increased with every step. Soon he could see rows of small evergreens and a number of hardwood trees lining the shore. With hope he hurried forward. "I put my foot on shore for the first time in the name of Jesus, silently and with strange feelings."

"After we had landed, near the spot where I afterwards built my own house, we discovered that there was a belt of evergreens, nearly all small, and also a scattering of hardwood trees, along the whole shore, but this belt was not very wide. Soon we entered a beautiful tract of woodland all hardwood (maple, beach, ironwood, some basswood and oak, of the last very few) and the deeper we penetrated into the woods eastward, the more beautiful it became—the trees [were] tall and straight and there was so much space between these beautiful hardwood trees that it appeared to us possible that one could drive with horse and wagon right through, without clearing a road.

"About half a mile east from the shore, Brother Melchior Jacobs removed the snow (about one foot deep) and dug into the earth with a piece of wood. Taking the black loam up in his hands, he made the statement that it was not only good but rich soil. Larsen praised it no less. It was very strange that Brother Melchior did not at that time encounter any stone and little did we dream of the extensive layer of limestone just a few feet under the surface.

"From the East we traveled toward the North about a mile and found the same kind of soil and the most beautiful timber. I might compare the trees with organ pipes and from the top of these trees there came to our ears a 'soft murmur,' which appeared to me to be a good omen. That we all felt very much enthused goes without saying. Well satisfied we traveled westward over the slightly rolling surface, with no big hills, until we were very close to the shore and the evergreens, when we encountered a sharp declivity, but Larsen informed us that there were several places where the land was not so steep and where roads could be built.

"When we again returned to the ice, or, rather, to the shore, Larsen called our attention to the fact that we ought to discover the markings on the trees showing where the section line ran and after some search we located it down by the shore near the spot where later our church was built. While the brethren made this spot more conspicuous for later use, without being noticed, I quietly stepped aside in among the small evergreens and kneeled down upon the white snow. The Savior knows how fervently I prayed on that spot for the first time. I received full assurance that right here would our Atoner plant his little congregation and never forsake it in spite of all meager circumstances. I returned to my companions and told them that I was solemnly assured that here was the spot for our congregation and the brethren present acquiesced enthusiastically in this statement."

Andrew and his followers would stake their lives on the wilderness overlooking Eagle Harbor. The search for Ephraim had ended.

Milwaukee and Green Bay

1

VOYAGE TO AMERICA

Zululand! This African country was the focus of Andrew Iverson's dreams. As a young Norwegian, training for missionary service with the Lutheran Church, his plans revolved around going to Africa "to work among the heathen."

In January 1849, Andrew was living in Stavanger, Norway, and finishing up his studies at the Norwegian Lutheran Mission School and Society. He and two fellow graduates were looking forward to leaving for Zululand in March, when he received an unexpected visit from his mentor and confidante, Reverend Stephanus Due, who made the surprising suggestion that Andrew abandon his idea of working in Africa and travel instead to America. Due explained that there was an urgent need for mission work among Scandinavians who were living in the Milwaukee area of the newly-formed state of Wisconsin.

Andrew responded to this suggestion with little enthusiasm. Due, however, informed him that it was not likely the Diaspora would send him to Zululand, but rather would discipline him by sending him to a very strict Lutheran Mission School in Germany. The Diaspora, the governing body of the Lutheran Church, hoped that such a move would encourage Andrew to give up his beliefs in Moravianism, which compared to Lutheran beliefs, were more evangelical and less doctrinaire. Andrew and the two students destined for Africa had already been persecuted for Moravian views that some considered heretical and alien to the Lutheran Church. Although all three of them had been cleared in a formal hearing, this early incident underscored the strength of Andrew's feelings and beliefs. He was aware that his zeal could work both for and against him in the church.

Despite his disappointment in not being sent to Zululand, Andrew recognized the importance of "this urgent and serious call" and agreed to give it "mature consideration, with earnest prayer." He and Due met and prayed many times, but several weeks went by without "any clear decision as to what really was the will of God in this matter." When he was unable to "arrive at any satisfactory solution and definite decision," Andrew allowed the drawing of lots to make the decision for him. The lot was cast and his destiny was to serve God in Milwaukee. He took the drawing of the lot to be "Christ's own command," and "his mind was immediately at rest." His future was now in God's hands.

To Andrew's relief, the Norwegian Lutheran Mission Society gave him permission to go to Wisconsin as a Moravian missionary, wholly independent of the Society, and he began his preparations for leaving Norway. On the morning of March 23, 1849, he said goodbye to his friends who would soon depart for Africa. On the afternoon of the same day he married Laurenze (Laura) Hansen, a member of Due's Diaspora Society. It was the day before her 25th birthday. One month later they sailed for America.

****

On the 28th day of April 1849, Andrew, his new wife, and Rasmus Hansen, his wife's 17-year-old brother, set sail from Stavanger on board the *Ebenezer*, a ship bound for New York. Stavanger is a modest-sized port city on Boknafjord, along the southwest corner of Norway's jagged coastline. The *Ebenezer* was the only ship scheduled to sail from Stavanger to New York that season.

The *Ebenezer* was a small and relatively new sailing schooner captained by H.C. Clausen, an experienced seaman with whom Andrew was to forge a close relationship during their voyage across the Atlantic. This schooner was an emigrant ship, and most of these transatlantic workhorses were built sturdily of cedar, locust, and live oak. Their three masts were designed to carry as much sail as possible, and a crew of 20 to 36 men were involved in keeping such vessels in trim and on schedule.

As the *Ebenezer* eased away from Stavanger's deep water dock, the ship's rails were lined with the 74 men, women, and children making the voyage. Two of the children were only six months old and the oldest adult was 60. Most of the passengers had never ventured far from home and certainly none had crossed an ocean. Many wept as the crew worked aloft to unfurl the sails, allowing a gentle breeze to carry the ship westward. Ten or so excited, and somewhat bewildered, children watched and listened with awe as the ship began to groan with movement. The biggest adventure of their lives was beginning.

Gradually the coastline began to fall away, but after the ship had sailed only a few miles the wind died. With its load of disappointed passengers, the *Ebenezer* was forced to drift into a nearby harbor, where the captain ordered the sails furled and the anchor dropped to await better sailing conditions. The becalming of his ship was decidedly frustrating for the captain, because he was responsible for all on board and continually had to balance the amount of provisions and water available against the time spent without headway. The vessel lay at anchor for several days while the equally frustrated passengers tried to amuse themselves as best they could. Fortunately for Andrew, several relatives and friends heard that the ship was becalmed nearby and took advantage of the occasion to visit it and again pray with the Iverson family for a safe voyage. Little did they know that the Iversons, and all others on board including the captain, would spend a great deal of time in prayer before this voyage was over.

The layout of the *Ebenezer* was like most other schooners sailing the Atlantic with emigrants aboard. On the top deck there were small cabins for those who could afford them. Andrew managed to secure one of these cabins for his family by talking directly with the owners of the ship. Most emigrants could not afford such quarters, and they crossed the sea as steerage passengers, or "tween decks" as seamen put it, because steerage space was located between the upper deck and the cargo hold in the bowels of the ship. On emigrant ships steerage was always crowded with impoverished families willing to tolerate this dark and claustrophobic space for a chance at a new life in America—a nation of promise and opportunity.

On ships much larger than the *Ebenezer*, as many as 800 emigrants could be crammed into steerage along with their meager belongings and foodstuffs for the trip. Cooking was allowed on a single grating on the main deck, weather permitting. Water was available to all on board, but it was often foul smelling and equally foul tasting. Food was provided for the crew and cabin passengers but steerage passengers were on their own. Access to steerage was usually by fore and aft hatchways that were closed and sealed during inclement weather. There were usually no portholes to illuminate the space between decks. During daytime, some stray light came in through open hatches; dimly lit lanterns provided the only other light. Two tiers of wooden platforms along the ship's sides were divided vertically into small sections or "bunks," and most families traveling in steerage could afford only a single bunk on which to sleep and store their possessions.

Finally, on the first day of May of 1849, after five days in port, Captain

Clausen responded to favorable winds and ordered the anchor raised and the sails unfurled. The *Ebenezer* slowly resumed its westward journey. "The first week of our voyage passed very pleasantly and swiftly, for our schooner was a very speedy sailor. Our Captain was not only a very experienced man but also a good man, with the fear of God implanted in his heart and for that reason I had a splendid opportunity of holding meetings for the emigrants on deck, when the weather permitted it."

Conditions on board the *Ebenezer* were more civilized than on many emigrant ships. The fact that the ship was new also made a difference, especially to the passengers in steerage, for in such closed quarters odors from cargo were pervasive. On older ships, lingering odors from old cargo, such as animal hides, hung heavy in the steerage space where there was little air circulation.

There were usually toilets on the upper deck, but in steerage such facilities consisted of a few buckets, with or without seats, surrounded by some kind of privacy screen. When passengers were seasick during storms, or when a shipboard epidemic of diarrhea broke out, the toilet facilities were awash in filth. It was very common for passengers, especially children and older people, to vomit in their crowded bunks.

Although storms could have devastating consequences, they were often the least serious problem faced by emigrant ships. So little was known about human disease in the early 1800s that a transatlantic voyage was always a race against time in order to arrive before the outbreak of one or more contagious illnesses. With several hundred people on board, some of them diseased or in poor health, epidemics were common during voyages. Cholera outbreaks occurred frequently, and ships' doctors were powerless to stem the spread of the disease or even properly care for those afflicted. Typhus, known as "ship fever," was another dreaded disease. Spread by lice, this disease imperiled emigrant ships, since most were infested with these tiny blood-sucking insects.

Andrew's ship was spared epidemics, but it was not spared the violence of being caught in overwhelming storm conditions. Things went well for the first half of the voyage, but in mid-Atlantic the ship began to encounter one violent storm after another, each one increasing in intensity. Although storms were frequent occurrences, tumultuous weather always carried great risks for those on board wooden ships powered by wind against cloth.

To the passengers, especially emigrants traveling between decks in steerage, a storm was a frightening experience. Finding themselves sealed in a darkened space in the hold of a ship that was being tossed about like a cork was terrifying. Being seasick along with scores, sometimes hundreds, of other trapped souls, and being assaulted by the din of adults screaming, youngsters crying, and nearly everyone praying, was a test of human endurance. Surprisingly enough, the great majority of those who made such journeys survived and went on to live normal lives.

Two-thirds of the way to America, the *Ebenezer* encountered a hurricane that drove the ship and its occupants to the edge of destruction. High winds shredded the sails as if they were tissue paper, but since minimal sails are necessary to maintain a heading to prevent capsizing, crewmen were pushed to the brink of endurance as they worked the rigging and fought to save themselves and their ship.

"At day-break on the 23rd of May, a huge breaker rolled over our ship with such a tremendous weight that it shook like a leaf. The enormous damage that this wave caused cannot be described in its details but the destruction was horrible." The lifeboats were smashed and flung overboard, the railing was torn away, and the main hatchway collapsed causing water to roar into the hold so rapidly that the crew was "horror-stricken" and believed all was lost. At the height of the storm the first-mate reported that the schooner was half full of water and things looked hopeless. The crew drew on what little physical reserves they had left and worked feverishly to contain the damage, with the furious manning of the pumps receiving first priority.

After quickly surveying the destruction from the vantage point of the deck, Andrew returned to his cabin to read his Bible and pray fervently, after which he claimed that his mind was completely at rest. He appealed to God to "spare all those unprepared emigrants who were on board from destruction and perdition," and he also reminded God that "he had been selected for this voyage to America to be His witness there." Laura was present during his prayers, and she was also at rest, "although the terrible storm howled with unabated fury and the waves rolled mountain-high about us and death and destruction stared us all in the face."

Captain Clausen called on every measure of his previous experience in dangerous seas as he barked orders to his crew on behalf of the safety of all on board. Fortunately, the ship's hull remained tight and temporary repairs could be made while the crew fought to outlast the storm. The pumps managed to bring the water level in the hold down to an acceptable level, and the storm sails held as the ship altered course back toward Europe to run with storm winds from the west. By the next morning the storm had blown itself out, and the battered ship and its desperate occupants began to feel the winds of survival and hope.

After the storm abated, the exhausted Clausen sought out Andrew and another respected passenger, an older gentleman, to seek their advice. The captain "explained in detail the condition of our ship and stated that we were still nearer America than England—although during the storm we had been obliged to sail eastward a considerable distance ...." He discussed the options and asked for their thoughts on what to do next. Should they continue westward and hope for the best, or turn the ship around and take advantage of the westerly trade winds to seek repairs in England?

Andrew felt that if God could guide their heavily damaged ship safely to England, He could just as easily guide it safely to America. After all, though battered, the *Ebenezer* was still seaworthy. The older passenger also felt that they might as well press on to New York, and upon reflecting on the advice he had received, the captain ordered the crew to turn the ship westward and again set sail for America.

The *Ebenezer* enjoyed a few days of favorable winds while the crew attempted to repair the damage done to its deck fittings and rigging. The weather again took a turn for the worse, however, and the ship was buffeted by still another violent storm. Finally this storm passed and a week or so of steady wind and good weather carried them to New York. Early on the morning of June 13, 1849, Captain Clausen awoke Andrew and requested his presence on deck to see a most welcome sight. In the distance Clausen pointed out the dim outline of New York and the shore of Sandy Hook. Andrew immediately hurried back to his cabin to inform Laura, and the two of them knelt in prayer to praise God for his blessings. That afternoon, there was great rejoicing as everyone crowded the deck of the *Ebenezer* and listened to the rattling of the chain as the anchor secured the tired ship in New York Harbor. Andrew described the sound of the chain as "... sweeter music and more impressive to us than the finest organ's most musical selection."

When he set foot on American soil for the first time, Andrew was overcome with deep feelings of "both joy and sadness." His long voyage to the New World was over; he had been tested, and he had survived. He felt buoyed by the trust his fellow immigrants had placed in him as their spiritual leader during the dangerous voyage, and he looked forward to accompanying many of them to Milwaukee. It was just as well he had no way of foreseeing that there would be many more tests of his spirit and endurance.

****

Before his group departed on a Hudson River steamer en route to Troy, New York, and subsequently to Milwaukee, Andrew received a letter from church officials informing him that the situation had changed in Milwaukee, and the prospect of establishing a Moravian church there was not good. If Andrew were willing to serve as a Lutheran minister, however, a position could likely be found for him. Andrew was bitterly disappointed, as was Laura, and he reminded himself that he "never could and never would become a Lutheran pastor." After seeking guidance from God, he decided that he must continue his journey to Milwaukee without delay.

Andrew, Laura, her brother, and a large group of Norwegians from his ship, traveled up the Hudson River by steamer to Troy, where they contracted for the use of a canalboat to take them to Buffalo, New York. Andrew and his family "enjoyed the favor of having a beautiful and comfortable cabin placed at our disposal in the bow of the boat, while the 74 emigrants were obliged to accommodate themselves as best they could in the midst of all their boxes and baggage in the large compartment. Here it was almost unbearably hot so that I very much feared some outbreak of sickness, especially as we had heard in New York that there were a good many cases of Asiatic cholera in the country."

Indeed, the slow trip up the canal in a horse-drawn boat was miserable due to sickness on the part of a number of the immigrants. One person on board showed symptoms of cholera, and Andrew, who was interested in homeopathic medicine, was glad he carried his bag containing herbs, potions, and other "medicines" of the day. As he labored to minister to the health needs of the immigrants, he took the opportunity to minister to their souls as well. He talked "earnestly and confidentially with the immigrants" and many of them were described as being deeply touched, as "evidenced by their flowing tears." Andrew's mission work in America had begun.

After 10 long days on the canal, the group arrived in Buffalo on June 24, 1849. There they encountered another Norwegian, Ole Larsen, who ran a boarding house, and he invited Andrew and Laura to stay overnight at his establishment as his guests. Larsen, a widower, operated the business with his two daughters, and Andrew was pleased to learn that they were disposed toward the Moravian faith. The next day, after thanking Larsen for his kind hospitality, Andrew and his group departed for Milwaukee on a Great Lakes steamship. The four-day trip was uneventful except for one death due to cholera.

On June 29, 1849, the group finally reached Milwaukee and was met by several fellow Moravians. The trip from Norway had taken two months. Andrew and Laura said farewell to most of their fellow immigrants, who planned to travel on to Chicago, and many tears flowed as they wished each other well.

Although officially without a church of his own, Andrew made good use of his days in Milwaukee. He was becoming fluent in German in addition to his native Norwegian, and he worked hard to learn English. He made friends with many of his fellow Scandinavian immigrants, among them Zacharias C. Wathne, a widower he first met in Stavanger, and Andrew and Anne Nelson, husband and wife from Christiansfeld, Denmark. Wathne and the Nelsons would play important roles in helping Andrew establish the village of Ephraim a few years later.

Andrew and Laura rented housekeeping rooms in an area of Milwaukee where many Scandinavians lived, and Andrew found a schoolhouse where twice each Sunday he held church services in Norwegian. There he preached his first sermon in America to a capacity crowd, and he wondered how many of the 200 people in attendance had come out of curiosity "to see and hear the young preacher." He was 25 years old. That afternoon he preached a second sermon to an equally large crowd. "It was a real revival sermon. Many, many tears flowed but I feared that perhaps only feeling and emotions were present." Later, however, he discovered that his message induced several people to accept the word of God and change their lives.

Andrew was a riveting speaker, and his sermons were often spell-binding, playing on the emotions of his listeners in an effort to carry them to a higher level of spirituality. Among his first converts in America were two young Swedes. Their awakening occurred in August of 1849, when his message touched everyone present, and the two men responded with "great trembling and violent weeping." After the service, when all the tears had been wiped away, Andrew learned that they were tradesmen who had attended out of curiosity. But they acknowledged that their eyes had been opened, "so that they saw they were poor, lost sinners and that the word of God had softened their hearts." Later, according to Andrew, one of the converts confessed that the night before the service he had a dream in which he envisioned many of the details surrounding the occasion, and that he felt an irresistible force compelling him to travel to the south end of Milwaukee to attend Andrew's church meeting. Andrew accepted such mystical experiences as the way of the Lord.

Moravian missionaries were charged with keeping a record of their activities, and Andrew was fully prepared to do just that. Even before his church was formally established, he stopped at the Arnold and Wilson Book Store on Wisconsin Street and purchased a sturdy journal in which to record events of the congregation. In a beautifully flowing hand he inscribed it: *Kirke Bog for den Norske Brödremenighed* (Church Book for the Norwegian Brotherhood). He then carefully apportioned it into sections, labeling them *Döpte* (Christenings), *Egteviede* (Marriages), and *Döde* (Deaths). It was a book he would keep with him for much of his life as a missionary.

After a month or so in Milwaukee, Andrew was afflicted with a strange malady that he attributed to the change in climate. He felt weak and exhausted, barely able to walk, and he was dejected and despondent. Although this continued for over six weeks, he somehow managed to find enough strength to preach his sermons. Then one Sunday after several weeks of depression, as he arose at the end of a silent meditation at one of his services, a dramatic change occurred and his weakness and depression dropped away. "As if in the twinkling of an eye, I felt as if a hand touched me, first on top of my head and further, clear through my whole body, ending under the soles of my feet. As if by a miracle, in that very moment, I stood there completely restored and healed and my body, just a few moments before so weak, was now endowed with more than ordinary strength." He then delivered his sermon with great fervor in an unusually loud voice. The impact on the congregation was substantial: "some sobbed and wept and the faces of everyone present were as if bathed in tears ...." His ability to deliver a powerful sermon in a charismatic manner was never more evident. His faith and strength had returned, but it was mainly his faith that had helped him cope with his mood swings.

In the autumn of 1849, a German named Friedrich Fett visited Andrew. He was the first missionary appointed by the Moravian Home Mission Society in Bethlehem, Pennsylvania. Although Fett spoke little English or Norwegian, one of his tasks was to investigate newly settled areas and provide the administrative office with information about living conditions, religious affiliations of the settlers, church needs, and recommendations about placement of ministers. His other responsibility was to serve the spiritual needs of the growing number of German immigrants in the area.

Fett was an outgoing person and his approach to religion was emotional and evangelistic, much like Andrew's. They enjoyed each other's company, although after their first meeting Fett reported to Bethlehem that he found Andrew to be a "childlike Christian, in whom there is no guile (31)." As a result of Fett's recommendation to Bethlehem, Wisconsin's first Norwegian Moravian Church was formally established in Milwaukee, with Andrew as leader of the congregation of 18 adults and two children. Within a short time, Fett and Andrew grew to trust each other, and as a result Fett went out of his way to assist Andrew and his small group of followers.

On the last day of December, Andrew and Laura had their first child, a girl named Anna Munda Laurenze. She was baptized by Fett on January 6, 1850—her baptism was the first performed by the congregation.

When spring came Andrew received word that he was to be ordained officially as a minister in the Moravian Church. Upon hearing the news, he "wept hot tears of submission and obedience...." Traveling to Bethlehem for the ordination ceremony, he passed through Buffalo, New York, and sought his old friend, Ole Larsen, but Larsen was nowhere to be found and no one knew his whereabouts. Later Andrew learned that Larsen had remarried and moved to the Great Lakes area.

Andrew was euphoric during his visit to Bethlehem. He later described his first view of the village in lavish, almost mystical, terms. "What an impression this sight afforded me! The surrounding country seemed to me to be exceptionally beautiful, more beautiful than any landscape I had ever beheld in my life ... It was as if I had been transplanted in a delightful dream, and it is impossible for me to describe the peculiar sensations and emotions which arose and overwhelmed my soul. It seemed to me that I was disembodied and a few tears rolled slowly down my cheeks." At his ordination on May 6, 1850, he was nearly overcome with emotion. "Overwhelmed by my feelings, I burst violently into tears so that my whole frame shook. Dear Brother Schultz, who stood by my side, was astonished when he noticed me, but I explained to him that this music seemed to me to be supernatural and fascinating, yes, almost heavenly."

"Dear Brother Schultz" was Reverend Henry A. (H.A.) Schultz, a key figure in the Moravian Home Mission Society office in Bethlehem and editor of several of the church's publications. He became a mentor to Andrew and remained his friend for many years. He admired Andrew's courage and missionary zeal and later demonstrated great faith in his young protégé by loaning him money to buy land on which to establish a Moravian colony.

Over the ensuing years, officials safe in the home office in Bethlehem came to look forward to Andrew's reports about braving blizzards and trekking through the frontier wilderness to carry the message to remote communities. In his capacity as editor, Schultz was pleased to publish many of Andrew's colorful writings. These reports from the frontier enlivened Church communications that generally made for dull reading. Although not a sophisticated writer, Andrew knew how to play to his administrative audience in Bethlehem. Perhaps he was not as naive as Fett suggested.

2

CONFRONTATION

As he relaxed on the train carrying him on the second leg of his journey back to Milwaukee, Andrew's thoughts returned to the emotional and tiring trip he was now completing. After his exhilarating ordination at Bethlehem he traveled to Philadelphia and then to New York, where he was introduced to Otto Tank, a fellow Norwegian who had arrived from Europe only a few days earlier. He remembered being awestruck at his first sight of the imposing Tank. Standing six feet four inches tall, with a powerful chin, this self-assured and wealthy man was a commanding figure. "When I saw this great giant, who was bound to instill respect, I almost became frightened, but he appeared to receive me with open arms and soon expressed his great joy in having met me."

Tank, like Andrew, was a Moravian missionary who had come to America under the auspices of the Church. Speaking in Norwegian, he talked with Andrew at length and drew him into his confidence as he described in detail what he hoped to achieve on behalf of his countrymen. He told Andrew he had come to America for the express purpose of assisting Scandinavians and fellow Moravians locate land and establish economically viable communities. Tank said he intended to purchase land, tracts of which would be sold to his countrymen at low interest rates, and that he hoped to establish a community where all could live together cooperatively. There would be farms, factories, and shops so that everyone would have work.

Andrew felt his enthusiasm rise as Tank told of his plans—and of his hopes that Andrew might be part of them. He realized that his struggling congregation, so desirous of leaving Milwaukee and settling on their own land, could be greatly assisted by Tank, and he wondered if it would be possible for them to work together in establishing Moravian roots in Wisconsin. He also remembered thinking that "It seemed to be altogether too good to be true ...."

Tank had listened carefully while Andrew described the circumstances in Wisconsin. He had talked about his little congregation of Moravian settlers and their collective hope of finding a permanent place to establish themselves. Soon the two men were discussing the possibility that they might join forces. During his nearly two-week stay in New York, Andrew had taken the time to contact Bethlehem, seeking permission to invite Tank to Milwaukee for the purpose of helping the Moravian settlers find land. Church leaders had given a qualified yes to the arrangement. Now Tank, along with his wife, Caroline, and their seven-year-old daughter, Mary, shared the train with Andrew as it rumbled westward toward Wisconsin and the future.

Andrew hoped the decision to let Tank help the congregation was the correct one. As he had listened to Tank back in New York, Andrew had grown to feel comfortable with his new friend and excited about his offer to buy land for the congregation. His enthusiasm was tempered, however, by the memory of a warning Church officials had given him. They told him to be cautious of Tank and to keep them informed about the situation, but Andrew was not entirely clear why the Church was wary of Tank. He knew only that Tank had been a Moravian missionary in Surinam, South America, where it was rumored he had found gold, and that the Church thought his business methods there were questionable. Andrew was not the only one puzzled by Tank. Church officials, too, understood him poorly. Because he came from a wealthy family and was highly educated, he was unlike most of the missionaries the Church was accustomed to supervising. Although he was a devout and tireless worker, his superiors were somewhat distrustful of him and transmitted this distrust to others. Andrew's ambivalent thoughts about Tank were interrupted by the arrival of the train at New Buffalo, Michigan. There he and the Tank family boarded a steamer for the final portion of their journey, which would take them to Chicago and then on to Milwaukee.

As their little group stepped off the steamer in Milwaukee it was impossible not to contrast the tall and dignified Tank, who was 50 years old, with the much younger Andrew, who came barely to his shoulder. But an observer would have quickly noted Andrew's piercing eyes and fervent manner and concluded that this was an intense young man to be reckoned with. They were given an enthusiastic welcome by Laura and members of the congregation. Friedrich Fett was also present in the greeting party; he spoke warmly to Andrew and Tank and welcomed Tank as a fellow Moravian missionary.

Tank's arrival was noted by local newspapers, one of which reported that he had brought $1.5 million dollars worth of gold with him. It was no wonder that his appearance in this city of 20,000 people aroused curiosity and interest. He was an extremely wealthy man, and the source of his wealth was a subject of intense speculation, as was his past life. In fact, his past life was probably more intriguing than any speculation in which the local press indulged itself.

Tank, born in 1800, was the only son of one of the wealthiest and most politically influential men in Norway. He was raised in an elegant home, received the finest education available, and traveled widely in Europe. Although his father was a worldly man, his mother was a devout woman who belonged to the Moravian Society. She derived great comfort from her faith and imparted her sense of religion to her son. Following a number of years of travel and study, Tank became a convert to Moravianism and joined the Moravian colony at Christiansfeld, Denmark. Around the same period of time his father experienced business losses so overwhelming that he was forced to apply for a government pension—the Tank fortune was completely gone.

The Moravian colony at Christiansfeld was a highly successful communal village. The structural harmony within the colony, where everyone was equal and worked toward the good of the whole, made a lasting impression on Tank, and he began having thoughts of someday establishing a similar colony in America. In 1838, while living at Christiansfeld, he married his first wife, Mariane, who was chosen for him in the traditional Moravian way—by lottery. She was the well-educated daughter of a Moravian missionary and had recently served as the principal of a girls' school in Switzerland.

In 1842, Tank was ordained as a missionary and he and Mariane, who was pregnant, were sent to Surinam. His assignment was to carry out missionary work among the slaves on Dutch plantations and assume charge of the mission's stores. The work in Surinam was grueling and the living conditions wretched, but Tank displayed a tremendous capacity for working in the intolerable heat. The mission economy flourished under his direction, and he was indefatigable in his efforts to minister to the sick and improve conditions for the slaves. A few months after their arrival Mariane gave birth to a daughter, Mary. Unfortunately, less than a year after arriving in Surinam, Mariane died of a tropical fever, leaving the grieving Tank with an infant to care for. He requested an immediate transfer out of Surinam, but before a replacement for him could be found the mission's superintendent died. Tank stepped in and filled the superintendent's position for the next two years (1846–1848).

His years as superintendent were filled with ceaseless activity. He established a carpenter shop, a cobbler shop, and a smithy. A bakery and grocery store thrived, and he had plans for a lumbering industry and other business projects. He increased the size of the mission substantially and he frequently visited the interior of Surinam, which appealed to his sense of adventure and his love of natural beauty. It was during these visits that he was on the lookout for gold. Although it was widely rumored that he found it, this was never confirmed.

In 1847, five years after he arrived in Surinam, Tank and his young daughter departed on a trip to the United States. The purpose of the trip was to investigate the treatment of slaves in that country as well as in the West Indies, and he assumed his absence from Surinam would be temporary. His departure, however, was greeted with relief by his fellow missionaries, who did not care for his ambitious schemes nor his increasing interest in freeing slaves.

After visiting America, Tank made his way to Holland where he reported to government officials on the deplorable living conditions and treatment of slaves on Dutch plantations in Surinam. The government responded by contacting Surinam asking for further information. The missionaries there had grown uneasy with Tank and were also pressured by plantation owners who did not want their slaves freed. As a result, the missionaries provided an evasive reply about the slaves' situation and went on to portray Tank as an unstable individual. Their disclaimers made it impossible for him to return to Surinam. And Church officials, already ambivalent about Tank, became even more cautious in their dealings with him.

Tank therefore found himself in Holland without a congregation to serve, in questionable standing with the Church, and with a motherless seven-year-old daughter to raise. As he traveled the country renewing acquaintances, he was fortunate to meet Caroline van der Meulen in Amsterdam. She was the daughter of a wealthy clergyman and had been a friend of Tank's first wife, Mariane. Otto and Caroline had much in common, and following the death of her father in 1849, they married. She promised to follow Tank anywhere in the world except to South America. Because Caroline had inherited a substantial fortune from each of her parents, Tank was again an extraordinarily wealthy man and Moravian Church leaders again found him a force with which to reckon.

The newlyweds traveled to Norway on their honeymoon, and while there they discussed with friends Tank's long-held dream of establishing, in America, a Norwegian community that would combine worship, agriculture, and higher education. This dream had begun during his years at Christiansfeld, and he was now in a position to make it come true. He had heard of a struggling Norwegian Moravian community in Milwaukee, and he determined to go there to investigate. In 1850, Tank, Caroline, and Mary departed for New York, with Milwaukee as their ultimate destination.

Thus the stage was set for the development of a complex relationship between Andrew Iverson, the evangelistic preacher from a Norwegian farm family, and Otto Tank, the aristocratic and wealthy missionary from one of Norway's most notable families. From the very beginning of their association, Andrew had been somewhat suspicious of Tank and his intentions. Andrew was more emotional than intellectual, more mystical than realistic, and now he was obliged to deal with a towering figure of a man who was handsome, intelligent, articulate, and wealthy, and who seemed to hold out golden promises to Andrew and his congregation. Although Andrew was not particularly handsome, not very large, and certainly not wealthy, he had fire in his eyes and a missionary zeal that would serve him well. He was also justified in being a little wary of Tank, for the two of them were headed for confrontation.

****

It took quite a long time to unload the Tank party's baggage from the steamship. While waiting, Tank observed his surroundings with interest. He noticed that the Milwaukee waterfront was crowded with buildings, mostly frame, but here and there were a number of larger buildings made of an unusual cream-colored brick. Wooden sidewalks bordered rutted streets filled with heavily loaded horse-drawn wagons. Milwaukee seemed to be a thriving city, teeming with activity.

Omnibuses from numerous boarding houses and hotels were on hand to meet the steamship, and their drivers were busy soliciting business for their lodging establishments. The Tank family chose the largest and finest hotel the city had to offer. Once their bags and trunks were collected and loaded onto his hotel's omnibus, Tank said good-bye to Andrew. He had previously made arrangements to meet later with him and his followers.

It was with great excitement that Andrew introduced Tank to his small congregation. He had also invited Fett to attend the gathering, which was conducted entirely in Norwegian, so it was necessary to provide a translator for Fett, who spoke German. Andrew greeted everyone and opened the meeting by explaining the congregation's wish to move away from Milwaukee. He said they wanted to live in the country, where each could farm his own plot of land. He went on to say that there were other problems with living in the city, such as the "dangerous temptations" it presented, and the fact that some settlers "who were workingmen were often cheated out of their wages ...."

Each male member of the congregation was given an opportunity to speak and express his opinion. Everyone who spoke described the congregation's plight in similar terms and said that they were "very anxious to secure a location out on a tract of land and the financial condition of our brethren was also made clear." Tank did not address the group until everyone had his say. He then presented his plans in detail. When he finished, members of the congregation "wept for joy, blessed him and looked upon him as an angel sent from heaven, sent by the Lord, sent to help during these hard times."

Tank promised to "search for a good tract of land and, when located, buy it for the congregation and there establish a little brethren-village with workshops, factories, and farms all around so that everyone could be employed at something." The congregation listened, enraptured, as they heard their countryman say that he would sell them tracts of land at low interest rates and would extend payments over a period of years. Tank warmed to his presentation as he recalled his stay at Herrnhut and his dream of establishing a similar colony in America. He was greatly encouraged by the eagerness with which his plans were received, and he told the gathering he would purchase horses and a carriage the very next day so the search for appropriate land could begin immediately.

Fett listened intently during the meeting. He was so impressed with Tank's plans that he asked whether he would be willing to assist poor German congregations in a similar manner. Tank responded with an emphatic yes. Andrew, buoyed by a tide of hope, allowed himself to feel optimistic about the future. At the same time, however, he recalled the Church's warnings about Tank and reminded himself to contact Bethlehem as soon as possible and inform the administrative office of the latest developments.

As promised, Tank bought an expensive carriage for six and a team of fine horses. After hiring a congregation member as driver, he left Milwaukee on May 30, 1850, to search for suitable land in the "interior of Wisconsin." Completing the search party were Caroline and Mary Tank, as well as Fett, who had asked to accompany them on this "journey of exploration and investigation."

After the Tank party departed, Andrew and his congregation attempted to settle back into their routine. This was difficult, partly because they were eager to hear good news from Tank and partly because of increasing anxiety about a recent outbreak of cholera in the city. The summer of 1850 was very warm and an increasing number of cases of "deadly Asiatic cholera" were being seen all over the country. There were reports of 1,400 cholera deaths in Cincinnati that summer, and General Sam Houston lay seriously ill with cholera in Texas. Newspapers were filled with page after page of advertisements for patent medicines guaranteed to ease the suffering of those afflicted.

Because it is spread by contaminated food and water, cholera is capable of exploding quickly into a full-fledged epidemic wherever sanitation is poor and living conditions are crowded. This was the case in some parts of Milwaukee in

1850. The city had been incorporated only four years earlier and was experiencing rapid growth as immigrants from the eastern states and Europe came crowding in. Some of the immigrants were infected with cholera, which Andrew knew to be a frightening disease characterized by massive and constant diarrhea, dehydration, and collapse. Many years later it would be learned that cholera is caused by a bacterium and it would be many years after that until antibiotics became available to treat the disease effectively. Andrew remembered clearly his first encounter with cholera on the canal boat taking him from New York to Buffalo. His knowledge of homeopathic medicine enabled him to "successfully treat" a fellow passenger, but shortly thereafter he saw a steamship passenger die from this extremely contagious disease.

Now, back in Milwaukee, the danger of cholera would affect him in a much more personal way. Just a few weeks after his return from New York a group of 12 Moravians, newly arrived from Norway, joined his congregation. Many came down quickly with cholera and three died. When his seven-month-old daughter, Anna Munda, became ill he was greatly distressed. Despite the ministrations of a local homeopathic physician, her condition gradually worsened, and Andrew sought solace in prayer.

The congregation, meanwhile, eagerly awaited word from Tank, but the only communications they received were discouraging, stating that he had not yet located suitable land. Finally, late in July, Fett returned to Milwaukee alone and called the congregation together for a meeting. He explained that the Tank party had traveled from Milwaukee to Delafield, Watertown, Oshkosh, Neenah, Appleton (where they stayed at the newly-established Lawrence University), Little Chute, and Green Bay. Fett was convinced that appropriate land was available in the Green Bay area, but he was frustrated by Tank's indecision about what land to buy. He suggested that the congregation go to Green Bay and implore Tank directly to buy land and live up to his promises. Most of the congregation agreed with Fett's advice, and Andrew concurred. His daughter's health was deteriorating steadily, and her physician advised them to leave for Green Bay as soon as possible "as the climate up there was much healthier than in Milwaukee and he considered this change as the only possible solution ...."

After hasty investigations, Zacharias Morbek, a member of the congregation who spoke English, located a small steamship, the *James Wood*, that made weekly trips between Milwaukee and Green Bay. The congregation hurriedly arranged to leave within the week, and Andrew wrote to Tank informing him of their plans and time of arrival in Green Bay. He also advised Church officers in Bethlehem of the imminent move.

On August 1, 1850, the congregation spent most of the day loading their belongings onto the boat, and early in the evening 27 adults boarded. Anna Munda, who was gravely ill, was tenderly carried on board by one of the women of the congregation and placed in a little stateroom where she could be cared for by her grieving mother. Despite black clouds and threatening skies, the boat departed as scheduled at eight o'clock in the evening, but several hours later a violent storm erupted. As midnight approached, lightning split the sky over Lake Michigan, followed by thunderclaps and rising wind. The boat began to pitch and roll as it pushed its way through the whitecaps. The storm increased in intensity while Anna Munda grew progressively weaker. Andrew knew the end was near. "Our grief was deep and tears flowed abundantly. A half hour past midnight, our most precious Anna Munda expired and the Great Friend of children had taken her soul to himself in eternal glory."

Andrew scarcely noticed that the storm abated before dawn. In his grief over the loss of his child, he turned to God for comfort, as well as to the other members of his congregation. Two of the women "took charge of the little lifeless, emaciated body, to prepare it for its narrow resting place, while Brother T. Davidson hurriedly constructed a very plain coffin on the deck. When this was finished and brought in, we placed our first-born little treasure in it, and through a flood of tears, we took a last look at our departed angel who had been with us scarcely seven months ...." "After that the coffin was quietly set aside on [sic] a quiet spot on board, where it remained undisturbed during the whole voyage."

Although fair weather prevailed for the rest of the three-day trip, members of the congregation were quiet and subdued. The steamer was not fast and the voyage seemed interminable, as their course took them from Milwaukee north over Lake Michigan, through the treacherous Death's Door Passage between Washington Island and the Door peninsula, then south into Green Bay waters.

Tank was on the dock to meet the boat, and after greeting Andrew and Laura he expressed shock that they had suffered the painful and sad experience of losing their first-born daughter. Two days later Tank conducted Anna Munda's funeral service. Following his address and reading of the liturgy, he and his wife and daughter accompanied the entire congregation to the burial site. Anna Munda was buried in a cemetery "close to departed Christian Indian children, designated by several raised graves." She was the first Anna Munda—Andrew and Laura would subsequently have two more.

After receiving Andrew's letter announcing the date of their arrival, Tank hastened to prepare for the the congregation. In order to provide housing and a place for worship, he rented a large, old house belonging to the Indian mission of the Episcopal Church. The two-story building was spacious enough to accommodate everyone. In the big kitchen there was a new stove, installed by Tank himself, and upstairs an ample dining room contained long tables and benches. Andrew and Laura moved into two rooms on the first floor directly across from two rooms assigned to the Tank family. Andrew was quite content with the living arrangements, declaring that though "these rooms could not be called beautiful, they would prove very serviceable."

Andrew wasted no time in scheduling worship. He was so eager to begin his mission work that on the evening of their arrival he held a service in the dining room. Thereafter the dining room became the gathering place for the congregation and the site of daily morning and evening devotions for as long as they lived in the mission house. The little group also agreed upon a communal household management system. "At five o'clock in the morning a bell sounded in all the hallways and all the brethren and sisters who were well arose. A half hour later a bell rang again and then all were gathered in the large dining room." After a brief devotional service, breakfast was served, and then the men went to work outside while the women dealt with household matters.

Only a few days after the congregation arrived, Tank called everyone together to announce that he had located suitable land on the west side of the Fox River, and that he was purchasing close to 900 acres for $7 an acre. He planned to divide it in the best way possible for those who wanted to farm, and he explained that he would try to provide work for those who were not farmers. The congregation was delighted with the news.

Shortly thereafter Andrew had an opportunity to inspect the property and was "very well satisfied with the land and its location." He noted that there was a small amount of river frontage and 20 cleared acres extending inland. The rest consisted of woods. Tank intended to lay out a village on the riverside portion and sub-divide the remaining land for farming. He hired a surveyor to lay out lots.

Of the 900 acres purchased by Tank, 210 acres were to be conveyed to Andrew's congregation. The prices set by Tank varied from $20 an acre for lots on cleared land to $10 an acre for lots far back in the woods. Because Tank had paid only $7 an acre, some of the settlers considered these prices excessive and expressed their unhappiness to Andrew and Fett. They did not, however, mention their displeasure to Tank.

When all the lots had been laid out, Tank again called everyone together, this time to discuss his plans for the settlement. He wanted to be sure that each man had a suitable job. "He desired to know who wanted to engage in farming and who wanted to continue as tradesmen and common laborers ...." "All the conditions with reference to credit and the methods of payment he explained very carefully." But nothing was put in writing. "Tank stated at the time that no written contract was necessary between brethren." They called the new settlement Ephraim, a Biblical name meaning rich or abundantly fruitful.

Throughout the fall of 1850 activity was intense as most men of the congregation cleared land and built houses, while others fished and a few worked outside the settlement. "Everyone was engaged at something, and for a time it appeared that everything was going well." Tank's energy seemed endless. He opened a store and extended credit to the settlers. He started a school for children and organized another for adults. He often arose early to help with construction projects and he preached at some of the Sunday services, including one in October at which 16 new members were received into the congregation.

Most of the preaching was enthusiastically handled by Andrew, who was also in charge of the twice daily devotions. He was a popular and emotional speaker whosc "meetings were well frequented and the words about the sufferings on the cross and the blood of Jesus were not in the least an empty voice." His role as a traveling missionary became as important to him as his own congregation, and he undertook arduous journeys to spread the word of God to far-flung settlers. This usually involved holding services in someone's house or other temporary preaching place. Andrew believed fervently that "the Lord anointed me with the Holy Spirit to preach salvation and Christ the Crucified as the only Savior." This passion for ministering to remote congregations would continue throughout his life as a preacher.

As the Green Bay settlement took shape Andrew kept in touch with Bethlehem, and he reported in detail on the growth of the community. Upon hearing of their remarkable progress, Church officials "became very enthusiastic and gave up their former scruples and doubts concerning Tank ...." Shortly thereafter Tank was notified of his appointment as the Church's fourth Home Missionary in the area.

Throughout this period of organization and growth, Fett lent support to the small community. Although he remained busy ministering to his German congregations in Green Bay, he found time to visit the Norwegian congregation and offer advice and encouragement. He was present at many of their important celebrations, including presiding at the service instituting the new congregation, as well as at their first wedding ceremony. Andrew considered him to be a trusted confidant.

In the beginning, things went along smoothly in the little commune of Ephraim. Although not all the men were industrious and some of the fishermen and sailors were reluctant to work in the fields, they were in the minority, as were those who were lax in paying up their credit at the communal store. But by and large the settlement functioned harmoniously through the fall of 1850.

By late fall and early winter many settlers had left the mission house for their own newly constructed homes, and in late November the Tank family moved into a renovated house situated on the shore of the Fox River. Andrew and Laura remained at the mission. As December approached a few people began to complain to Andrew about Tank, saying they found his sermons cold and not inspiring. Even more worrisome was their anxiety over not having written deeds to their lots. It seemed to them that Tank "made first one change and then another in his arrangements as regards land and lots and other details, and as time went on these changes became more apparent. If a brother made a reasonable objection and reminded Tank about the original arrangements, terms and promises, he flew into a snorting rage and was unwilling to make anything right."

As these concerns became more widespread, a general air of uneasiness settled over the colony. The Christmas season was approaching and instead of joy the settlers felt anxiety. Finally several leaders in the community came to Andrew and asked him to "remonstrate with Tank against this injustice and insist that the original terms should be binding ...."

It was several months before Andrew was able to find just the right moment to speak with Tank, although he did have a number of opportunities to discuss the situation with Fett. Like Andrew, Fett often felt diminished in the presence of the wealthy and highly educated Tank, and he resented the fact that he was occasionally treated as a subordinate. There was little warmth in the relationship between the two men. Fett was suspicious of Tank's motivation, finding it peculiar that a rich man should be living in such an uncivilized area—he wondered what Tank's real motivation was. He did not hesitate to share his mistrust and suspicion with Andrew.

In March 1851, an apprehensive Andrew finally called on Tank and presented the congregation's case. Tank became furious and "would make no concessions and even used insulting language against the brethren." Rebuffed, Andrew left feeling both frustrated and angry. After hearing his report, the congregation decided on a new plan of action. "The result was that five of the most experienced brethren were appointed to call on Tank and make absolute demand for written and legal contracts for land and lots, in accordance with his original verbal promises."

The next day, while Andrew and the congregation remained in the mission house praying that reason would prevail, the committee of five called on Tank at home. During the long, uneasy wait to be admitted to his presence, the men could not help noticing Tank's many fine books and beautiful furniture, all in sharp contrast to the simple furnishings in their own living quarters. At long last they were permitted to enter his study. "Brother Zacharias Morbek was the spokesman and presented to Tank, in a very sensible manner, the reasonable demands of themselves and their congregation. This produced a storm which was terrible to endure, but the brethren remained calm."

Finally, after his anger seemed spent, Tank began to talk to his callers in a more composed fashion. For a long time he chatted "about this and that," apparently collecting his thoughts. Individual ownership of lots meant that he would have to give up his dream of a thriving communal colony, and it seemed to him that the people he had hoped to help were ungrateful for his generosity. Finally he looked at each of his visitors in turn, and speaking with obvious reluctance, he told them to return in four days and "he would give a written and legal contract to each individual ..." who desired it.

Exhilarated, the five returned to the mission house to let the congregation know that their visit had met with success. Upon hearing the good news there were wide grins and much backslapping among the settlers. Their five representatives were praised for a job well done—they had persuaded the wealthy Tank to accept the congregation's terms.

Four days later a large group of settlers met outside Tank's house, their hopes soaring. They would be free and independent landowners at last. "They had to wait a long time before Tank showed himself and when he finally opened the door and stepped out, he was in a furious mood and in a thunderous voice he shouted that he never would give anyone a written contract for land or lots ... It did not help in the least that a brother reminded him about his promise made four days ago. He left them as a madman and slammed the door behind him." After glancing at each other in disbelief, members of the group moved quickly away from the Tank residence and trudged back to the mission where they told Andrew and the rest of the congregation what had happened. As they discussed what to do next, Andrew advised against acting hastily and suggested that the entire congregation meet with Fett and get his advice. Meanwhile they agreed to pray about the matter.

When informed of the situation Fett displayed no surprise at Tank's attitude, but he became very angry about Tank's treatment of the settlers and "expressed himself in unmistakable language ...." The word spread quickly and the entire "congregation was grief-stricken and burning prayers were sent up to the throne of Grace." A general meeting was held, attended by Andrew, Fett, and the men of the congregation. Sorrow reigned and many of the men wept. There was unanimous agreement that the congregation would have nothing further to do with Tank. Three individuals were assigned the task of preparing a written petition to Tank requesting that he cancel all verbal agreements regarding distribution of the land. All land would revert to Tank. The congregation wanted only to distance themselves from their wealthy benefactor and his golden promises.

The three petition writers returned apprehensively to Tank's house and presented him with the document. "They found him silent and when the petition was handed to him, he read it with apparent pain and anxiety, but, after some hesitation, he answered in a subdued voice that he would acquiesce in the demand."

The congregation realized immediately that they would have to leave the mission house, which was owned by Tank, and that those who had built houses would have to give them up. It was a sad and fearful time—they would have to move again—they must start over.

The congregation's poignant last meeting was held in the dining room, site of so many morning and evening gatherings over the past year. It was where Andrew had preached his first sermon in Green Bay, and where they had shared so much: their hopes, their fears and, perhaps most important of all, their spirituality. It was a moving and sorrowful occasion, and "many warm tears were shed." The congregation was now forced to scatter, with some renting rooms in Fort Howard and some in Green Bay. Although they located an abandoned church in which to hold their Sunday services, everyone missed the morning and evening gatherings they had shared.

The collapse of the communal colony after less than a year brought pain to all participants. Many of the families suffered financial losses when the closing of their accounts with Tank took place, and all suffered disillusionment as their hopes of being self-sufficient landowners faded. Andrew, Tank, and Fett all wrote letters to Bethlehem, each with a different version of events, each blaming someone else. But there was nothing church leaders in Bethlehem could do—the damage had been done.

Tank had made a great financial and emotional investment in Ephraim, and he was devastated to see his long-held dream of establishing a commune slip away amidst bitterness and misunderstanding. Although an ordained missionary, he never again involved himself intimately with a religious cause. Andrew, however, felt fully justified in the actions he took, which he was convinced were necessary to preserve the integrity of his congregation. It would be many years before he realized that perhaps he had not fully comprehended Tank's vision—perhaps he had acted in haste.

The Ephraim Years
1853 - 1864

3

CARVING A VILLAGE FROM THE WILDERNESS

The years 1851 and 1852 were difficult ones for Andrew and his dispersed congregation. Following the break with Otto Tank many families moved to Fort Howard where church services were held in a "very dilapidated building." Although the congregation remained largely intact, living quarters of the members were widely scattered, and they missed the closeness they had experienced in the past. By the middle of 1852 they were giving serious thought to establishing a community of their own. There were, however, two serious problems: they did not know where to look for land, and even if they found it, they had no money with which to purchase it.

Andrew knew that finding a suitable location for the little congregation would not be easy, but he soon received help from a surprising source—Ole Larsen. Andrew's friend, previously the owner of a boarding house in Buffalo, had moved with his family to Fort Howard in 1851, and he and Andrew had resumed their friendship at that time. About a year later the Larsens moved 75 miles north of Fort Howard to Door County, a 50-mile-long peninsula extending northward into Lake Michigan, with the broad waters of Green Bay to the west. Here Larsen purchased Eagle Island and "was carrying on a business in fishing and firewood." In the fall of 1852, he made a visit to Fort Howard and told Andrew about the beautiful, heavily forested, government land that lay near his home. He offered his assistance should Andrew decide to investigate this area, which fronted on Eagle Harbor along the west side of the peninsula. Andrew was elated and "treasured this piece of news in my heart."

Because he wrote frequently to Church leaders in Bethlehem, they were well aware of Andrew's situation in Wisconsin. Most of his letters were addressed to his friend, editor, and supporter, H. A. Schultz. Schultz had grown to feel paternalistic toward Andrew and he admired the young preacher's enthusiasm for pioneer life. Late in 1852, Schultz responded to Andrew's plight by agreeing to loan the congregation $500 with which to purchase land; the loan was be repaid over a ten year period and required a legal bond in the name of Andrew M. Iverson.

Andrew was overjoyed when he received word of the loan, and he immediately spread the news to those he trusted. At last he had the means to establish his Moravian colony, and equally important, he once again had control over his destiny. The aftermath of the prolonged battle of wills with Tank was over. Tank's strong mindedness and cultural sophistication had grated against Andrew's stubbornness and unrefined nature. Now members of his small congregation would look to him alone for both spiritual and worldly guidance. He relished his new position of influence and independence. His prayers had been answered and he praised God for His blessing.

Andrew promptly dispatched a letter to Schultz in Bethlehem, "informing him of our poor congregation's joy over his beneficent offer, which was received with great thanks." He also told Schultz that they "had been informed about a locality not far distant where there was rich government land and good fishing." When the promised $500 arrived, Andrew immediately began making plans for the "long, weary journey over the ice." Congregation members Gabriel Wathne and Abraham Oneson volunteered to accompany him, and on a cold February day in 1853, with the prayers of the congregation following them, the three men set out on foot to investigate the land Ole Larsen had praised—the land that was to become Ephraim.

****

Thus Andrew Iverson, Gabriel Wathne, and Abraham Oneson, joined by Melchior Jacobs in Sturgeon Bay, undertook the fateful expedition that resulted in their arrival at Ole Larsen's home in February, followed by their day-long exploration of the available government land around Eagle Harbor. That day their future was determined when, during Andrew's prayer for guidance, the Lord assured him that this was the spot for his little congregation. Tired but excited, the group stood along the shore and imagined a Moravian colony overlooking the beautiful bay. "Well satisfied ... we returned over the ice ... and reached our friend Larsen's home where a splendid dinner awaited us. Before partaking of the meal, however, I offered sincere thanks to the Lord for all His mercy and guidance bestowed upon us."

After dinner "a lively conversation took place. Diagrams and charts were unfolded and studied. I discovered that with the $500 which we had borrowed we could probably acquire a tract of land a mile along the water-front and running back three-quarters of a mile." Larsen generously agreed to use his horse and sleigh to take Andrew on the long trip to the land office at Menasha to purchase the tract. Jacobs accompanied the party as far as Sturgeon Bay and Oneson and Wathne got off at Fort Howard. The congregation at Fort Howard had been awaiting news of the expedition, "and there was great joy when they learned of our successful reconnaissance." Larsen and Andrew then left Fort Howard for the three-day trip to Menasha, where Andrew used most of the $500 loan to purchase 425 acres of government land. This was the wilderness land along Eagle Harbor that was to become the community of Ephraim. With Andrew's guidance, the name of the village was chosen by the congregation. "I suggested several Biblical names from which they chose the name 'Ephraim,' a name which has remained to this day." (It is curious that in his recollections Andrew fails to mention that the Green Bay settlement had also been named Ephraim)

In the spring of 1853, planning for the move to Eagle Harbor began in earnest. Andrew was 29 years old when he undertook the great effort necessary to shepherd his small flock northward. Ole Larsen had agreed that the congregation could use Eagle Island as a base camp from which to row to shore to fell trees and clear land for the settlement. Andrew and his family had been invited to share the Larsens' house, and others would erect temporary shanties on the island.

Andrew gave a great deal of thought to how to subdivide the land. He decided that town lots should be about one and a half acres in size, while larger outlying tracts of about 10 acres could be used for farming. Members of the congregation agreed with his overall plan, and in his spare time he used his artistic skills to make a fairly detailed map of the newly purchased land. On his plan he "laid out the congregation's village in blocks and lots, with streets and roads." Later, when the county surveyed the area, Andrew's plat map was accepted, with only a few modifications, as the official survey of the village boundaries (see Figs. 2 and 3).

The manner in which Andrew laid out the proposed village was in many ways very similar to the design used by Tank for the Green Bay colony, although Andrew probably did not take time to consider that Tank deserved any credit. In spite of the similarities of the two village plans, there was one very important difference—in the new Ephraim the settlers would have titles to their land.

IVERSON'S PLAT MAP OF EPHRAIM

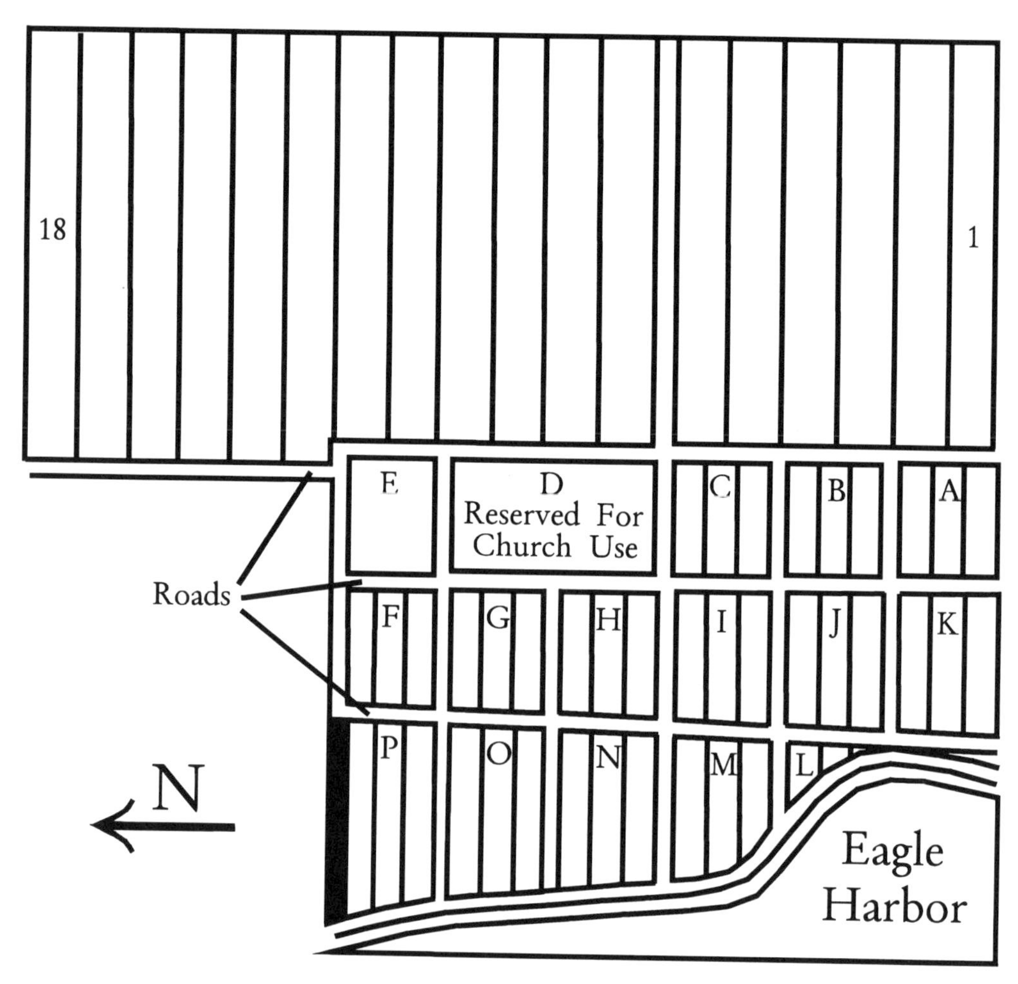

FIGURE 2 — Diagram based on Andrew Iverson's original plat map of Ephraim. The original plat is recorded in Deed Vol. B, p. 301, in the office of the Register of Deeds in Sturgeon Bay. All the parcels are numbered. Fifty-eight lots are shown, plus large lots D, designated for church use, and E, which was intended for public use. The roads laid out by Iverson exist today and some retain their original names, although Willow and Church Streets have been partly abandoned. Four north-south streets are shown, beginning with Norway at the top, Dane and Moravia in the center, and Water Street along the shore at the bottom. For further detail, see Fig. 3.

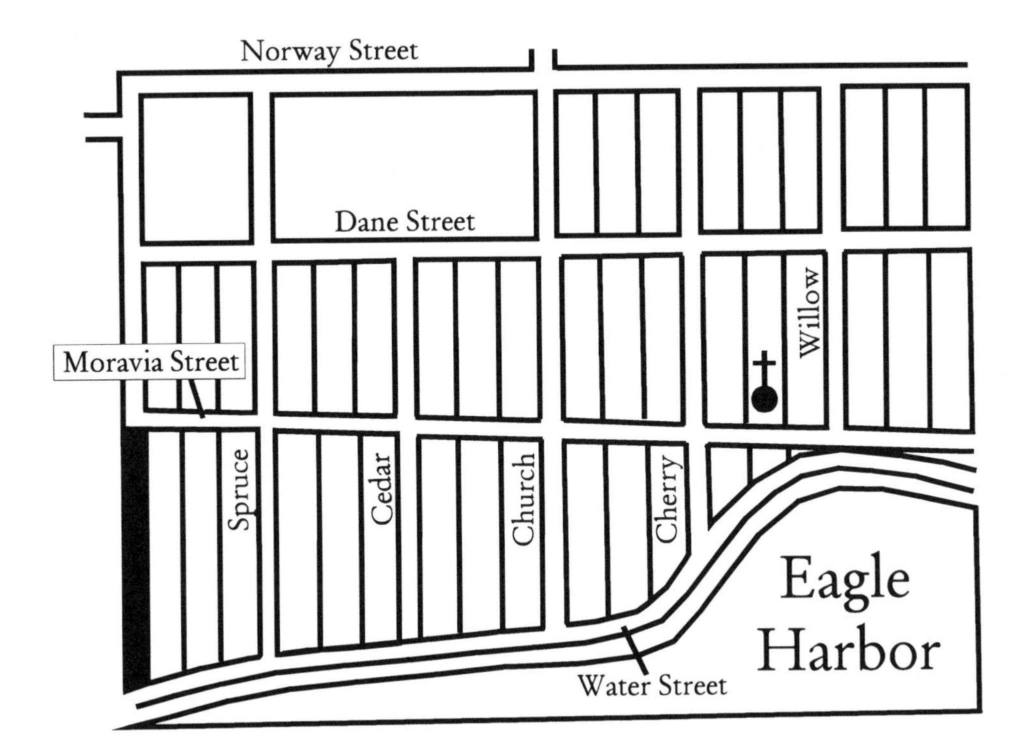

FIGURE 3 — Detail of Fig. 2, showing the streets laid out by Iverson and the present site of the Moravian church building. Before 1883 the church was located along the shore near the intersection of Church and Water Streets.

****

By mid-May of 1853 preparations for the move to Eagle Harbor were complete. Congregation members Zacharias Wathne, Henry Johnson, and Abraham Oneson planned to join Andrew in the move, along with H.P. (Hans) Jacobs of Sturgeon Bay. Others were to come later. Andrew's family, which now included his 10-month-old son, Alfred, was the first to depart. Laura and Alfred and all their belongings left Green Bay for Eagle Island on the little steamer *Columbia*. Andrew, however, sailed from Green Bay on a sailboat he designed and built himself. His sailing ship, constructed during the summer and fall of the previous year, was his pride and joy. It represented hours of thoughtful effort and was the product of Andrew's superb carpentry and woodworking skills. He describes its construction as follows.

> "As early as the spring of 1852 I had considered the construction of a large sail-boat, with a 24 foot keel, designed according to the rules of shipbuilders which I had studied somewhat while residing in Norway with my brother-in-law who was a master shipbuilder. Moreover, I was experienced in the handling of all kinds of tools and hundreds of times this ability stood me in good stead. This piece of work progressed slowly but the boat was not finished before late in the fall [and was] a real wonder to the many spectators. An American boat-builder who critically inspected this boat while still on land expressed the opinion that its lines were absolutely correct and he ventured to say that the boat would be a good sailor and never capsize. This prediction proved to be true for shortly afterwards we launched it on the Fox River and with its three masts and four sails it shot away like an arrow to the amazement of many. Some refined Americans made the statement that it was worth $200.00. It remained on land for the winter and in the spring of 1853 I made a few improvements and as soon as the ice had disappeared, I launched it again. I gave it the name 'DUEN' (The Dove). Furthermore, I had whittled out of wood a Dove, natural size, which I had placed in the bow of the boat."

The morning after his family departed on the steamer, Andrew and Gabriel Wathne loaded up *The Dove* and sailed from Green Bay to Eagle Island, arriving the same evening. Over the next few weeks, more of the colonists arrived at

Eagle Island and quickly erected shanties for themselves and their families. Andrew and his family stayed in the Larsen cabin in a large room with an attached lean-to as a kitchen.

Although he was eager to begin staking out lots on their newly acquired land, Andrew waited for the arrival of H.P. Jacobs, who was the one member of the group with substantial mathematical skills. As a graduate of the Royal Academy of Navigation in Denmark he had sailed both the Atlantic Ocean and the Great Lakes as a ship's navigator. As soon as Jacobs arrived, Andrew organized a party to travel across the bay to begin staking out lots. This involved making careful measurements with a chain rod and pocket compass, using the section lines as boundaries, and then defining individual lots by blazing trees with an ax.

After several days of hard work, nine streets and 43 building lots had been marked, including 10 acres set aside for church purposes. The congregation looked forward to someday building their own church. Two lots were set aside for Andrew and his family, and the settlers agreed that anyone intending to build a house could have one lot fronting the water and another one in the rear. Each of the small village lots would sell for $4.00. Lots were selected for clearing by Zacharias Wathne, Henry Johnson, H.P. Jacobs, and Abraham Oneson. Andrew considered these four men to be "the first pioneers in Ephraim."

Even while measuring and marking village lots, the settlers began the strenuous task of felling trees and clearing the densely forested land. Work crews rowed over from Eagle Island carrying axes, two-man crosscut saws, ropes, and other tools, along with enough provisions to last the day. H.P. Jacobs found the forest to be so dense that when his boat reached shore he had to step out with an ax and clear a place to unload. Andrew, assisted by two unmarried members of the congregation, began clearing his property. Others worked equally diligently on their own parcels, and sweating workers created great piles of brush and tree limbs. The forest rang with the thumping of ax blades as they bit into the stout trees lining the shore, and joyous yells accompanied the toppling of trees.

By afternoon of the first day plumes of smoke from burning piles of brush announced that a wilderness had begun to give way to man's hand. The trimmed trunks of larger trees were carefully set aside to provide walls for the primitive log buildings that would soon begin to dot the clearings. Family members back on Eagle Island watched the smoke rising from the distant shore as gaps in the forest began to appear. It was an exciting time, and in the evening the men returned to Eagle Island to share the excitement with their families and to talk about the future.

Day after day the settlers labored with renewed spirit, eager to leave the island for their new life in Ephraim. They shouted words of encouragement back and forth. Zacharias Wathne was the first to complete a log house for his wife and two sons. It was a primitive structure with log walls, a bark roof, and no windows, but to the Wathnes it seemed "very comfortable." After months of turmoil and uncertainty they at last had their own home on their own piece of land. The second house was built by Abraham Oneson, who had fully recovered from his scare on the ice a few months before. A carpenter by trade, Oneson carefully constructed a two-room log house that, for the moment at least, was the finest house in Ephraim.

The third house to be completed was Andrew's. Members of the congregation were of the opinion that the Iversons' house "ought to be the best and the largest." Andrew did not disagree. Acting as his own architect, he drew up a plan that included two brick chimneys and eleven glass windows. The house measured 24 x 36 feet and was to be situated up on the hill at the south end of Eagle Harbor with a splendid view to the west.

The construction of this superbly built house was a cooperative effort. For most of the summer of 1853, Andrew's helpers were Even Nelson and Peter Weborg, who made regular trips from Fish Creek, about four miles south of Ephraim. Nelson was a fine barrel maker (cooper), who was also known for his ability to hew logs with great speed and precision. Every log used in the house was hewn flat and fitted carefully into place. Neighbors made shingles for the roof, and Andrew himself made the doors, windows, and trim pieces. He gave special thought to the entry door that would welcome his neighbors, and he decided the door should open to the north, because most of the villagers lived in that direction. Beside the front door he set a vertical tier of four small windows through which neighbors could be seen as they came to visit, and at night a welcoming lamp could be placed inside on the bottom sill. As did other settlers, Andrew constructed primitive tables and chairs to use until he had time to make nicer furniture.

Andrew and his family moved into their house in November. Its completion was significant to everyone in the small settlement, because until a church could be built, the dwelling's main room would be used for church services. This room, with its exposed ceiling beams, reminded many parishioners of the homes they left behind in Norway. Well over a century later the house continues to watch quietly over the harbor as a monument to the lives of the hardy Moravians who made a community for themselves in such an isolated place.

****

As autumn of 1853 drew to a close the settlers made final preparations for the long winter ahead. They stockpiled provisions, carefully examined the condition of log walls, and forced additional chinking into place between logs wherever needed. They spent many hours cutting and stacking firewood near the four completed houses. Winter began to set in before all the settlers had finished their homes, and those with unfinished houses were invited to move in with those who had shelter. Eighteen people spent that first winter in Ephraim. There were five couples, four children, and four unmarried men.

By late November there were a few snow flurries, and it was with awe and considerable apprehension that members of the little community watched a skim of ice form on the bay and then break up into a slurry of shoreline ice that became, almost overnight, thousands of hexagonal plates. As they walked along the shoreline on a still day the settlers could hear the swishing sound of the plates of ice rubbing against each other as the bay began to slowly freeze over. By mid-winter, three and a half feet of snow covered the ground and the tiny settlement was now utterly isolated in a frozen land alongside a thick sheet of groaning ice.

That first Christmas in Ephraim was a special occasion for the settlers. On Christmas day the group was joined by the Ole Larsen family from Eagle Island and the families of Even Nelson, Peter Weborg, and Asa Thorp from Fish Creek. Andrew, Laura, and their two-year-old son, Alfred, warmly welcomed villagers and friends for services in the living room of their new home. On that festive occasion, Andrew preached a sermon of thankfulness and everyone participated in Holy Communion. The next day two church meetings were held as the Moravian settlers continued to share in the joy of the season and count their blessings—they had their independence, their own property, and a beautiful and bountiful area in which to live.

As winter progressed, the men continued to cut timber and clear land whenever weather permitted, and once the bay froze over they spent a great deal of time fishing through the ice. Often they were successful in catching large quantities of fish that provided meat for the table. Excess fish were salted and placed in barrels, most of which were made by cooper Even Nelson, and transported over the ice to Green Bay on Ole Larsen's sled. There the fish were traded for provisions or sold for cash. Although there was considerable snow that winter, their first as a community, the weather was relatively mild compared with winters to come, so it was possible to work outdoors on an intermittent basis. Fortunately, they had stockpiled enough provisions to last all winter, and the steady catch of fish, along with an occasional deer or rabbit, provided meat to supplement their potatoes and bread.

Time passed swiftly—soon the snow melt began to trickle toward the creeks and the bay ice glistened with wetness. The settlers' spirits rose as the days grew longer and sunshine began to drive away the grayness of winter. Those doing chores out-of-doors paused, then watched, and listened as flocks of geese began to appear overhead, honking directions to one another as they flew north. Spring was coming and the trillium would soon bloom. Andrew and his flock had survived their first winter in isolation.

****

When the Moravian Church ordained Andrew as a Home Missionary, it charged him with visiting and "preaching the story of the cross" to his countrymen, not only in central Wisconsin, but also in Illinois and Minnesota. He had to relinquish his mission work in Minnesota because of the great distances involved, but he was expected to make other evangelistic trips as often as possible without shirking his responsibilities to his own congregation.

There is no doubt that Andrew was committed to a traveling ministry, for he willingly undertook many taxing trips, often traveling great distances on foot. Although not a large person, his wiry frame was vested with physical endurance that easily equaled his spiritual stamina. In 1853 alone, while in the midst of clearing land and building houses in Ephraim, he found time to make four trips to the Cooperstown and New Denmark area, two to Mishicot, three to Fort Howard, and one to Chicago.

In the summer Andrew frequently sought passage to Green Bay on a southbound sailing ship; in the winter he occasionally accompanied Ole Larsen and his pony-powered ice sled on trips to Green Bay to sell fish. After arriving in Green Bay he would continue his mission work on foot—to Fort Howard, New Denmark, and Mishicot. It was 20 miles from Fort Howard to New Denmark and another 10 or so miles to Mishicot. He often returned to Ephraim from Green Bay on foot. The return trip would take two or three days, with stops along the way to spend the night with acquaintances who had built log houses in the wilderness. Such houses were few and far between, and winter weather could change quickly and imperil any unprepared traveler. There is no doubt that Andrew's travels on foot were arduous and that he frequently exposed himself to considerable danger.

****

The first spring in Ephraim (1854) was a time of intense activity—there was much to be accomplished and not many months of warm weather would be available. Logging and land clearing continued and once again smoke from burning piles of brush rose over the settlement. The fifth house was erected during the spring and a sixth house appeared that summer.

As soon as weather permitted, settlers began planting small vegetable gardens in recently cleared areas. They set out potatoes and corn in abundance but included other vegetables as well. The crops were planted with anticipation and hope. Everyone believed the soil to be fertile and they expected an adequate, or even abundant, harvest. The seeds germinated on schedule, but many of the tiny plants were devoured by insect larvae. Although most of the potatoes and corn were spared, the overall harvest was dangerously meager.

The crop failure was a cause of grave concern, because lack of provisions would mean an occasional long hike to Green Bay by men of the village. Without trails or roads, they would have to follow the rocky shoreline, and this required several days of travel. If they were lucky, after buying provisions they would find a schooner captain who would drop them and their supplies off at Ephraim. If they were unlucky, they would have to return to Ephraim on foot, carrying bags of food on their backs. When they encountered storms, finding shelter to keep flour and other staples from getting wet was always a problem.

During the summer seven more Norwegian families arrived to settle government land north of Ephraim. Andrew's congregation initially considered the new arrivals to be rude, uncultured, and even ignorant. "However, they came repeatedly to our services and what astonished them for a long time was that the preacher in Ephraim delivered his sermons extemporaneously and that he did not read his sermons from a paper." Andrew preached in Norwegian in a loud, strong voice, and his style was animated and vigorous. He worked hard to deliver his sermons in a simple manner and with great emotion. When he fixed his piercing gaze on worshipers, there could be no doubt that here was a man of God with a powerful message to impart. On some Sundays that summer more than 50 people, young and old, attended services in his living room.

In the spring and summer of 1854, while the settlers continued to clear land, Andrew again made trips to Fort Howard, New Denmark (Cooperstown), and Mishicot. Although New Denmark was settled mainly by Danes, he made numerous friends in the area. During the summer, members of his New Denmark congregation suggested that he might consider moving his family there for the coming winter. They were aware of the crop problems in Ephraim, and they also knew that Andrew and Laura were expecting a second child in November. The congregation told him that if he would come, they would find housing and even provide maintenance funds.

Andrew was appreciative of the offer from his followers in New Denmark, and the more he thought about it the better he liked the idea. It would provide him with a respite from the harsh frontier life in Ephraim, for he became somewhat depressed when he thought about another lonely winter on Eagle Harbor. In a letter to Bethlehem dated August 23, 1854, he wrote that "only a few of our brothers and sisters are left at the present time and if there were not so many of our countrymen around us who regularly come to our meetings, I would consider it a sin to stay here alone." Since he put so much emotion into his preaching, he felt the need to minister to a larger audience than would be available in isolated Ephraim, and in New Denmark he would have the opportunity to preach to a hundred or so believers.

Andrew also told church leaders in Bethlehem that he and his family suffered from the "pressing poverty" of life in Ephraim, and he complained that his clothes "are so worn that I am ashamed to let myself be seen in Green Bay." In addition he expressed unhappiness that some of the settlers had sought better living conditions elsewhere. Church leaders in Bethlehem responded to his complaints by granting his request to spend the winter in New Denmark, with the understanding that the assignment was only temporary.

It was with sadness, and undoubtedly some guilt, that Andrew presented his last sermon in Ephraim before departing for New Denmark. The separation was "touching" and everyone was "bathed in tears" as they said goodbye in October 1854. Zacharias Wathne had agreed to conduct services in the Iverson home, and God willing, during the course of the winter Andrew would pay Ephraim a long visit.

The Iverson family departed on a northbound steamer which took them around the tip of the peninsula and then south to Manitowoc. They traveled the rest of the way to New Denmark in ox-drawn wagons, a distance of about 20 miles. The oxen moved slowly over the rutted and bumpy roads, and the trip was extremely stressful for Laura, whose baby was due in just a few weeks. Two and a half-year-old Alfred, however, arrived in a "very lively" state.

Since housing was scarce in New Denmark, the Iversons stayed in the home of a fellow Norwegian named Peter Peterson. Peterson and his wife Mary had lived briefly in Michigan and from there they had moved to New Denmark. Mary had joined her husband-to-be in America, crossing the Atlantic with Aslag and Halvor Anderson, two brothers from Norway. In Michigan the Anderson brothers worked with Peterson at a sawmill. Although they lost contact with one another after Peterson and his wife left for New Denmark, fate would reunite the Anderson brothers with their old friend several years later.

Andrew greatly enjoyed his winter ministry in New Denmark. He preached in a large building that served as a combination school and town hall, and his congregation was made up of about a hundred men, women, and children, many of them Danes of the Lutheran or Baptist faiths. He also gave weekly confirmation instruction to five young people. He was disappointed, however, that in spite of the fervor of his preaching so few souls were publicly converted by his efforts. On November 5 he received an early Christmas present when his wife gave birth to "another little charming daughter" who was named Anna Munda Eleonora, in honor of her sister, Anna Munda Laurenze, who had died on the ship traveling from Milwaukee to Green Bay.

Sometime in January Andrew's contentment was shaken by bad news. The schooner preparing to deliver supplies to the settlers in Ephraim had become trapped in ice at Green Bay, meaning that his friends would have to struggle along as best they could with what they had on hand. It would be a long winter for them, and Andrew began to think seriously about his promise to return to Ephraim for a visit. His spirits had been lifted by his warm reception in New Denmark and the opportunity to minister to larger groups of worshipers, but his thoughts often turned to Eagle Harbor and Ephraim, his "real and dear home." He worried about the hardships his countrymen might suffer as they waited out the winter, and he felt guilty about not being with them to bolster their spirits.

Without roads, the only way to travel to Ephraim in wintertime was over the ice, so his trip had to await word that Green Bay was frozen along the Door Peninsula. By the time January slipped into February, Andrew began asking travelers about ice conditions on Green Bay. Although he did not relish the long, difficult trip back to Ephraim, Andrew was worried about his friends and eager to find a way to visit them that winter. After all, he had made them a promise.

4

1855 AND 1856

When Andrew decided to honor his pledge to friends and parishioners in Ephraim that he would return for a visit during the winter, he never guessed that the journey would nearly cost him his life. Toward the end of February 1855 he received word that Green Bay was solidly frozen, and he began preparing for the long trip back to Ephraim. Bundling up in his warmest clothing he said goodbye to his family, and early in the morning he left New Denmark on foot. He arrived at Fort Howard at the end of a long day and spent the night with friends.

The next day he heard that several sawmill workers were leaving the following afternoon by horse and sleigh for Sturgeon Bay, and he quickly made arrangements to join them. Although the trip took two days, with an overnight stop at Bay Settlement (about six miles north of Fort Howard), they were in excellent shape and in good spirits when they arrived in Sturgeon Bay on a Friday. Andrew stayed in Sturgeon Bay on Saturday and after preaching on Sunday, he spent the night with H.P. Hanson. Hanson was a friend and fellow Moravian whose house was located near the edge of the ice-covered bay a mile or so from town. Andrew planned to leave the next morning and walk over the ice of Green Bay all the way to Ephraim, a distance of almost 30 miles.

During the night the temperature dropped and a raging blizzard developed, trapping everyone inside their houses for three days. It was obvious that venturing out for even a short time could be life-threatening. By Wednesday evening the intensity of the storm had diminished enough for Andrew to consider resuming his trip northward. Unfortunately, there was a serious problem—over four feet of snow had fallen.

Hanson argued that it would be foolhardy to try to reach Ephraim on foot, but Andrew was eager to get on with the journey. He pondered the situation—he was close to Ephraim and yet it seemed far away, especially under the existing conditions. When he discovered that his host had a fine pair of seven-foot-long Norwegian skis, he began to think about making an attempt to reach Ephraim in spite of the waist-deep snow. As a boy Andrew had often used such skis, and he knew their length would buoy him up and help him move through the snow and deep drifts. Although Hanson was willing to loan the skis, he argued that making the trip alone would be very hazardous, because there were no settlers along the many miles of shoreline between Sturgeon Bay and Fish Creek. Despite Hanson's warning, Andrew was determined to proceed "provided the weather was good."

Thursday morning the sky was clear but the temperature was bone-chilling. After a hearty breakfast and lots of coffee, Andrew paused to pray and ask God to provide him with strength and protection. He pulled his flannel-lined "Indian Rubber" boots over several layers of socks, struggled into his overcoat, and pulled on the warm cap that would protect his ears from frostbite. Mrs. Hanson had stuffed his backpack with provisions, and once the pack was in place, he said a fond goodbye to his hosts, slipped on his skis, adjusted his gloves, and pushed through the drifts out onto the frozen bay. He made good progress all that morning and about noon he paused to eat lunch, or "dinner" as it was called in those days. He used some large blocks of ice as a picnic table, said a short prayer, and then enjoyed the generous meal prepared by Mrs. Hanson. The beautiful snow-covered setting elevated his spirits as he anticipated seeing friends in Ephraim. He missed having a cup of hot coffee to go with his meal, or even a drink of water, but the only available water was that on which he stood or the drifted snow on its surface. After eating Andrew stiffly lifted himself off his ice chair, adjusted his backpack, and pressed on. He was glad to get moving again, for while he was sitting the cold had begun to penetrate his sweat-soaked clothing.

By the time he reached the deserted bay called Egg Harbor, Andrew was tiring and becoming increasingly thirsty, a feeling that was impossible to quench by eating snow. As his legs weakened his pace diminished, and he often had to stop and rest before he could continue. At the same time his thirst continued to grow in intensity. By now he was becoming alarmed—and very tired. He knew he might never get up if he lay down to rest in the deep snow, so he forced himself to keep going.

Daylight wanes early in February in northern Wisconsin, and just as dusk was becoming darkness and the sun's reassurance was about to be lost to the frigid winter night, Andrew looked up from his misery and saw Even Nelson's house in the distance, about two miles ahead. Thank God! His prayers were about to be answered. He had nearly reached Fish Creek.

In his struggle over the past few hours, he had failed to notice that clouds were appearing overhead and that the wind had begun to blow from the northeast. The intensity of the wind picked up quickly, and with little warning Andrew found himself enveloped in a blizzard. Leaning into gale winds and blowing snow, he fought to maintain his bearings and stay upright on his skis, which now felt like great weights suspended from his legs.

When he was able to look up he caught a glimpse of light from Nelson's house, but before he could give thanks he felt an agonizing pain in his right knee just before it stiffened and locked into place. This was the most pain he had ever suffered, and he stood there with tears in his eyes, unable to move, with the storm swirling around him. He knew he was now in serious trouble, for he might well freeze to death within sight of Nelson's warm cabin. He rubbed the knee vigorously and just as vigorously he prayed for his life. "I turned to the Lord of Life and Death, my savior, in deep prayer and told him in childish innocence of my present predicament and danger, [and] just as I uttered the 'amen,' I discovered that I could move my right knee again. With great joy I began to move onward, exerting my exhausted strength all I could, [with] Nelson's lamplight beckoning to me encouragingly. But alas! I had hardly advanced one-twelfth of a mile before the same very painful stiffness again seized me, and there I stood, unable to move again."

Andrew fought to keep going in spite of the pain and stiffness in his knee that at times forced him to stop and wait until limited movement returned. During such stops he prayed and gasped for air, not daring to sit down. At about 10 o'clock in the evening, many hours after first seeing the light of the Nelson cabin, Andrew reached the shoreline just below the steep hill leading up to the house. He raised his head and "shouted" out his thanks to God as he quickly removed his skis and lay panting on the bank. Resisting the urge to just lie there and allow the spreading numbness to smother his pain, he tried to get to his feet and make his way up the trail. After falling several times he gave up and began to crawl toward the house. Slowly he inched his way along through the snow, dragging his stiff leg and raving "like a drunken man," until he reached the house. The light was still on as he pulled himself up and knocked feebly. Nelson opened the door and stared in disbelief at the staggering ghost that lurched over the threshold and threw itself into a chair. He quickly recognized Andrew, who in a throaty mumble begged for water. Nelson and his astonished wife wasted no time in meeting his request.

After warming up and drinking his fill of water, Andrew recounted his adventure. The Nelsons were dumbfounded—there was no doubt in their minds that Andrew was lucky to be alive. When their visitor pulled off his boots and socks, they discovered that most of his toes were bleeding where the ski straps had rubbed off the skin. After a cold bath, a meal of potatoes, eggs, bread, and strong coffee, Andrew expressed his deepest thanks to his hosts. He joined them in a brief and subdued devotional service, then eased himself into bed. It had been a close call, but he had survived.

Late the next morning Andrew decided that in spite of his painful toes he would be able to continue the few miles to Eagle Harbor. He was eager to be in his own home. Nelson and his neighbor, Peter Weborg, who both had skis, traveled with Andrew to Ole Larsen's place on Eagle Island. When they arrived at the island, Larsen greeted them with great pleasure and was astounded to learn that Andrew had been alone on the ice when the blizzard hit and had barely made it to the Nelsons' house. Larsen and his wife were greatly concerned about Andrew's welfare, for they always treated him as if he were a member of their own family. After making certain Andrew was comfortable, Larsen told him that the congregation in Ephraim was in good health and spirits. With special pleasure, he mentioned that his daughter, Pauline, had been holding classes for children of the Ephraim area. She conducted schoolwork in both Norwegian and English.

Even though Andrew admitted he was quite tired, by late afternoon he declared that he could wait no longer to see his friends in Ephraim. Larsen accompanied him across the snow-covered ice. At their first stop, the house where Pauline Larsen was teaching school, Andrew was warmly received. He took the opportunity to make a little speech to the children and offered a prayer. After visiting briefly with his daughter, Ole Larsen returned to Eagle Island. Andrew skied alone along the bay to visit other homes, most of which were almost buried by snow. He was enthusiastically received at every house. There was much handshaking and laughter as Andrew greeted each settler. Later that evening he held a special prayer service, and in his recollections Andrew recalled what a wonderful evening it was as "we fell upon our knees and [humbly offered] prayers of thanks and deep sincerity, mingled with many tender tears ...."

Over eight days, Andrew visited homes and had heart-to-heart talks with his friends. He also held frequent services, and he wrote that they were "heart-touching and blessed, especially when we celebrated Holy Communion." Andrew felt strongly about the importance of bringing the word of God to impoverished settlers, and part of his message was that earthly poverty was nothing compared to the suffering of Christ in behalf of man. Ever the evangelist, he often reminded the colonists that their earthly hardships were of little consequence and that their faith would provide reward. Andrew loved his followers in Ephraim. They were his friends and they shared a common heritage. They had been through a lot together, and he was willing to place himself at risk in their behalf. After all, they had believed in him enough to follow him into a wilderness to try to establish a better life for themselves.

On the last day of his visit Andrew conducted a farewell service and prayer meeting where "our tears flowed again." He promised his followers that, God willing, he would return soon with his family. The next morning he began the trip south in the company of four sturdy settlers who wanted to ensure his safe travel to Green Bay. The snow had acquired a hard crust and their Norwegian skis skimmed the surface as if it were glass.

The party moved easily and with great speed, but when they were within three or four miles of Sturgeon Bay, Andrew received a grim reminder of how dangerous it was to travel alone in sparsely populated Door County in the wintertime. As the group took a brief rest about a half-mile out from shore, Andrew saw what he thought was a large dog sitting in the snow along the shoreline. The dog looked strange and it seemed to be slowly moving its head from side to side. How on earth had a dog managed to find its way to this remote place? Andrew recalled seeing a deserted house about a half-mile back, but no one lived in the area. The five men skied toward the slowly moving animal and their eyes widened as they discovered "a man, completely exhausted and frozen, sitting in the snow, with bare hands, frozen stiff, but moving his head which was covered with a black cap."

Under Andrew's direction, they made a crude litter out of light cedar posts found along the shore and covered it with overcoats. They placed the frozen man on the conveyance, and each member of the group supported part of it as they slowly made their way on skis back to the deserted log house. The snow was three to four feet deep and the drifts were even deeper. Once they reached the primitive shelter, they used pocket knives to cut away the ice that encrusted the barely breathing man. Next they cut away his dilapidated footwear and socks, only to make the grisly discovery that both feet were frozen solid. Andrew and another member of the party decided to ski as quickly as possible to Sturgeon Bay to find help, but their frantic effort was in vain. The frozen stranger had died by the time a team of fresh horses pulling a sleigh could make it back to the deserted cabin the next morning.

The man's name was Green, according to papers Andrew found on the body before he conducted a funeral service for him. He was a lighthouse keeper in Baileys Harbor, and he was trying to reach Green Bay to receive his pay. Instead, he paid a terrible price. Andrew realized that he and the lighthouse keeper had something in common—each had subjected himself to the dangers of winter travel in an isolated area. Only one of them had survived. Andrew was both thankful and lucky.

A number of days later he returned to his family in New Denmark, on foot in deep snow. Word of his ordeal had already reached them, and they praised God for his preservation. In his recollections, Andrew summed up the days after his return as follows: "During the following two months of my stay in New Denmark, nothing unusual happened."

****

During the remainder of his stay in New Denmark, Andrew spent a great deal of time preparing five young people in his congregation for confirmation in the Church. As he began to think about his return home to Ephraim in the spring, he also devoted time to visiting with parishioners in their homes and thinking about his sermons. He was still frustrated with his inability to elicit visible signs of conversion among his churchgoers, although he "fervently prayed for it."

On the other hand, his instruction to the five youngsters, and their response, gave him much pleasure. He recalled that their tears often flowed as he talked to them about making a commitment to Jesus. No doubt Andrew's piercing eyes and intense manner, as he communicated with them on a personal level, elicited both awe and emotion in his young charges. "On a Sunday forenoon in the latter part of April 1855, before a large gathering and under deep solemnity, at the conclusion of the service which brought streams of tears, these five young and promising persons confirmed their covenant with the Holy Trinity ...." Andrew was in peak form that day, and "After this gripping scene there were persons present who wept audibly so they shook with emotion ... I am frank to say that never before had the settlers experienced as solemn an occasion as this was."

Near the end of April 1855, Andrew loaded his family's belongings into an ox-drawn wagon. He then assisted Laura, who carried Anna Munda, onto the top of the loaded wagon and helped Laura's maid and young Alfred on board. The wagonmaster cracked his whip and the wagon began creaking north toward Fort Howard. As the ox leaned into its load, Andrew followed behind leading a cow that had been given to him by the congregation in thanks for the spiritual leadership he had provided. When he described the departure scene in one of his reports to Bethlehem, church leaders greeted his description of the slowly moving procession, cow in tow, with laughter.

After spending a few days in Fort Howard, the Iversons managed to get themselves and their cow on board a northbound steamer early one morning. That same afternoon they docked in Ephraim, where a jubilant "Welcome Home" awaited them. Andrew greeted every settler with a warm smile and a handshake. He was delighted to be home. Even his cow was given a friendly reception and shown to its new quarters in the small stable built into the hill under the first floor of the Iverson residence.

Settlers spent the summer of 1855 planting crops, expanding the cleared land areas, repairing and building log homes, and extending the village even further into the surrounding forests. Andrew obtained some rocky pastureland for his cow, and he found time to gather stones from the pasture. He used these, and the ones he had saved from the excavation beneath his house, to make a stone fence along the primitive road that bordered his property to the west. Each stone was thoughtfully placed, for Andrew wanted the fence to last a long time. The beautiful wall he constructed still stands—a testament to his artistic talents and construction skills.

Andrew made several preaching trips to New Denmark and Mishicot that summer, traveling much of the way on foot. Fortunately, good weather provided a bountiful crop of potatoes and corn. Autumn passed into winter and Andrew again made trips to Fort Howard, New Denmark, and Mishicot. The deep snow he often encountered made these journeys difficult and dangerous, but he accepted such challenges as part of his mission and was sustained by his faith in God and Church. In recalling these journeys, such as a 12-mile trek from New Denmark to Mishicot in deep snow with the temperature well below freezing, Andrew remembered the warm receptions he received rather than the rigors of the trip. As an evangelist he drew strength and confidence from the knowledge that he was needed. He was God's shepherd and his flocks were scattered in the wilderness. He would go to great lengths to find them.

On one of his winter trips to Mishicot, Andrew became infuriated when he learned that his spiritual territory was being encroached upon by a few Lutherans who had moved into the area. When he heard rumors that they were trying to persuade people to stay away from his services, he began to view these stubborn interlopers as enemies.

There was growing competition among the various frontier faiths for new recruits, and with the arrival of more settlers from Scandinavia and Germany, the competition grew keener. Andrew had tremendous confidence in himself and his beliefs, but he also understood that the spirituality of others was often capricious and required constant reinforcement. The evangelist lives to convert souls, and Andrew prayed for converts. During his sermons he wept and thundered to convince listeners that his message provided the means to salvation. He wanted to be certain that his followers needed him, for he surely needed them. And to be challenged by Lutherans was the greatest threat of all. Hadn't he suffered enough at the Mission School in Stavanger when he was persecuted for resisting Lutheran indoctrination? How could he forget the anger he felt when an effort was made to send him to the strict Lutheran school in Dresden to "cure" him of his Moravian beliefs? Nevertheless, Andrew was only too willing to do his own proselytizing. When invited to Lutheran territory to preach, he welcomed the opportunity and enthusiastically accepted the challenge of delivering the word of God to those of other persuasions. Perhaps a few conversions would come from his efforts.

Andrew's letters to the Bethlehem Home Mission Society indicate that he made several preaching trips in January and February of 1856. On January 20, accompanied by two friends, he used a horse and sleigh to travel over the ice to Chambers Island, a distance of about five miles from Ephraim. In a letter published in *The Moravian*, he said he had received an invitation from a Norwegian family there, and when he arrived he was surprised to find that even the American settlers on the island had assembled to hear him speak. Although Andrew had not expected to preach to a large group, after enjoying an "excellent" dinner, he conducted a "lively meeting" which was so well-received that he was invited to preach again as soon as possible.

Four days after returning from Chambers Island, Andrew left again for Fort Howard, New Denmark, and Mishicot. It was difficult going, as were most of his winter trips. He traveled to Fort Howard with a friend who owned a horse and sleigh, but the ice was heavily cracked and had heaved into great piles. It required tremendous exertion by the horse and a great deal of zig-zagging to move through the ice walls. The tired horse and equally tired travelers finally plodded into Green Bay on January 26, two days after leaving Ephraim.

By the end of February, when Andrew finished his preaching circuit, he had been gone almost a month and was eager to return home. He considered himself lucky when he found a settler with a horse and sleigh who agreed to take him from Green Bay to Sturgeon Bay. Sad to say, he discovered that his luck was short-lived. This is how Andrew described the experience in one of his letters published in *The Moravian* (45).

> "But [when it came time] to start, on the 23rd of February, I saw that my driver was drunk. I had very little appetite to go with

him, but no other means of conveyance was to be found, and disagreeable as my position was, I was forced to submit. The poor fellow, however, had respect for my person, and after we had left Greenbay [sic], he commenced a great talk about the Moravians. When we came near to Bay Settlement, he got into a dispute with another German driver about the road. Their rage broke out in a flame, and I thought it would end in a terrible fight. Had it not been for my baggage, I would have left the sleigh and walked off. Insupportable as it was to me, I had to sit calmly there for three quarters of an hour, until they got through with their quarrel. That day we got no farther than Bay Settlement, where I persuaded my driver to stop with me over night at the house of a very friendly family with which I was acquainted. The next morning my driver was sober; and as the day was fine and the air not cold, we had quite a pleasant ride, arriving at Little Sturgeon Bay, by three o'clock, P.M. Here I passed the night. The following day, the 25th, I went afoot over the rough ice to Big Sturgeon Bay, leaving my baggage to be sent on after me in a day or two. Immediately upon my arrival, I appointed a meeting for Wednesday evening, the 27th of February; but on Tuesday, I was taken so sick that I feared I should not be able to keep any meeting at all. On Wednesday morning I felt miserable; yet exerting my little strength, I was able with the Lord's assistance to hold service twice, twice [sic] to administer the holy communion, and to baptize two children; all which transactions were performed at different houses, because no better arrangement could be made. I could not speak above a whisper. Though I felt feverish and had a headache, I nevertheless set off on the following morning, the 28th, for home, drawing a handsleigh after me on which I had about 100 pounds weight of baggage. The distance I had to travel was at least twenty-six miles. At half-past eight o'clock, P.M., I reached my house, but felt so ill that I had to go to bed immediately. It was a fortnight before I recovered my strength; then, however, I felt as well as at any time of my life, and so my health has remained ever since. Oh, how much I am indebted to the Lord for this blessing."

In June of 1856 Andrew once again prepared to travel south to spread the gospel. Details of this event-filled trip, which included the entire Iverson family, appeared in a letter published in 1857 in *The Moravian*. Laura was usually left alone during Andrew's mission travels, but this time she prevailed upon him to take her and the children with him as far as Sturgeon Bay. They would remain there with friends until he returned from his journey.

On the morning of June 7, the Iverson family and three Norwegian men left Fish Creek in an open sailboat bound for Green Bay, with a stop at Sturgeon Bay. The vessel had no cabin or other kind of protection, and after sailing a few miles they were caught in a downpour that drenched everyone on board. Unfortunately there was little wind and the boat was too large to row, so they remained becalmed in the rain for several hours. The rain finally stopped and their spirits began to lift, but after a few hours they were soaked again by a second storm.

By evening the water-logged crew and passengers had managed to make their way into Egg Harbor, only a few miles south of Fish Creek, where the Iversons spent the night with some "American friends." The next day the boat made it to Sturgeon Bay, but Andrew became ill and had to rest for a few days. In the meantime, the men who had sailed the boat from Fish Creek decided not to go to Green Bay after all, and Andrew was obliged to look for another south-bound boat. He eventually found passage with two men who were planning to sail to Green Bay as soon as the wind was favorable. Several days later Andrew said good-bye to his family and continued his journey south. When he finally arrived in Green Bay, 10 days after leaving Fish Creek, he was "trembling with cold," having spent the entire previous night sitting on the sailboat's deck "in the chill air."

Despite this trying journey, Andrew spent only three days in Green Bay. Then, staff in hand, he set out on his long walk to Cooperstown and Mishicot. He describes the trip in *The Moravian* (47).

> "On Friday, June 20th, I left Green-bay [sic] for Cooperstown. The rays of the sun poured down, on that morning, with fearful power. I travelled, as upon previous occasions, afoot, carrying a large carpet bag on my back. If the heat was so great in the early part of the day, you can imagine how it felt by noon—I cannot tell how much I suffered before I reached my place of destination. More than once I sank down, exhausted, by the wayside, panting for breath; while the perspiration flowed in large drops from every part of my body. To give you some idea of it—(and I speak nothing but the bare truth)—my large carpet bag, filled with clothes and books to the thickness of nine inches and more, was

steamed all through; not a single article in it was left dry,—all were wet, as if they had been put into lukewarm water. Whenever I lay down at the wayside, I was tormented by the musketos [sic]. At last I came to Cooperstown; my face and hands were so swollen from heat and the bites of the musketos that I did not look like myself. A home missionary, however, must make up his mind to suffer the painful, as well as to enjoy the good things that fall to his lot. At Cooperstown I was welcomed with the same cordiality as usual: there was no lack of kindness, and I certainly stood in need of it; I had even to borrow a full suit of clothes, for all my own clothing was not in a fit condition to be seen."

After preaching many times, visiting many homes, and offering spiritual guidance to all who requested it, Andrew completed his mission work on July 7. A good friend walked with him from Cooperstown back to Green Bay, carrying his carpet bag. After a few days in Green Bay, he took the steamer *Michigan* to Fish Creek, arriving a little after midnight on July 10. The following morning he walked through the woods to Ephraim, but upon reaching his house, he found it empty—his family had not yet returned from Sturgeon Bay. Two days later he and a friend who had a sailboat set out to pick up Laura and the children. He arrived in Sturgeon Bay on a Saturday, and the next day he preached a sermon and performed a marriage ceremony. Early on Monday, July 14, Andrew and his family boarded the friend's sailboat for the trip back to Ephraim. The trip north was a repetition of the earlier trip south, for again they were caught in a heavy downpour and had to wait out the storm in Egg Harbor. Once underway they worked against a head wind and sailed until midnight. It was an exhausting trip. The Iversons did not arrive in Ephraim until July 15, nearly five weeks after leaving home. Needless to say, they were relieved to be back.

In early summer of 1856, a Norwegian merchant named H. Thompson arrived to visit Ole Larsen about business of mutual interest. The merchant was a trustee of an Evangelical Lutheran congregation in Chicago, and he knew of Andrew and his ministry. Since the Lutheran congregation would be without their minister for a few months, Thompson invited Andrew to travel to Chicago and serve as a temporary replacement. He gladly accepted the invitation after receiving approval from Bethlehem, and he traveled with his family to Chicago, where they stayed in the merchant's home. Every Sunday, morning and evening, Andrew preached to several hundred Scandinavian Lutherans, and he recalled that he "was careful not to say one word against other congregations ...." In addition he held meetings during weekday evenings, which meant that he preached, in some form, seven days a week. Only someone as energetic and as devoted as Andrew could sustain such a pace, and in spite of the intensity, he thoroughly enjoyed his two months in Chicago.

Upon returning home to Ephraim, the Iversons discovered that several newly arrived Scandinavian families had settled in their neighborhood. Immigrants from Germany, Poland, and even Iceland had also begun to settle on the Door peninsula, and many more were expected. In the fall of 1856, several German families settled east of Ephraim. This was the beginning of what was commonly called the "German Settlement," an area of several hundred acres populated by farm families. The influx of settlers reminded Andrew that Ephraim was growing and was likely to become a business hub for settlers scattered throughout the area. The demand for spiritual guidance would certainly grow, and it occurred to him that his large parlor would soon have to give way to a church building. He did not have much time to ponder the changes occurring in Ephraim, however, for within a few weeks of his return, he was "obliged to start out on another mission trip to Fort Howard, New Denmark and Mishicot."

Late that fall he made yet another mission pilgrimage to Fort Howard, New Denmark, and Mishicot. Andrew was never at rest, despite the fact that these trips required great effort, yielded few converts, and brought little if any financial reward. Because the congregations in New Denmark and Mishicot were made up of poor settlers, Andrew did not expect much payment for his efforts. In fact, he told the two groups that he would like them to give what they could on every other visit. During his fall visit, Andrew understood that no collection would be taken for his services.

During his stay in Mishicot, he was walking toward the outskirts of the village to visit members of the congregation when he encountered a man who was on his way into town. He recognized the man as a bitterly outspoken critic of the Moravian cause and, in every way, an "enemy" in the competition for the souls of settlers. In his recollections, Andrew describes the incident this way:

> "I approached him fearlessly, in a friendly manner, and soon [we] greeted each other with a 'Good Morning' and a handclasp. His face showed this time nothing but friendliness and kindness and after exchanging a few words about each other's health and the weather, he began politely to express his amazement that I was able to travel so often and such long distances to see such few

> people who could contribute very little to my pay, etc. I answered him kindly but firmly that money did not in any way enter into the calculation in my coming to Mishicot, except to win souls for Christ by true conversion and in order that they might be saved, etc., and also that my friends there had done more for my support than I could expect. This answer seemed to strike deep. Before I could realize it, he pressed a banknote into my hand and begged that I would not refuse such a small gift and after I thanked him with deep feeling, we parted and said 'Good Bye.' I discovered that I had been presented with a three-dollar banknote and how very strange! It was a lesson to me that the Lord could bend even the hearts of our enemies; I praised His name and to His honor is this fact reported here."

****

As the leaves on the maple, birch, and aspen trees began to change color and days became shorter and nights cooler, the settlers of Ephraim hastened their preparations for the coming winter months. Their thoughts turned to the Christmas season and to projects that could be completed indoors. Mothers worked long hours mending winter garments and making new ones as required. Wintertime would present the settlers with an opportunity to take stock of their lives and their community and to reflect on the past year's events even as they made plans for the future.

Before returning to Ephraim from Mishicot and Fort Howard, Andrew purchased many provisions for his family and arranged to have them delivered by steamer. Once home, he joined other members of the village in preparing for the coming winter months. That summer the vegetable gardens had yielded a fine crop of foodstuffs to put up, and Andrew was proud to note that his garden alone produced 130 bushels of potatoes.

With the addition of new settlers that summer, Ephraim began to take on the appearance of a thriving village. It was a tightly knit community, for everyone was keenly aware that the colony was still an isolated oasis bordered by water on one side and dense forests on the other. They needed each other to survive, and the original settlers helped the new arrivals establish themselves. Everyone worked diligently through the autumn, anticipating the coming season when they must be self-sufficient. It was important for the new settlers to know about the severity of winters in Wisconsin and for them to understand that there would be periods when blizzards isolated them in their houses.

The year of 1857 arrived with bitterly cold winds from the north. As snow and cold enveloped Ephraim, villagers modified their daily routines to accommodate the weather. They replaced cotton garments with woolen ones, men began to wear their wool flannel underwear, and women put on quilted petticoats under their long dresses for extra warmth. They made last-minute repairs to heavy wool socks, sweaters, gloves, and mittens so they were ready to use. People moved more slowly, not only because of the heavy clothing and boots required to venture outside, but because there really was no hurry.

Winter would be here for a long time so villagers spent a great deal of time close to warm stoves. Women often sewed, knitted, or quilted during the long hours indoors; men sat around the fire and swapped stories as they smoked their pipes, drank coffee, and planned their next fishing venture out on the ice. During daylight hours, instead of blue sky they saw mainly smoke against a gray sky, and the light waned in early afternoon. Even as cold tightened its grip on the village, the settlers were sustained by the knowledge that once the light of day began to lengthen after the new year arrived, warmer weather was only a few months away.

By the end of January 1857 the ice cover on Green Bay was thick enough to support horsedrawn sleds and sleighs; its thickness was significant, because the ice was the villagers' winter roadway to the outside world. One beautiful day near the end of that month, Andrew and two young men of the village traveled 20 miles over the ice of Green Bay to Marinette and Menominee, neighboring lumbermill settlements along the border between Wisconsin and Michigan. There Andrew planned to visit his friends, the Lindquists, and conduct church services. After giving two sermons to the mainly Swedish residents of the area, he was asked to return as often as possible to "look after the need of their souls." Andrew willingly added these communities to his list of preaching places.

During the winter months, settlers in Ephraim and the surrounding area had time to ponder how quickly the wilderness was giving way to pockets of civilization. Lumber barons were financing the harvesting of forests in Door County. While settlers continued to clear land to establish their homesteads and farms, the cutting of large trees to serve the lumber industry became a dominant economic force. Many smaller trees were also felled, cut to length, and shipped south as cordwood (because it was sold by the cord) to be used as fuel. The building of Chicago and Milwaukee was well underway, and tremendous quantities of lumber were needed to sustain their growth and fuel their furnaces. A surprising amount of this lumber came from the Door County area, and lumbering provided jobs for many settlers. As Chicago and Milwaukee grew, the great forests of Door County diminished.

Before Ephraim was founded and before lumbering became the economic engine of the peninsula, the modest economic base that existed was related to fishing. In the 1840s and early 1850s, fishermen populated Washington, Detroit, and Rock Islands at the tip of the peninsula. By the middle 1850s, however, the influx of European immigrants began providing manpower for the growth of lumbering in northeast Wisconsin, and sawmills and settlements appeared. Ephraim was not the only one of these settlements that became a permanent village. By the winter of 1857, Baileys Harbor was well-established as a small but active lumbering community, and six lime kilns were operating near the harbor. Settlers were beginning to populate the Sister Bay area, and land in and around Egg Harbor and Fish Creek was being cleared and settled. Growth and development of Door County had begun.

As more and more people settled the area, communities began to think about organizing themselves and establishing some kind of governmental structure. Ephraim, Fish Creek, Egg Harbor, and Baileys Harbor petitioned the State to organize themselves as the Township of Gibraltar. Presumably the characteristic rocky bluffs and outcroppings of the area inspired the name. Permission was granted by the State, and Andrew, to his surprise, was elected to the office of Town Superintendent of Public Schools. He accepted the responsibility.

Sometimes Andrew wondered whether he had too many responsibilities. He was expected to minister to the spiritual and community needs of Ephraim and simultaneously to maintain missions at Fort Howard, New Denmark, Mishicot, and the Marinette-Menominee area, as well as to conduct services at various preaching places around Door County. Now he would also be expected to minister to the educational needs of school-age children in the Township of Gibraltar. What about his obligations to his wife and small children? He sometimes worried about his wife, for she often did not feel well and seemed to have a frail constitution. It was important to Andrew that so many people needed him, but how would he find time for them all? Andrew prayed that God would help him find a way.

5

GOOD TIMES AND BAD TIMES

The early settlers of Ephraim were sturdy, hard-working pioneers who suffered the hard times and praised God for the good times. There were plenty of both during the period from 1857 to 1859. These were eventful years, and the community was tested in many ways. Villagers looked to Andrew for leadership during both good and bad times, and he tried his best to be there when needed. In addition to his devotion to Ephraim, Andrew the evangelist continued to travel a wide area spreading the Lord's word to other communities. In spite of his many commitments, he would recall the period as one of growth and accomplishment for himself and his village.

From 1857 to 1859 more and more immigrants joined those already established in the area; among the newcomers were additional farm families from the Pomeranian Province of what would later become the Republic of Germany. They came because immigrants who had settled east of Ephraim wrote to family and friends in Europe about the availability of land and the opportunity to be part of a growing nation free of oppression. The established settlers went out of their way to welcome the newcomers, and Andrew's congregation continued to grow.

Andrew usually conducted church services in Norwegian, because this was the language with which most of the villagers were comfortable, but he could also preach in German and English. Church meetings at his house were crowded events, with people gathering around as best they could. On April 8, 1857, seven adults were confirmed. On May 28, after much preparation by Andrew, seven young people were added to the growing fold. Andrew always took a special interest in bringing children and young adults into the church, for in them he saw promise for Ephraim's future.

The winter of 1856-57 was a difficult one for Door County settlers, not so much because of the cold, but because it seemed to go on and on. After February, provisions began to dwindle rapidly, and meals often consisted of potatoes, a little bread, and occasionally some meat, usually fish. Finally in early May ice left the harbors of Green Bay and ship traffic could resume. On May 8 a ship from Chicago loaded with $8,000 worth of supplies arrived in Sturgeon Bay; others soon followed carrying much-needed provisions to the remote coastal villages of Door County.

The settlers hoped their food supply would be replenished by a bountiful crop of garden vegetables, but they were to be disappointed. The summer of 1857 was so hot and dry that vegetable and grain crops struggled to survive. Settlers again began to worry about how they were going to provide food for their families during the coming winter.

The congregation's spirits rose when Andrew announced with pride that a fund-raising drive in Bethlehem had raised a small amount of money to be used for a church building in Ephraim. As soon as the funds arrived, Andrew met with his congregation and asked families to contribute any amount they could toward construction of a church. To his surprise the total amount collected was enough to allow the congregation to begin work on a building measuring 24 feet wide, 40 feet long, and 16 feet high.

Men of the congregation vigorously debated the location of the church. Andrew had already surveyed an area just north of his house on the hill, and he argued that this should be the site for the church. He was strongly opposed by several parishioners who wanted it built along the shore in an area called the "commons." They insisted it would be too expensive to carry timbers and boards up the hill and far more convenient to build it along the shore. Although Andrew longed to have the church on the hill where "all could see it," he yielded to his opposition to keep peace in the congregation.

Andrew engaged the services of a flat-bottom schooner, operated by Captain David Clough of Chambers Island, to pick up and deliver lumber from Cedar River, just north of Menominee, Michigan. When Clough arrived in Ephraim to begin the three-day trip, he informed Andrew that he had no crew. As a result, Andrew was obliged to take an unexpected voyage as the ship's one and only deck hand—and cook. "The friendly mill-owners in Cedar River gave me a good discount when the amount was figured out and I was invited to take my meals in their house while the boat was being loaded with lumber and Capt. Clough was then obliged to be his own cook." When the ship returned to Ephraim, villagers assisted in unloading the supply of lumber Andrew had carefully selected to become part of God's house in Ephraim. Since suitable foundation stones were not available along the shore, it was necessary to transport stones to the site on a sled pulled by the only pair of oxen in the village. Andrew took the opportunity to remind several of his friends that for what it cost to bring in the stones, the lumber could just as cheaply have been taken up to the site on the hill where foundation stones were abundant.

The congregation could not afford skilled carpenters, but several members agreed to help with the framing, although they required Andrew's constant supervision as he worked alongside them during the hot summer months. In a letter to church leaders in Bethlehem, Andrew mentioned that if they had been on the scene during construction of the church, they would have "seen the poor spiritual leader of Ephraim, at the same time the chief carpenter at the church building." With steady effort, even in Andrew's absence, workers managed to frame the building and complete the roof by autumn. They also constructed a steeple that Andrew, the architect, felt was "too small according to my drawings and my taste...." Little could be done about the undersized steeple, however, for building funds ran out and construction of the church had to be abandoned—its completion would have to await better times. For the moment, villagers had to deal with the more immediate problem of food shortages. As early autumn approached, the community had to face the fact that the unusually hot summer had resulted in dismal crop yields. There was growing unease about how they were going to obtain food and other supplies for the winter ahead. They were running out of time.

Andrew did what he could to bolster morale in the village, and he spent many hours thinking about how to obtain provisions for winter. Finally he persuaded all but one of the men of the village to sail with him to Green Bay on a large boat owned by Ole Larsen to seek a way to obtain badly needed supplies. On the journey south, Andrew prayed for a way to deal with the food shortage, for he knew his leadership was especially important to the community at this time.

Timing and perhaps the Good Lord answered Andrew's prayers. Shortly after arriving in Fort Howard, he received word that an Irish merchant there, a Mr. Gray, had just purchased a large schooner and was contracting for cedar fence posts to be shipped to Chicago in the spring. The merchant and his son had known Andrew when he resided in Fort Howard, and they trusted the young Moravian minister. Andrew informed the merchant of the village's needs. The businessman was sympathetic, and after some discussion they reached an agreement that by spring Andrew's congregation would have fence posts ready for pick-up by the schooner. The contract would provide Andrew and the settlers with advance credit in the merchant's store amounting to one-third of the total value of the fence posts they would prepare. Contracts were drawn for every male villager who accompanied Andrew, and Andrew himself signed a contract for 2,000 fence posts and agreed to assume responsibility for seeing that the entirety of the contract was satisfied.

The happy group set out to use their credits to obtain the needed food and supplies, with flour, sugar, salt, and coffee at the top of most lists. Many also bought a bit of tobacco. Some needed to replace worn-out items of clothing and most bought cloth that could be made into apparel. As settlers loaded their newly purchased goods on board Larsen's boat there was laughter and banter, and the trip home was a triumphant one.

One man from Andrew's congregation had stubbornly chosen not to make the trip to Green Bay. He was angry and upset, claiming he had no money and could not get credit anywhere. And he blamed Andrew for his predicament. Later that fall members of the congregation made one more boat trip to Green Bay for provisions, and again the man refused to join the group. Instead he continued to accuse Andrew of not assisting him in his hour of need. Although Andrew was taken aback by his parishioner's childish behavior, he endured the tongue lashing. Later he asked two of the church Elders to join him in meeting with the bitter colonist in hope of convincing him to cooperate in making preparations for the winter. They met with him for two hours, but he continued to insist that he would not cooperate in any way and that Andrew had failed him.

Finally Andrew gave up, exhausted, and prepared to leave. He turned to the man, and as tears filled his eyes, he said softly, "I forgive all the wrong you may have done me and my earnest prayer is that some day you will be standing by my side, saved, at the Throne of the Lamb." In an instant the settler "burst violently into tears, threw his arms about my neck and cried out in a sobbing voice: 'I acknowledge that I am the cause of all wrong and that I have sinned! Oh, forgive me, please, for everything!'" Every member of the little group then began to cry. Andrew implored everyone to kneel as he prayed for forgiveness for all sinners. Afterward the other settlers agreed to share their provisions with their repentant brother and his wife, who humbly accepted the offering and thereafter treated Andrew with consideration and kindness. Peace returned to the congregation.

****

In late autumn of 1857, the settlers began cutting and trimming the cedar fence posts they promised to have ready in the spring. Christmas and New

Year's celebrations were joyous affairs, with the gathering on New Year's day being so well attended that Andrew and Laura's house was completely packed with listeners. During a quiet moment after the final service, he thought about what an eventful year 1857 had been, the highlight of which was seeing his church begin to rise along the shore.

Andrew was thankful for many other things, too. Laura had given birth to their second son, whom they named John Huss, and his other children were well. Although the crops had failed, the Good Lord heard his pleas and no one would starve that winter. More and more people were choosing to settle the area, and this pleased him greatly because he knew his beloved Ephraim must grow to assure its future. He was confident that he was making a difference in the lives of many people, including those in his far-flung missions. He felt secure, and he was thankful for the Lord's blessing. He prayed he would continue to have the energy and endurance to meet his many responsibilities.

Whenever the weather permitted during the winter of 1857-58, villagers were busy cutting, sawing, and stacking hundreds of fence posts. Andrew carefully tallied each one, in addition to working to produce his own quota of 2,000 posts. After cutting posts to size, the men hoisted them to their shoulders and carried them down to the beach where they stacked them neatly. During breaks in the weather the crisp winter air carried the sounds of axes shaping cedar trees into fence posts, as well as the never-ending sounds of axes preparing wood for fuel. At the end of a long day of cutting and trimming posts, Andrew would stagger home "so tired that I could scarcely stand on my feet." In addition to making fence posts, he continued to visit his four mission stations and lead prayer meetings for his Ephraim congregation during the week. Each Sunday, he held services, including church school, in his house. There were also preaching places nearby where he held services regularly. In spite of his work load, Andrew recalled the winter as a very happy time when "Christ was our helper."

As soon as the ice disappeared from the bay in the spring, Andrew and a large group of villagers crowded aboard Ole Larsen's boat bound for Fort Howard. On arrival, they sought out the merchant who had ordered the posts and informed him that the entire order was now stacked carefully on the shore in Ephraim, ready for him to pick up. The settlers then received the remainder of their pay in the form of supplies and clothing. When the merchant's schooner stopped in Ephraim, it had already taken on so much cargo at previous stops that only about half of the fence posts could be loaded. The rest were left near the beach to be picked up later. For several years the piles of posts simply lay there, weathering away, until they were destroyed in a timber fire. Why they were never picked up remains a mystery.

****

Shortly after returning from one of his journeys to New Denmark and Mishicot, Andrew received a letter from the Home Mission Office in Pennsylvania. The letter announced that his friend and mentor, H.A. Schultz, would soon visit Ephraim. Andrew was first flabbergasted and then beside himself with excitement. He could hardly wait to show his fatherly friend what he had accomplished. Schultz planned to arrive on the steamship that sailed from Buffalo, New York, to Green Bay, disembarking at its Fish Creek stop.

In May of 1858, Asa Thorp from Fish Creek appeared at the door of the Iverson house just as Andrew was finishing breakfast. Thorp informed him that his visitor from Bethlehem had arrived. He was traveling with his daughter Mary and they had just stepped off the steamer; now they were awaiting transportation to Ephraim. Andrew immediately dashed down to Zacharias Wathne's house and asked him to round up some strong men and take the best boat available and row down to Fish Creek—as fast as possible! Andrew accompanied Thorp back to Fish Creek on foot using the crude path that existed between the villages. The path ran through two swampy places where a foot or so of standing water was encountered regularly; however, it was possible to manage the area without wading by walking along logs lying beside the path. Andrew and Thorp negotiated this water hazard in record time, arriving in Fish Creek shortly after the row boat from Ephraim docked.

Schultz and his young daughter, who appeared to be about 12 years of age, greeted Andrew enthusiastically. Schultz was looking forward to seeing Ephraim. Because he had faithfully published Andrew's communications about his mission work and the founding of the village in *The Moravian*, he was eager to sample the wilderness life Andrew described vividly in his letters. He was also eager to see what kind of village his $500 loan had helped establish. As they prepared to return to Ephraim, Schultz let it be known that he had a great fear of small boats. Andrew reassured his visitor and noted that the weather could not be better for safe passage on the bay. As soon as the villagers loaded the steamer trunk and other pieces of luggage into the row boat, they helped Schultz and his daughter aboard. Andrew himself took the tiller while the other men dug the long oars into the water to begin the trip north to Eagle Harbor.

As the boat glided along, Schultz and his daughter kept up a running commentary on their adventure, noting with awe the speed of the boat, the clearness of the water, the rugged shoreline, and the beauty of the area. What a thrill it was to be part of a wilderness experience! As the boat rounded the point off Nicolet Bay near Eagle Island, the great bluff came into view and the village could be seen in the distance. Schultz and his daughter were quiet for a moment as they took in the panoramic scene. They were enthralled, and Schultz cried out "Ach, es ist Alles wonderschon!"

During the week or so that Schultz spent in Ephraim, Andrew and the colonists talked with him at great length about life on the frontier. Schultz visited every family and joined many of them for dinner, asking question after question about the status of their lives. Andrew spent many hours with his visitor and reported in detail all that had happened as he labored to serve the Lord and his fellow man. It is an understatement to say that Schultz was supportive of Andrew's efforts. He was more than that—he had tremendous admiration for Andrew, and he felt toward him as he would his own son. He was greatly impressed with Andrew's dedication to the word of God and his evangelistic efforts to make Moravian teachings available to isolated settlers in a rugged land.

One Sunday during his visit, Schultz preached three times at Andrew's house, choosing to deliver his message in English rather than his native German. The house was packed for each service, and after the sermons Andrew summarized the message in Norwegian since some of the worshipers did not understand English. On several occasions, Schultz congratulated Andrew for the spirituality of his congregation. He also let Andrew know that he was pleased his loan of $500 had been used so well.

During the night before Schultz and his daughter were scheduled to depart for Fish Creek and the steamer trip back to Buffalo, the wind picked up from the northwest and the bay became covered with whitecaps. Since Schultz was not fond of either water or boats, he became agitated and fearful about trying to reach Fish Creek by water. Andrew could not convince him that there was absolutely no danger and that he and the settlers had been out in waves 10 times larger than those that now filled the bay. Finally Andrew decided the luggage should be taken to Fish Creek by boat while he and Zacharias Wathne accompanied Schultz and his daughter on foot. After saying goodbye to the congregation, the two visitors followed Andrew and Wathne along the primitive road south of the village, beside the bay, then up the hill and into the forest, southward toward Fish Creek.

Things went well until the party reached the first of the swampy areas, where Schultz refused to take a detour off the path to avoid the water. He was fearful that if they ventured off into the surrounding forest they would get lost and never find their way back to civilization. Hoping to reassure him, Andrew explained that he had used the detour many times and that they could not possibly get lost. The anxious Schultz was not persuaded. He finally decided he might be able to walk on the wet logs if Andrew was strong enough to carry his daughter. Andrew agreed, and the party hesitantly resumed their journey, with Andrew struggling along carrying Schultz's daughter in his arms as he slowly made his way through water 16 inches deep. They traversed both swamps in this manner, and after a few rest stops the party finally reached Fish Creek. The boat from Ephraim, of course, had been there quite a while following an uneventful sail from Eagle Harbor.

After Andrew and the others from Ephraim said a warm goodbye to Schultz and his daughter, they set sail for the return trip to Eagle Harbor. Everyone breathed a sigh of relief now that the intense and eventful visit with their guests from Bethlehem was over. Later Andrew learned that back in Bethlehem when Schultz described their trip through the swamp, the story was greeted with hoots of laughter.

Only a few months later, this same swampy and poorly marked path caused Andrew further distress when he found himself walking back to Ephraim from Fish Creek after disembarking the steamer from Green Bay. The steamer arrived at dusk and Andrew immediately started the trek north. As night fell he realized that a lantern would have made the hike much easier. He described his journey in a letter to *The Moravian*. "The only way I could discover that I had not lost my way, was by the sound of my footsteps, and by feeling the trees for the marks which had been hewn into them to indicate the road. I turned aside from the road several times, but always succeeding in regaining it again." About three hours later when he finally reached Ephraim, he "very much rejoiced in finding all well."

****

One of Ephraim's most industrious new residents was Peter Peterson, who encouraged by Andrew, had moved to the village from New Denmark. He helped establish commerce in Ephraim by using a small boat to operate a freight and trading service that served settlements up and down the coast. He later built and operated a general store. One of Peterson's greatest contributions to Ephraim's early growth stemmed from his friendship with Aslag and Halvor Anderson, brothers he had known in Norway, who had emigrated on the same boat with Peterson's wife-to-be. In the spring of 1858, the Anderson brothers made their way to Ephraim to visit their old friend. Peterson and the two brothers talked at length about business opportunities in Ephraim. Aslag and

Halvor were particularly interested in learning that a considerable portion of the land Andrew had purchased on behalf of the Church remained unsold.

Peterson introduced the Anderson brothers to Andrew. Aslag made the following offer: if the congregation would sell them land at the original price per acre, they would agree to build a large, deepwater pier for the village. Villagers would have free access to the pier, which would provide docking for large sailing vessels and steamships. Aslag himself would operate and maintain the dock. Andrew realized that such an economic lifeline to the outside world would be of tremendous benefit to the village, and he agreed to discuss the matter with the male members of the congregation. Meeting at Andrew's house, the men discussed every detail of the offer. They agreed that a good dock that allowed large schooners and steamships to serve the community would greatly increase their chances of selling cordwood, fence posts, shingles, and salted fish. In addition, the sale of the property would enable them to partially repay H.A. Schultz the $500 he loaned them in 1852. They unanimously decided to sell 166 acres of land to the Anderson brothers.

The news was conveyed promptly to Aslag and Halvor. Aslag received title to 110 acres of land for $124.67, while Halvor received 56 acres for $65.39. The transaction was witnessed by Peterson, Ephraim's Justice of the Peace, who was delighted that his trusted friends had decided to join him in Ephraim. Andrew also asked for and received a written statement from the principals agreeing to certain obligations and responsibilities toward members of the community regarding dock access and use.

The Andersons quickly cleared some of their land, and at the same time Aslag began assembling timbers for the dock. He started work on the pier in 1858 and finished it in 1859. Aslag played the predominant role in its construction, with help from Peterson and other villagers who were hired to lend a hand. Halvor occasionally helped out, but he was primarily interested in establishing a farm on his land, located up the hill from Aslag's property. Andrew was very supportive of the hard-working Anderson brothers. It is a testament to Aslag's enterprise that during construction of the pier and dock he also managed to build a general store nearby. Later, around 1870, he built a house and barn across the road from the store. Being located close to the dock, Anderson's Store became a focal point for area commerce. In addition to farm equipment and hardware, the store carried groceries, dry goods, clothing, hats, caps, boots, shoes, furniture, crockery, glassware, paint, oil, etc. Eventually it also provided telegraph service and acted as agent for the various ship lines serving Ephraim and the surrounding area.

Peter Peterson and Aslag Anderson played key roles in creating commerce in Ephraim, and the village slowly began to develop a modest economic base. Andrew deserves credit for encouraging Peterson to move from New Denmark to Ephraim, because it was the arrival of Peterson that set in motion events that led to the building of a "municipal" dock and the development of early business establishments. It bothered Andrew, however, that Peterson was a staunch Lutheran, and this certainly shaded Andrew's feelings about the many contributions Peterson made to the village. Later, when Peterson led the effort to build a Lutheran church in the village, Andrew spoke bitterly of him, calling him his "archenemy."

****

On December 2, 1858, the congregation consecrated their small cemetery, located up on the hill behind Andrew's house. On the same occasion they buried a six-week-old child. The burial service had special meaning for Andrew since he had converted the parents in the interval between the infant's birth and death. He empathized with the mother and father, who were now left with only themselves and their faith. Almost all the settlers in the area joined the parents around the tiny grave of the child, their grim faces reflecting shared thoughts about the fragility of life in this isolated outpost.

During December, sometime after returning from preaching trips to New Denmark and Fort Howard, Andrew began conducting special prayer meetings. They were held separately for men and women, since women were not allowed to pray publicly with men. Prior to Christmas, Andrew redoubled his efforts to bring meaning to the sermons he would be delivering as the year drew to a close. During one of his services, he was preaching so vigorously that a blood vessel ruptured in his windpipe. As he stood at the pulpit, blood stained the corners of his mouth, and the congregation gasped while he paused to wipe it away. According to his recollections, however, he "continued [his] sermon to the end just as if nothing had happened." In a letter published in *The Moravian* in March of 1859 Andrew elaborated on the incident as follows.

> "In the forenoon service of the 4th Sunday of Advent, while preaching, my feelings became so high wrought, and I spoke so loud, that I ruptured a bloodvessel in my chest. The blood began to flow so very profusely from my mouth, that the whole congregation became exceedingly alarmed. I myself did not notice it until after I had closed the discourse. I quickly gave out a hymn, and during the singing sat down to rest and recover.

> While sitting in the pulpit, my mouth filled several times with blood. I was not at all alarmed, on the contrary my heart was filled to overflowing with love for the Savior and precious souls. After the congregation had sung the hymn, I concluded with a prayer and the benediction. After the close of the service, I left the church and retired to my own house, where I took some medicine. My dear wife was very much alarmed, and I had not a little trouble in consoling her. My whole system seemed to be in an uproar. After resting awhile the hemorrhage ceased, and I felt relieved. At 3 o'clock in the afternoon I was enabled to preach a second time, but found it necessary to speak in a lower tone of voice than was my wont." "During several days of the succeeding week I was very feeble, and obliged to take good care of myself. On Christmas day, especially in Communion, I was much refreshed in body and spirit." "Several of our unconverted neighbors have been accustomed to suspect my sincerity, and were in the habit of declaring that I meant it not so earnestly as I said, but since this accident [they] are disposed to think otherwise."

About a year later, when preaching in Menominee, he began spitting blood again. In a letter to Bethlehem he indicated that the hemorrhaging was probably because he had "preached too loud."

****

In his new post as Town Superintendent of Schools, Andrew realized quickly that a great deal of work was involved in organizing the new school districts. He knew it was important for young people of the area to receive a good education, and he took his new responsibility seriously. After learning as much as he could about state school regulations, he set out to establish boundaries of school districts and provide each district clerk with a boundary description. He was also responsible for examining prospective teachers and issuing certificates of qualification. During the term of instruction, as determined by the district, he was required to visit schools and send written reports to the State Superintendent of Education. For his efforts, he received $1.50 a day—a welcome supplement to his meager church income.

Andrew sent out word that communities should provide him with petitions of organization. A response came quickly from Fish Creek (School District #1), followed by petitions from Ephraim (District #2), Egg Harbor (District #3), and Baileys Harbor (District #4). Shortly thereafter the districts were renumbered such that the Ephraim (Gibraltar Township) district became District #4. The school district officers were elected, and soon efforts were underway to raise enough money to build schoolhouses.

The first official meeting of District #4 was held in Ephraim on June 21, 1858, at three o'clock in the afternoon at Andrew's house. The group elected Andrew as chairman and Lacaria Morbek as secretary. They also selected Peter Peterson as district clerk, H.P. Jacobs as a director, and Martin Johnson as treasurer. Andrew kept the meeting moving along and the group passed several important resolutions. They decided that a tax of $120 would be levied for the construction of a schoolhouse—in the meantime, they would try to raise $50 to repair a house that could be used for classes for a period of three months. They further resolved that school would be taught by a female teacher for a three-month period beginning July 1, 1858, and that the rate of pay would be $4.00 a week.

Andrew was insistent that children of the community receive schooling, because education had been a cornerstone of Moravian doctrine going all the way back to John Huss. With Andrew's blessing, instruction had initially been provided by Ole Larsen's daughter, Pauline, apparently as early as the spring of 1854. Andrew had known Pauline in Milwaukee, and he had great respect for her teaching abilities. The fact that she was an exemplary Moravian was also important to Andrew. Until 1859 when a schoolhouse was built on a small piece of land above Andrew's house, Pauline provided instruction by rotating her classes between various homes in the district. In the beginning lessons were taught in both Norwegian and English, but eventually English became the language of choice at school. Children usually spoke Norwegian at home.

The schoolhouse, built on land Andrew donated, was completed around June of 1859 and cost $130. Andrew gave Pauline Larsen, who was by that time Mrs. Martin Johnson, her teacher's certification test, and to no one's surprise she passed with flying colors. She then officially became Ephraim's first teacher. In 1859 records indicate she was responsible for providing instruction to 21 female and 14 male children.

As usual, Andrew was constantly on the move. When he was in Ephraim he spent a great deal of time tending to both the spiritual and earthly needs of established and newly arrived settlers. He was involved in every aspect of village life, and he was always ready to assist others with their problems. He often combined his prayers on behalf of those who were sick or indisposed with recommendations based on his knowledge of homeopathic medicine. Helping others was a driving force in Andrew's life, probably because he derived a feeling of self-worth and confidence from being needed by others. He was a diligent messenger of the Church, continuing his travels from place to place, spreading the gospel. By 1858, he was serving at least seven communities and preaching places from New Denmark to Marinette.

Andrew was still willing to go to astonishing lengths to sustain these scattered missions, often traveling under miserable conditions. On one of his walking trips from New Denmark to Mishicot, a distance of 10 or 12 miles, he slipped and sloshed through mud that was ankle deep in places. Along the trail one foot slipped in the mud and became wedged between the roots of a large tree. Vigorous jerking and pulling finally rewarded him with freedom, but in the process the upper part of his old boot pulled away from the sole. As a result he had little choice but to limp along through the muck, his flapping boot filling with mud one moment and water the next.

When he finally reached Mishicot, sympathetic friends took up a collection and hurried to nearby Two Rivers to buy a new pair of boots for their visiting pastor. Breaking in a new pair of boots is always difficult, but with Andrew's boots the difficulty was compounded by the fact that the fit was poor. On his way back to Fort Howard after conducting services, his feet swelled so much he had to stop and spend the night in New Denmark. The next day he reluctantly put on his new boots, gritted his teeth, and set out once more for Fort Howard. His feet again became so swollen that he feared "the hard, stiff boots would split open." As he plodded on, the weather turned bad and he was caught in a heavy downpour. "Every step was accompanied by excruciating pain which almost seemed to pierce my heart ...." He was in so much pain that he nearly gave up. All of a sudden he decided to place himself at the mercy of God, as if he were a child. He prayed with all his heart. "I had no sooner ended my prayer, when a most miraculous answer took place—just as instantly; for in a moment the intense pain had vanished, totally and completely. My physical vigor was completely restored, and it was revealed to me that the hand of the Savior had for the second time touched me in a most wonderful manner. I burst out with a song of praise, rejoicing in a loud voice, and marched on, while water and mud splashed about me—and this was just like play to me."

During the remaining six miles to Fort Howard, Andrew felt no pain whatever. Upon his arrival he removed the boots from his swollen feet to discover that the constant abrasion had rubbed all the skin off his heels. Oozing sores remained. He returned to Ephraim by steamer wearing soft slippers; it took his feet two weeks to heal.

In July of 1859 Andrew curtailed several preaching trips and remained in

Ephraim to care for Laura, who was severely ill. For a period of time, she was not expected to live. Although she finally recovered, mysterious illnesses such as hers were common occurrences in the lives of settlers living in isolated areas. Andrew often expressed concern about his wife's ill health, but the record indicates that her indispositions did not often interfere with his traveling ministry.

Andrew made many preaching trips that year and also held a big revival in Ephraim. Aware that this was the colony's first revival meeting as well as the first one in the entire county, he wanted the event to be a memorable one—and it was fire and brimstone religion at its best. "Streams of tears flowed, even from the eyes of strong men ... and when different ones were willing to yield to Him and accept Him in a new living faith, their spiritual joy became indescribably intense ...." Olia Knudsen was a "narrow and untalented person" before her conversion during the revival meetings. After her conversion she was "filled with the Holy Spirit," and she was able to lead others in prayer using "a living stream of the choicest words and sentences [that] flowed straight from the depths of her heart and which, so it seemed, God with His own spirit had inspired." From a nearby room, Andrew overheard her speak in a ladies' prayer meeting conducted by his wife. He was so moved by her speech that he "wept violently and in all quietness." He worked day and night to make the event a success, and under his direction, the revival went on daily for several weeks.

That summer Andrew also found time to make trips to Chicago, where he held meetings and solicited funds with which to complete the church in Ephraim, and to La Salle County in Illinois. He had been encouraged to travel to La Salle County to meet with Endre and Herman Osmundsen, two well-to-do farmers from Norway. One of them, in fact, had resided for many years in Stavanger where Andrew attended mission school. From Chicago he took a stagecoach to Mission Point in La Salle County, a distance of about 70 miles, where the Osmundsen families and their friends greeted him as if he were one of their own. When they heard that Andrew had been sent as a home missionary by the Church, they requested that he hold services in several schoolhouses located around the Norwegian settlement. Andrew was flattered and agreed quickly, for he had found some "genuine Children of God and discovered that there was a burning desire to hear the true gospel preached." The shepherd had found another flock to tend.

Andrew's stay with Norwegian countrymen in Illinois was so successful that he wished he could remain and serve a "fixed mission field" among such hungry souls. In his heart, however, he knew that no matter how far his evangelistic ministry required him to travel, his home base would always be Ephraim.

****

Since one of the reasons for his mission trip to Illinois was to solicit donations to finish the church in Ephraim, Andrew was delighted that he received enough money to resume work on the building. He preached several times in Chicago and his merchant friend, H. Thompson, assisted him in soliciting funds. To his surprise they collected about $150, with Thompson being the major contributor. Some of the contributions were in the form of pledges—later Andrew wrote in his recollections that a sizable portion of the pledges were never paid.

With the growth of the village there was renewed interest in finishing the church building as soon as possible, and Andrew and the congregation worked long hours to complete the job. Andrew himself built the pulpit that even today remains a prominent fixture in the Ephraim Moravian Church. He painstakingly made a pillar on each side of the pulpit to support the oil lamps that would illuminate the lectern during evening services. Others completed the interior woodwork, as well as the chairs and benches, while still others undertook the task of painting the exterior. Andrew took great pleasure in knowing that his beautiful little church was the first one built in Door County, although he remained steadfast in his belief that it should never have been built so close to the water.

On November 18, 1859, several intrepid workers fitted a spire with an arrow to the top of the church steeple and the congregation rushed to complete the small amount of inside work that remained. The Home Mission Office in Bethlehem had sent a special contribution of money to be used to help furnish the church. A stove, lamps, and a steel church bell were among the items ordered by Andrew and his congregation in time to arrive before the bay froze. The church was finished in early December of 1859, and its dedication was set for December 18. An announcement of the grand event went to all Scandinavian and German settlers in the area, and "even to the Americans in Fish Creek."

As soon as the carpenters cleared away their tools and leftover scraps of wood, the women of the congregation moved in with dustcloths, rags, brooms, buckets of water, and mops. It was a joyous occasion as they carefully cleaned the inside of the building and polished its furnishings. The sounds of hammers pounding and saws rasping were replaced with the soft chatter of women at work. Some even hummed a hymn or two. Ephraim was proud of its new house of worship, which was painted a highly visible white.

Andrew was both excited and anxious about the dedication, but he kept himself busy handling the many preliminary details associated with the event.

The choir began practicing many weeks before dedication day, and Andrew often stayed up late composing church music and making copies to be used in the ceremony. Several feet of snow fell a few days before the dedication, causing him to worry, but he was relieved when villagers teamed up to break a road through the deep drifts.

Finally dedication day arrived. "On that memorable day for Ephraim, the weather was mild, with no wind, but the sky was somewhat overcast. Brother Gabriel Wathne had volunteered to be the bell-ringer and it was his understanding that the bell ought to be rung three times before services (according to Norwegian custom), at 9:00, 10:00, and 10:30 A.M. It made an unusual impression upon the inhabitants in Ephraim to hear the church bell ringing for the first time. It was a sermon in itself and not a few shed tears softly. Oh, how I prayed with eagerness again and again that morning in my home, and when I arose from my knees in my study at the ringing of the bell the third time, I went to the house of the Lord with a quaking heart. Upon my entrance, I immediately saw that every seat was taken, but not only by Scandinavians, and this surprised me. Our experienced choir with their splendid voices was in its place. Soon the entrance hymn was heard with its impressive harmony. The program was carried out just as planned, but although I remember much of it clearly, even the substance of the dedication prayer, it would be too tedious to go into a description and narration of everything. I just want to mention that during the Act of Dedication, surrendering the building to the Holy Trinity, the whole congregation arose to worship under wonderful impressiveness. It was sublime!" Nearly 130 worshipers packed the little church to attend this first service.

Later in the day, visitors began to arrive for the afternoon (3:00) dedication service. "At the hour of two, one could notice big sleighs, drawn by oxen, slowly nearing the church, the sleighs loaded down with people—one load after the other, as the bell was ringing. It was the Germans, our neighbors on the east, and the Americans from Fish Creek. I must admit that after my viewpoint at that time, I would much rather watch these small primitive means of transportation than if I had ever beheld king's carriages, drawn by the most stately horses.

"When I stepped into our dear sanctuary at a fixed time, I found the whole building packed full of people. How many persons were present I cannot say, but it was a great gathering for Ephraim. The meeting was opened with a Norwegian hymn, after which followed prayer; reading of a portion of God's word, after which, with inspiration from Above, I made a short talk in my mother tongue. When I finished, I announced a few verses of a hymn in

English, rendered in a charming way by our faithful Sister Pauline Johnson and a few others. After that I gave a talk in English to the best of my ability. However, the words flowed easily and the Americans present listened with deep attention and interest. After my talk, I announced a German hymn (I knew beforehand that the Germans thereabouts used Lutheran hymn-books and I had borrowed a copy for the occasion). Soon a mighty song began, the voices composing it being so strong that the sound to us became almost painful, while they believed they were singing with spirit and power, and so it was. It was not long before these loud voices faded away and I then felt inspired to speak in German. (Es war wohl sehr gebrochen) Our German neighbors snapped up each word with enthusiasm and some women wept. I continued this talk for sometime, as I felt that my own heart was blest. I then closed with a prayer in German, English, and Norwegian, followed by a Norwegian hymn, full of harmony, by the choir. Collection was taken (only a small amount was obtained), and then the apostolical benediction.

"But people were in no hurry to leave. My hand became tired with handshaking and we heard many congratulations. The Germans especially clung to me and implored me most earnestly that I would hold some service in German in the future at the church and assured me that I spoke German well. There was nothing to do but to promise this."

Completion of the church in time for Christmas of 1859 was a wonderful gift to Andrew. As he enjoyed Christmas with Laura and their three children, Alfred, Johnnie, and Anna Munda, Andrew felt blessed many times over. On Christmas eve all the children sang at the church service around a brightly lit tree, and some of the hymns had been composed by Andrew just for the occasion. Tears of thanks, joy, and humility welled up in his eyes as he watched the faces of beaming children responding to the "story about Christmas and the all-powerful love of the child-Jesus." On Christmas day when Andrew entered the sanctuary, he was surprised to see that a few seats on the female side were empty, probably due to difficulties with the deep snow. That day 33 people celebrated Communion during Andrew's services.

Andrew would always remember 1859 as a remarkable year for Ephraim. The village had grown, the church had been finished, a number of business establishments had begun to serve the community, and the village's fine new pier and dock had been completed. As a result of dock traffic and the establishment of the Anderson Store, several settlers found employment with Aslag Anderson. Now that Ephraim had a deepwater pier that was one of the best in the area, there was increased demand for cordwood, fence posts, telegraph poles, and shingles. Sale of such items to outside business interests meant a steady flow of dollars into the community. Andrew was hired by a large telegraph company in Illinois to execute and oversee contracts for the cutting and delivering of telegraph poles and fence posts. This arrangement, which lasted for several years, meant a small amount of additional income for Andrew and his growing family.

Andrew had every reason to count his many blessings in 1859 and every reason to be proud of his accomplishments. Two days after Christmas he celebrated his 36th birthday. He had been in America for only 10 years.

6

COMPETITION FOR CONVERTS

Happily, the winter of 1859-60 was free from the traumas of previous winters. As ice sealed over the bay and snow and cold limited outdoor activities, life in the small but now thriving village gradually slowed. On cold windless days the pervasive odor of wood smoke filled the air, and villagers crunched their way through the snow to care for livestock and to chop and gather wood for stove and hearth. On milder days, when they were not in school or doing chores, children skied or threw themselves onto hand-made sleds to slide, over and over again, down hills and roadways rutted by the runners of horse-drawn sleds and sleighs.

Keeping warm was not easy. Thick stocking caps or wool hats with ear flaps provided protection from the cold, as did mittens, scarves around the neck, wool pants, long underwear, and even two pairs of pants worn at once. The settlers completed their outdoor wear with layers of socks inside rugged rubber or leather boots, wool flannel shirts, well-worn sweaters, and heavy wool coats. Youngsters sometimes improvised. If they did not have a proper pair of mittens, they might pull heavy socks over their hands to keep them warm until the snow that matted to the yarn began to melt from their body heat. Villagers ordered some of their winter clothes from Green Bay or purchased them from ample stocks at the two general stores, one owned by Peter Peterson and the new one established by Aslag Anderson. And if the customer was short of cash, credit was available. Many clothes were made by women of the village who sewed garments from cloth that they selected carefully and treasured until needed. Knitting was also an important part of their everyday lives, occupying what little time existed between meal preparation, housecleaning, washing, tending children, mending, and keeping the fire going. At night, when most of the chores were done, women continued to knit by lamplight.

Villagers had simple meals, beginning the day with bread, jams or jellies, and boiled coffee. Instead of coffee, children drank milk, if available. A typical noon meal featured fried bacon or potatoes along with bread and coffee, and the evening meal consisted of bread, tea, or coffee, and perhaps fish. Red meat was a luxury for the early settlers, but after 1860 the arrival of immigrant farmers from Germany and the establishment of larger farms meant that more meat and sausage were available. Villagers were happy to be able to supplement food from their own gardens and small farms with produce, meat, and dairy products from farmers of the nearby German Settlement, who could then use the income to pay off their debts at Anderson's or Peterson's general store.

Andrew made good use of the church building that winter, and as usual he provided his congregation, and others as well, with assistance in any way he could. He looked forward to springtime because it meant he could resume his missions to other communities without having to battle cold and snow. He was continuing to experience competition for converts in his mission work as more and more people settled in northeastern Wisconsin. Preachers of many faiths were bringing their messages to settlers, most of whom welcomed spiritual encouragement to help them deal with the many hardships of pioneer life. Crop failure, disease, death, and long hours of toil sharpened their longing for meaning. Andrew understood this longing, and he was committed to helping these people find comfort and meaning in the Moravian faith. Although he was keenly aware of the evangelical competition in his widespread mission, he was certain that back in Ephraim he would always be needed.

No matter how mild the winter, villagers eagerly anticipated the arrival of spring. In late December they began to take note of increasing day length. If they could just make it through December, then survive January, February and March, signs of spring would begin to shake everyone out of their winter doldrums. With the gradual rise in temperature, there would be a synchronous increase in village activity. Spring would give way to summer, summer to autumn, and the cycle would repeat itself. Isolated as they were, villagers were always aware that their lives were controlled by nature's rhythm.

****

Once the spring thaw was over and firmer footing replaced the deep mud and standing water, Andrew began his mission trips south. After lots of rest during the uneventful winter, he was eager to spread the gospel again. One of his first mission trips in the spring of 1860 was to New Denmark. In his first Sunday morning sermon there he worked hard to elicit emotion in his audience and "some of them wept audibly as if they were in spiritual distress." He preached again that afternoon and was pleased with an even greater emotional response. He implored his followers to join him once again at the evening sermon when he promised to show them the way to salvation.

Andrew rose to the occasion for his third and last sermon of the day. He preached with great fervor about the wonderful love of Jesus for the lowly sinner and the importance of surrendering one's heart to the Lord. With loud voice and grand gestures he reached out to those who "openly confessed that they were lost sinners and who really were in deep spiritual distress." As sweat glistened on his brow he "exhorted the souls that were touched in this way not only to pray quietly, each for himself, but also audibly in meetings and publicly acknowledge their condition." Andrew wept with the weeping as he proclaimed the word of God. "That evening a new voice was heard in New Denmark. God's own spirit taught them to pray and confess and while weeping, one after another talked, which created amazement with some. I had to promise to remain with them for at least a week and meetings were held every evening. While on the road from the Town Hall to my lodging place, accompanied by some of those who were most troubled, in the peaceful, late hour of the evening, I again fell upon my knees with them along the roadside, where I prayed to the Crucified Christ that He would bring peace to their souls and assist them to believe that they might receive assurance of forgiveness for their sins." What an intoxicating evening! Andrew was exhausted but elated after a long day of doing that which he loved most—preaching the word of God to a receptive gathering.

He was ecstatic about the response he received from his friends and followers in New Denmark, and his visit in the spring of 1860 would remain one of the highlights of his ministry. It was one of the most exciting weeks of his life, and even when he was in his seventies he recalled vividly some of those euphoric moments. "When late in the evening I was returning to my place of lodging over the long trails through the woods, there was always a number of happy believers who surrounded me and rejoicing sang songs of praise to the Lamb of God, their sweet voices resounding through the deep woods under God's twinkling stars." "The light from the twinkling stars was no doubt reflected in many a tear-stained eye and more than one thought silently: If the joy of the soul can be so great here, how much greater will it not be in Heaven when we stand face to face with the precious Savior."

As the time approached for his return to Ephraim, he "repeatedly and very carefully reminded the converted not to cling to me as I was only a frail human being, nothing but dust and ashes." Nevertheless, it was clear to Andrew that he "had become in their estimation the apple of their eye and their heart's favorite." Andrew left New Denmark buoyed by the tremendous success of his efforts, but he would soon be reminded that religious allegiance can be fickle. The spiritual roots cultivated by Andrew were to bear fruit in New Denmark, but a young Baptist missionary from Neenah would be there for the harvest.

****

An outspoken Dane had been in attendance regularly when Andrew preached in New Denmark that spring. Andrew found him rather uncultured and "a zealous bigot who imagined that all true Christians could only be Baptists." They discussed religion on several occasions and the Dane insisted that baptism was necessary if one was to receive the word of God. After Andrew returned to Ephraim, his antagonist wrote to a young Baptist missionary in Neenah to tell him about the enthusiastic response Andrew had received. This convinced the Baptist missionary, who was eager to establish himself among the settlers, that New Denmark would be a fertile field for converts to his faith. Since Andrew had already heightened the community's awareness of the rewards of salvation, the young preacher decided to travel to New Denmark to argue his convictions.

The Baptist minister moved to New Denmark and worked tirelessly to convert members of the community to his beliefs. He was clever and resourceful, and he maintained steady pressure on those who seemed to waver. In many people who had responded favorably to Andrew's ministry, Moravian spiritual teachings were soon displaced by those of the Baptist Church. During that summer and early fall the young preacher baptized 24 converts by immersing them in the little stream flowing through New Denmark, and as a result of his unrelenting efforts, settlers in the community established a Baptist congregation.

Andrew was surprised and disheartened when he heard about the success of the Baptist preacher in New Denmark. He spoke of the converts as "The poor victims!" After all his hard work he felt betrayed by the community, and he had difficulty concealing his bitterness about what had happened. His feelings were somewhat assuaged when he learned later that some of the Scandinavians in the New Denmark area shared his anger about the gains made in behalf of the Baptist Church. Their response was to send out an invitation to a nearby Lutheran preacher they had once rejected, suggesting that the time was ripe for him to return to the community and try to establish a Lutheran congregation. Although Andrew considered the Lutheran preacher a bigot, he reacted with pleasure when he learned that his ecclesiastical competition arrived in New Denmark, mounted a bold attack on all sects, and persuaded a number of the Baptists to join his new Lutheran congregation.

The Lutherans also compromised Andrew's mission work in nearby Mishicot, where an "arrogant and devious" Lutheran preacher moved in to seek converts. This "haughty" Lutheran "preached severely against the brethren [Moravian] congregation and the sects, [and] established also a bigoted Lutheran congregation and by deceit and trickery gathered into his fold some families who had previously belonged to my mission."

By 1860 it was clear that Andrew no longer had his wide mission field to himself, and population growth in northeastern Wisconsin was causing the competition for converts to become intense. Earlier, when settlements were small and far between, a visiting preacher was welcomed with open arms, regardless of his faith. The lonely settlers needed not only the spiritual guidance provided by the visiting evangelist but also the welcome contact with someone from the "outside" world and the news he conveyed. Now that the wilderness was giving way to civilization, there was an accompanying increase in the number of preachers of every persuasion looking for proselytes. And a minister who was willing to remain in a community usually had a decided advantage over the preach-and-run evangelist, even one as skilled as Andrew. Although Andrew felt the competition, he took comfort in knowing he could count on the support of his Ephraim congregation.

As always, Andrew was prepared to go to extra lengths to make himself available to the early settlers. A trip he undertook in late August 1860 is another example of the energy he was willing to expend to spread the gospel. The trip began when he felt "called" to visit his small flock in Sturgeon Bay, so with a friend and his young son Alfred, he set out for that community in a rowboat. After rowing a few miles the wind picked up and whitecaps began to wash over the boat. Turning around quickly, the party arrived back in Ephraim shortly before a severe storm broke over the area. The next morning the weather was more settled, and they resumed the trip in spite of the choppy water. By rowing steadily all day, mostly with Andrew at the oars, they managed to reach Sturgeon Bay before evening. Andrew spent a week preaching and visiting parishioners, and then he rowed his little group back to Ephraim. Although the trip home took only one day, he reported in a letter published in *The Moravian* that by the time they arrived at Eagle Harbor he was "much fatigued from hard rowing at the oars for nearly thirty miles."

****

In spite of his losses in the battle for converts, Andrew knew that Christmas of 1860 would have special meaning for the community of Ephraim. The village had continued to grow and prosper, its citizens were feeling more confident about their ability to survive the winters, and they began to look forward to a secure future. Ephraim was becoming a center of business and the pier built by Aslag Anderson was a hub of commerce for miles around. A wise businessman, Anderson kept his general store stocked with provisions. From foodstuffs to wearing apparel, he had everything necessary to help the settlers survive the vagaries of nature. Although Aslag and his brother, Halvor, had been raised as Lutherans, Andrew enjoyed their support and Aslag's wife, Anna, was very active in the Moravian Church.

Christmas of 1860 was celebrated with a new bell in the church belfry. It was a replacement for the original bell that was cracked by Gabriel Wathne, the designated bell ringer. Wathne, who was very strong, took his assignment seriously and could make the nearby bluffs echo with his ringing call to worship. Fortunately, the new bell withstood his most vigorous efforts. As was traditional in Moravian congregations, a church "love feast" and Holy Communion were celebrated on Christmas Day. Special German services were held the day after Christmas for farm families of the German settlement. It was a time of togetherness and celebration.

Shortly after the new year arrived Andrew received a letter from several members of the new Baptist congregation in New Denmark. In the letter the writers attempted to justify their conversion, and they urged Andrew to visit the community again when he could. He recalled his response to the letter as follows: "At first I was undecided as to what was the best thing for me to do regarding this invitation, but after mature consideration and repeated prayer, I decided that I would once more go to New Denmark and defend the truth."

Around February of 1861, Andrew made the long trip to New Denmark, where he was received warmly. Fortunately, the new Baptist minister was absent on a trip. Although Andrew was apprehensive, he made every effort to be "as calm and composed as possible." His anxiety, however, was heightened when he began to suspect that his one-time followers were conspiring to convert him to the Baptist faith. To this end, several of the smartest and most articulate members of the congregation arranged to have a private conference with him. Since he knew what to expect, he was mentally prepared for the confrontation of faiths—in fact, he welcomed it.

The meeting began at 10 o'clock in the morning, with Andrew facing six young Baptists eager to convince him that theirs was the only faith that could guarantee redemption. After a song and prayer, the Baptists "began with tears to assure me that it was far from their thoughts to have lost their devotion for me, that they would always acknowledge and confess that the Lord had made me the instrument to lead them to conversion and the new life in Christ, but that later a brighter light had arisen to guide them and that they had followed their convictions."

Andrew listened patiently to what they had to say. Their arguments were hardly new to him and he knew exactly how he was going to respond. At long last he had an opportunity to speak. With blazing eyes and set jaw, he declared how much it pained him that their new beliefs had displaced the fellowship they achieved during his many visits to the community, and that he felt as if an unsurmountable wall had been built between them. He followed with a lengthy and articulate defense of his position and beliefs as a Moravian minister. At one point he paused and looked at his young antagonists. "They seemed to be so completely dumb-founded and so depressed that I felt sorry for them as I beheld them." As Andrew continued to speak his features softened and tears welled up in his eyes.

He concluded his remarks with the following comments. "It must be very plain to you that you have completely failed to shake my holy conviction. Nothing can do that. However, as I see that you have nothing more to say, it is my sincere wish that my present presentation of proof may have convinced you that our old belief concerning baptism is the correct one and further it is my wish that you may have sufficient humility and courage to publicly acknowledge that you have made a mistake and permitted yourselves to be led astray ...." Andrew also urged them to have the courage to return to the Moravian faith they once embraced with such enthusiasm. "I made these remarks while deeply moved, yes, while weeping. No definite answer followed, but I remember very well that one of the company said: 'Dear Brother Iverson, if you had been a resident among us, we would never have become baptists!' "

A few years later Andrew learned that the Baptist congregation in New Denmark failed to meet the test of time. It became divided by disciples of the Seventh-Day Adventists and later disappeared. He vowed never to return to New Denmark—he had invested tremendous physical and spiritual energy in the community and had little to show for it.

Andrew was depressed as he traveled back to Ephraim. To make matters worse, on the way home he learned that several members of the Moravian faith in Sturgeon Bay had left the fold. This was almost too much to bear. He thought about all the difficult journeys he had made over the years to spread the gospel and about the great love and understanding he had extended to those he visited in his widespread mission. How could it be that so many of his converts were so fickle in their allegiance to the Moravian faith? He needed to be home among people on whom he could depend.

****

The year 1861 brought a new addition to the Iverson family. On February 20, Laura and Andrew welcomed their fifth child, a son. They named him Lauritz Joseph Andreas and decided to call him Joseph. In early summer of that year Andrew traveled to Chicago to preach and then continued on about 60 miles southwest to Mission Point, Illinois (later named Norway because of the many Norwegians who settled the area). He had preached there before to large crowds, and he had many friends in the community. Upon his arrival he sent a message to all the nearby settlers that the next evening he would be holding services in one of the local schoolhouses.

His visit was so well-received that he stayed an entire week and preached every day. His faith in himself as an evangelist was restored by the enthusiastic and moving responses of people attending the revival gatherings. At the end of his visit he was told of a Norwegian settlement not far from Keokuk, Iowa, located near the state's southeastern tip. Brother E. Osmundsen, an older member of the Moravian congregation in Mission Point, pleaded with Andrew to visit the settlement and even offered to accompany him and pay all expenses. Recalling that he had lost most of his followers in New Denmark and Mishicot, Andrew decided to make the trip and perhaps gain some new converts.

A long stage ride carried the two men across the whole state of Illinois to the Mississippi River, where they took a steamer to Fort Madison, Iowa, and then a train to Keokuk. Arriving at Keokuk the next day, they boarded a wagon for the remainder of the trip to the Norwegian settlement, an eight mile ride over bad roads that wandered through valleys and steep hills. The rigorous trip was worth it to Andrew, however, for he was received enthusiastically by his countrymen at Mission Point. He stayed five days, sometimes preaching twice a day, and at the end of his visit he was asked repeatedly to move his family from Ephraim to their little community. Several Quakers who attended his services went out of their way to tell him how much his message inspired them, and they led him to believe that they were awakened by his words.

It was a tremendous boost to Andrew's ego to feel so intensely wanted, especially when members of the community said they would provide for all the needs of his family if only he would move to their area and become their minister. As he said farewell he promised to write often and visit them again the following summer. It was a triumphant departure. He was a successful evangelist again, with converts to prove it.

After a brief stop in Chicago Andrew returned, with lifted spirits, to his beloved Ephraim. He recalled that he "was received with great joy." He was exhausted, but it was a fulfilled exhaustion. He remained in Ephraim for several weeks but then departed on a mission trip to Sturgeon Bay. There he hoped to help his Moravian followers find a way to build their own church. It would take some work, but he was prepared to make as many trips as necessary to make the church a reality.

Later that summer Andrew embarked on a trip around the peninsula that he would remember to his dying day. As Superintendent of Schools for Gibraltar Township he was obliged to pay visits to the small public schools of the area. Traveling on foot, his first stop was in Fish Creek, where he inspected the school and spent the night with his friends, the Thorps. Early the next morning he walked to Egg Harbor, where he visited the school, gave an examination to the teacher, and completed other duties. Shortly before lunch, he decided to continue on to Baileys Harbor, even though it was an unusually hot day with no cooling breeze. Not being familiar with the eight mile trek to Baileys Harbor, he asked a stranger about a new road that had been cut through the woods. Although the directions were vague, he finally found the road and began the long walk through unsettled land toward his destination on the other side of the peninsula.

As Andrew walked, the sun's rays seemed to grow in intensity. His shirt hung wet upon his back, and he realized that he had rarely perspired to such an extent. It was a blistering hot day, with high humidity and little breeze, and he was miles from habitation without food, or more important, without water. Gradually he became aware that his thirst was growing more intense with each step, and he began to quicken his search for signs of a stream or spring, but there was no evidence of water anywhere. "My thirst became intolerable; my entire inner body seemed to be burning up; the little moisture in my mouth became thick and slimy and my strength was rapidly vanishing."

In desperation he stopped several times at depressions in the ground to dig little holes in an attempt to find water. He was willing to suck the moisture from damp soil, but there was none to be found. After several more miles he became frightened, for he realized his strength was fading as his thirst grew overwhelming. When his body finally failed to respond to what little will remained, he sank slowly to the ground. Lying there, dozens of biting mosquitoes covered his exposed skin, and he began to have thoughts that he might perish. He was feverish—his mind wandered.

As he lay there his desperate thoughts were momentarily interrupted by the following possibility: "Why not immediately tell your Savior in a childish way about your pitiable condition?" As soon as he said the "Amen" at the end of his short prayer, he was "seized with a mystical impulse—there was no voice and I seemed to have no thoughts—just a guiding impulse which I blindly followed." He recalled the experience this way:

> "I managed to get up on my feet with great difficulty and then following that mystic impulse, I began to walk slowly ahead a short distance over to the left side of the road. I judge the width of the road was about 18 feet, with very heavy, dense timber on both sides. As I approached, I discovered a large tree which had been felled and which was perhaps 2 1/2 ft. in diameter and 20 to 30 ft. long. This tree, in my opinion, must have been dragged by strong oxen and placed there close to the woods on the left hand side of the road. For a moment my powerless feet rested at the base of the tree. At that moment the before mentioned mystical impulse conjured me to mount the tree and walk along its entire length. There was no sound reason for my action, for on the right was the open road without obstruction. But I followed the mystical impulse blindly and after several vain attempts, made with the greatest efforts and under the greatest difficulties, I was at last able to mount it, as before stated, and move forward on its top with slow, careful steps. When I had covered about one half the length of the tree—without falling down—led by the same mystic impulse, my eyes were seemingly compelled to stare downward on the side of the tree toward the woods and what a miracle! I immediately became aware that there was a depression there, with a spring of the clearest water—a living fountain!"

Even before he knelt to quench his thirst, Andrew "shouted" out his thanks to God. With that he jumped down beside the spring and used his closed hand to bring water to his parched lips. He could only manage a little at a time, but gradually he began to feel his strength returning. Over and over he drank, and each time he thanked the Lord. He ignited some dry leaves with a match, hoping the smoke would drive away the mosquitoes that swarmed around him. As he lay there by the spring, the following thought echoed through his mind:

"The dear Lord Jesus had again saved you as by a miracle."

When he recovered enough to resume his journey he realized he could easily have died. If he had not obeyed the impulse to leave the road and follow the felled tree into the woods, he would never have discovered the spring. Once again God intervened to spare his life. Later he learned that the little spring was the only one along the entire distance of eight miles.

****

It was December of 1861; Andrew paused by the living room window of his white-washed house on the hill overlooking the bay. He had arisen early, concerned about the many preparations necessary for the Church's upcoming Christmas celebration. He wanted it to be a special occasion, particularly for the children in his congregation.

A little light snow had fallen during the night, giving the bumpy dirt road in front of his house a salt and pepper appearance. He could see the small walnut tree in the front yard standing black and leafless in the early morning light, and along the edges of the bay below him the first tentative plates of pack ice were beginning to form. The house was cold and he stepped outside the back door for firewood.

After carefully uncovering embers in the two wood stoves and adding kindling and logs, Andrew sat down for a moment to wait for the house to warm up. Sitting in a chair he had constructed himself, he began thinking about the Christmas season that was close at hand, and he reflected on its importance to the children of the congregation. "They were very well bred and they often gave me much joy. They were very prompt in their attendance at Sunday school and readily committed to memory quotations from the Bible as well as verses of different songs. They never whispered in school, where I often told them about the Great Friend of Children. But we never really had a gathering for the children except when Christmas came and of course this was their happy festival."

His thoughts were interrupted by the voices of his own children coming from their room down the hall. He could hear nine-year-old Alfred and four-year-old Johnnie, but the baby, Joseph, was still asleep. He could also hear the quiet voice of seven-year-old Anna Munda, the only girl in the family. His blue-eyed daughter was truly the light of Andrew's life. Born during his stay in Cooperstown, this spiritual and mystical child amazed and delighted him daily. Andrew, however, had little time to reflect on his "precious Munda," because the house was warming up, the children would soon be swarming in, and the duties of the day awaited him.

Planning for the children's Christmas service started early in December and involved numerous members of the congregation. Particularly tireless in her efforts was Pauline (Larsen) Johnson. Thanks to her, Christmas of 1861 promised to be an especially joyous occasion. "The Christmas tree was more beautiful, the gifts more numerous and more expensive than ever before."

When Christmas eve finally arrived, "the church bell chimes called softly the dear little ones and the young people to the Lord's house." As they entered the glowing white church on the shore, "the Christmas tree seemed to smile with its many lights and gifts and to beckon to the dear little children's sparkling eyes and every child must have realized that this was their festival and their celebration." Although the service was designed for youngsters, the entire congregation attended. It opened with the children singing a Christmas hymn in Norwegian, followed by a prayer, and a reading of the Christmas story from the Bible. Among the intent young faces, Andrew could pick out those of Alfred, Johnnie, and Anna Munda.

After another song, followed by recitations, Andrew began his Christmas message to the children, and "a peculiar holy mood seemed to come over all of us." His message concerned the Christ-child's wonderful love and how it could save each person from great sinfulness. "I can never adequately describe the overwhelming impression which seemed to seize the children during my talk. The power of the Lord was poured out, especially upon the children. During the discourse, violent weeping was noticed. Tears flowed in streams and some wept so violently that it seemed as if their little hearts would break. I had never witnessed anything like it."

Because the children were still crying openly as Andrew concluded his message, he urged them to sing a familiar Christmas hymn. "They obeyed but it turned out to be a strange song, for there was more sobbing than singing." While they were singing and sobbing Andrew made a decision. "A strong voice whispered in my heart: Here in this weeping flock of children, there most certainly must be one or more who, touched by the Holy spirit, is willing honestly and unreservedly to surrender their hearts to the Savior." He turned to the children and addressed them directly. "Dearly beloved children! Deeply touched, I have observed your tears, because the Spirit of God has made an impression upon your tender hearts, and I believe that the Christ-child himself has revealed to me that one or another among you has come to a definite decision to surrender to the dear Savior your heart as a Christmas present to Him."

He asked any children who "had resolved to wholly surrender themselves to the Lord Jesus" to come forward and put their right hand in his. "Suddenly an intense silence prevailed, lasting for seconds. No one made a move and at length I thought that they lacked courage to publicly step forward. Just then one of them arose and with measured, determined steps came right up the aisle to me and it proved to be none other than my own dear little daughter, Anna Munda, seven years old. I noticed her tear-stained cheeks, as she approached me and as she was holding out her little right hand. I burst into tears; I was overcome." Taking Anna Munda's hand in his, Andrew asked if she was sure that she wanted to give her heart to Jesus. "Yes, dear papa! Right here on the spot I give my whole heart to Him!" As the two of them knelt to pray, the sounds of weeping could be heard throughout the congregation. Parents' and children's faces alike were wet with tears. Andrew's "burning prayer, offered in faith, was most mercifully heard right on the spot and as we arose from our knees, my dear Munda's soulful eyes radiated with an inexplicable spiritual joy, and she told me that she could now truly love the dear Lord Jesus and that she was unspeakably happy."

After Anna Munda resumed her seat, Andrew asked whether there were other children who would come forward and surrender their hearts to Jesus. An infectious fervor now swept the congregation. Anna Munda "had with the grace of God broken the ice, for in a few moments all the children and not a few young people came forward and gave me their hand. I had them all kneel about me and, with annointment [sic] from above, I prayed for them."

Andrew was ecstatic with the success of the service. "Ephraim had never known such a Christmas eve." Anna Munda "left that house of God and went home a ransomed spiritual and believing child, almost as happy as an angel." When she finally "reached home from this remarkable gathering, she told whole-heartedly and joyfully her mother, who was physically so weak that she could not be with us at the church, that she had given her whole heart to the Savior, that she loved Him tenderly and that she was so happy." It was unfortunate that Laura's poor health had prevented her from attending church on that extraordinary evening when Anna Munda dedicated herself to God.

Andrew's bedtime prayers that night were filled with thanksgiving. His joy in his daughter knew no bounds. Her luminous spirituality would continue to touch not only her family but also members of the church. Andrew referred to her as "our heart's favorite ... in the home as well as in the congregation ... the bright and shining, but also the humble light." He knew his memories of Anna Munda and the remarkable Christmas eve of 1861 would remain with him in vivid detail for the rest of his life.

7

ACTS OF GOD

The year 1862 marked the beginning of a difficult period for Andrew. There were certainly moments of triumph, but tragedy continued to shadow him. His second major revival meeting in Ephraim was an evangelistic success, but the establishment of a Moravian Church in Sturgeon Bay was fraught with difficulty. Tragedy awaited him at home where events would be set in motion that led to devastating personal losses. In addition, competition for converts among various religious groups was escalating, and the discord between the North and South had now erupted into a full-fledged conflict called the Civil War.

At first Andrew doubted the war would have much effect on Ephraim, but when food prices began to increase and a Union officer arrived to persuade young villagers to enlist, he realized he was wrong. The young officer was Ole Larsen's son-in-law. As news of the battles of the Civil War reached Ephraim many of the teenagers and a few young men boasted about their desire to enlist and help fight the great war. When the recruiter appeared, however, most of these boastful patriots disappeared, but four conscientious young men from the village did enlist. Two of them were Moravians who were candidates for confirmation in the Church, and they stopped by the Iverson house to say goodbye before leaving for induction. After insisting that the two stay for breakfast, Andrew said a heartfelt prayer for Charly (sic) Morbek and Thorger Thorgersen that morning, for they were on their way to train briefly and then do battle. They fought side-by-side, but only Morbek returned. For many weeks Thorgersen battled for his life in a hospital, while Morbek remained at his friend's side reading the Bible and praying with him every day. Thorgersen never left the hospital. Andrew noted that he was "buried in the distant southland far from his dear home in Ephraim."

New efforts to establish a Moravian Church in Sturgeon Bay came to Andrew's attention early in 1862, shortly after he celebrated his 39th birthday. He responded to the news by walking to Sturgeon Bay using the newly cut wagon and foot road leading south, a distance of about 30 miles. The new road left much to be desired and he arrived exhausted, but after a night's rest he began his visits with the settlers who were hoping to establish a Moravian Church. He knew every member of the group, and he informed them that when at least seven believers expressed their willingness to abide by the rules of the Church, he would help them organize a congregation and build a church. Thereafter he preached on numerous occasions over a period of several days and then hiked back to Ephraim. Upon his arrival late in the evening he realized how tired he was. He did not seem to have the stamina he once had.

During the rest of the winter Andrew preached regularly in his own church, holding services as usual in both Norwegian and German. Sometimes he went to Fish Creek to hold services in English. As spring approached and the days grew longer, Andrew began to plan another major revival meeting. He decided that this revival would begin on Palm Sunday and continue through Easter if his preaching was well-received and if souls could be saved. He prayed that his second major revival meeting in Ephraim would be as successful as his first.

The revival began with a sermon on Palm Sunday to a church filled with Scandinavians and Germans. He delivered his message in a solemn manner, but at services held later that week he began to preach more intensely and expansively. The revival was to culminate on Easter Sunday, when he hoped to deliver his most powerful sermons. On Easter morning Andrew arose long before sunrise to begin preparation for his first sermon at five o'clock A.M. As he had breakfast and his usual cups of coffee, he thought over and over about the message he wished to deliver. He wanted his sermon to be forceful and persuasive, for many people from the surrounding area would be attending the services and he sensed that this was going to be a special day. After the first service he planned to preach again at mid-morning, followed by a German service and communion at three o'clock in the afternoon. He would preach again in Norwegian at seven o'clock that evening.

By the time the evening service arrived, Andrew was still enthusiastic and at his evangelistic best despite the fact that he had been preaching since daybreak. "At this service, something truly remarkable took place." There was an "outpouring of the Holy Ghost over the large gathering and many who were not previously converted became violently awakened from their condition and became deeply distressed for their souls' salvation. This very penetrating awakening caused me to prolong my discourse, for I was in no hurry to leave such an unusual service."

Andrew's heartfelt message was so moving that long after the sermon members of the congregation remained at the church to share in the joy of the moment. Andrew took time to speak to individuals who were "in the most distress," and he gently gave them guidance and sympathy, along with a prayer for each person who requested it. That night Andrew and the congregation decided that services should be held every evening thereafter, until further notice.

Finally, around midnight, Andrew made his way home, guided by the lamp left burning in the window beside his front door. Although near exhaustion, he was elated that his revival was a resounding success. Laura was sick and could not attend the services, but she was eager to know what unusual occurrence had kept him so late at the church. He told her that "The Lord mercifully baptized us with fire from above [and] many became awakened and the folks were deeply concerned about their soul's salvation [and] I could not very well leave before now." Laura said she had a premonition that something unusual would happen that evening. Despite his exhaustion, Andrew was so euphoric about the day's events that he had difficulty sleeping.

Evening services were continued as part of the revival for several weeks, and many people returned again and again to hear the charismatic Andrew preach. Settlers from the surrounding communities heard about the revival and made it a point to attend. Some of the services lasted until midnight or beyond, which meant that men, women, and children who lived three or four miles away did not get home until early in the morning. At some of the services, "streams of tears flowed and audible sobbing was heard as if hearts would break." "During the services, there were many cries for help and many prayers were poured out over wounded hearts, but nothing fanatical occurred and everything transpired in an orderly manner." The revival of 1862 was an exhilarating time for Andrew, and its success was among his greatest evangelistic achievements.

In early summer Andrew walked to Sturgeon Bay to conduct services, and he was pleased to learn that his small group of followers was now ready to form a Moravian congregation. Bethlehem had previously granted Andrew permission to establish a church there, and on a Sunday afternoon he administered holy communion to 14 people. Before he returned to Ephraim he had the group elect three Trustees, and he advised them of the rules for subsequent elections. Andrew was thankful that he was instrumental in establishing yet another Moravian congregation within his mission following, and he hoped it would grow in spite of the constant proselytizing going on between denominations. He reminded himself to be on guard.

Shortly after returning to Ephraim Andrew felt "called" to leave on yet another mission trip—this time to Illinois and Iowa. After spending several days in Chicago, where he held services, he traveled on to Mission Point, Illinois. There he learned that a young Lutheran minister was trying to establish a congregation in the small community of Scandinavians. The minister, however, was not well liked because he was "ambitious and domineering, wanted to monopolize everything and to capture the country for Lutherdom." In addition to everything else, he was not even a good speaker. Andrew was stirred to battle. He decided it was time for him to provide the community with a spiritual reawakening to the Moravian faith. "I do not recall now how many times I preached during that visit, but I remember well that the hunger in their hearts was great and as for myself these meetings were soul-searching." The competition for converts was unrelenting.

Andrew next traveled to Leland, Illinois, where he found a number of friends and spent three weeks visiting and preaching. From Leland he took the train across Illinois to the Norwegian settlement in Keokuk, Iowa, that he had previously visited. He conducted services there every afternoon for about a week and also took the opportunity to see the sights along the bluffs overlooking the Mississippi River valley. "It is impossible for me to describe how these very impressive and remarkable views affected me, for they were very elevating and peculiar. I sat transfixed there for a long time, unable to say a word, for such wonderful views produced silence and amazement." It was a moving and mystical experience.

Although Andrew was in a happy frame of mind when he returned home to Ephraim, he soon realized that problems had arisen in his absence. The first problem he encountered was in Sturgeon Bay, where he learned there were disagreements among members of the new Moravian congregation. A small log church had been under construction for several years and now a few people who had worked on the building questioned whether it should be affiliated with the Moravian Church. As he feared, his efforts to establish a congregation in Sturgeon Bay were being undermined by members of other faiths. He traveled immediately to Sturgeon Bay and called a meeting to decide the fate of the church building once and for all. Thirteen people showed up to consider the matter, but only 11 were qualified to cast a vote. Eight people voted Moravian, two voted for the Friends' Society, and one voted Methodist. The result of the vote was declared legal and binding. The log structure would be a Moravian Church and plans were made to finish the building. Andrew saw to it that there was a written record of the meeting, noting the votes for and against, and he signed the document along with the three trustees. Problems in Sturgeon Bay were resolved for the moment, although later the signed document fell into the hands of someone other than a Moravian and was never seen again.

Problems were also arising in Ephraim. Some members of Andrew's congregation were dissatisfied with his long periods away from the community. Some whispered that he had behaved in an inappropriate manner with members of the opposite sex. Others complained that he was often too strong-minded and obstinate, and a few objected to Andrew's emotional preaching style. In addition to problems in his congregation, he was stung by efforts among a growing number of Lutherans in the area to establish their own church in his Moravian community. He began to refer to leaders of this effort as "archenemies." He and his friend Peter Peterson had grown distant, for Peterson was a devout Lutheran and hoped that someday there would be a Lutheran Church in Ephraim. Every so often Andrew felt as if his efforts were no longer appreciated in the village and that God was testing him. His life seemed to swing back and forth between one high and low point after another. Little did he know that in the near future he would suffer a crushing blow that would test him to his limits.

****

Although the revival meeting in the spring of 1862 was a great success and enhanced Andrew's position as Ephraim's spiritual leader, a series of events occurred that spring that brought his character into question. These events involved Andrew's curious relationship with the wife of Tobias Morbek, a friend and member of the Moravian congregation.

Morbek had recently moved from Eagle Island into his newly completed house at the south end of the village. He was a widower before he married his present wife, Elizabeth, who was quite a bit younger than her husband. During the move she became ill. Andrew, who had known Morbek for some time, was concerned about "Sister Morbek's" illness and he went out of his way to be helpful.

Sister Morbek had become very interested in religion, and Andrew hoped that through his spiritual guidance she might regain her health. She seemed to respond to Andrew's counseling and he felt "obliged to talk to her daily ...." Often these sessions became rather emotional, with tears flowing freely. Under Andrew's healing ministrations, Sister Morbek recovered gradually from her malaise—she proclaimed herself "touched by God's wonderful love and she felt herself unspeakably happy." Her happiness lasted about a week, and she said that she really did not think she had been sick at all—just weak from loss of sleep. She looked at Andrew and added with a smile, "Sleep seems to be entirely unnecessary to me for all through the nights I am in constant communion with my Savior and praying to him, and, Oh! it is such a happy time!" Morbek seemed quite relieved that his wife felt better, and he appreciated Andrew's efforts to help.

Because Andrew believed in homeopathic medicine, he often carried various extracts and remedies that he used to treat settlers, and he regretted that he did not have any sleep-inducing medicine at that time. Although still concerned about Sister Morbek's condition, he concluded that she was recovering and left Ephraim to attend to unexpected business in Green Bay and Fort Howard.

When Andrew returned a week later, his first stop as he came into town was the Morbek house. He was eager to find out how Sister Morbek was doing. Her distraught husband immediately pulled Andrew aside to tell him that his wife had not slept at all since Andrew departed for Green Bay and that her mind had been affected because of her inability to sleep. Andrew was shocked, for he had assumed that when he returned he would find her continuing to improve. When he went in to see her she was overjoyed with his presence, but it was obvious that her mind was wandering because she talked in a disconnected manner about one religious subject after another. Andrew was taken aback to find her in this condition. He realized she had slipped into a deranged state, but he was at a loss as to what to do.

After Andrew reached home he called together a few trusted members of the congregation and they prayed and wept together in behalf of Sister Morbek. Andrew lamented that he "could not understand why the Lord permitted such [things] to happen." After a prolonged period of prayer Andrew arose and happened to walk by the window overlooking the bay. Suddenly his gaze fixed on something that could hold the answer to his prayers. Anchored off shore he saw a small sloop that he recognized as belonging to Dr. Willey, a physician from Fort Howard with whom Andrew was acquainted. The physician had visited Ephraim in the past and his return at that moment brought Andrew renewed hope for Sister Morbek. He immediately rushed down the hill to find the good doctor.

After explaining the circumstances, Andrew accompanied the doctor to the Morbek house. The agitated Sister Morbek was not pleased to see the physician, and she said emphatically that she was no longer ill and did not need his help. Dr. Willey attempted to convince his new patient that she was indeed ill and tried to give her a spoonful of the medicine he used in such cases, but Sister Morbek adamantly refused. The doctor told her pointedly that she would only get worse without his help, and her husband begged her to take the medicine, but to no avail. She would have none of it. Finally Andrew stepped forward, took the spoon and medicine, and in a quiet but earnest voice said that it was his sincere belief that the medicine would be good for her. As he held her gaze with his intense look, he asked her once again if she would take the medicine. With resignation she finally said, "Yes, for your sake I'll take it." And she did. Thereafter during the course of her illness Andrew was the only person from whom she would take medicine.

Dr. Willey later informed Andrew that "this case was one of 'temporary insanity,' superinduced by strong religious feelings and especially because of the prolonged lack of sleep ...." According to Andrew, Willey prohibited all outside visitors and urged him to be in attendance as much as possible, since Sister Morbek would take medicine from no one else. The doctor remained in Ephraim a few days, and after he departed Andrew called on the patient as much as he could, spending a great deal of time at her bedside over a period of several months. Gradually Sister Morbek improved, and by the end of the summer of 1862 she had recovered her mind completely and had no memory of her previous mental condition.

As a result of the strange interdependent relationship between Andrew and Sister Morbek, rumors about the couple began to spread. This occurred in spite of the fact that the relationship was apparently sanctioned by her husband, Tobias, and that there was no real evidence that it was overtly sexual. Regardless, for many of the townspeople there was something too intimate about Andrew's preoccupation with the ailing Sister Morbek. It was as if he were obsessed with her—even his friends whispered speculation about what was going on at the Morbek house.

Although he does not mention it in his recollections, Andrew himself began to experience various kinds of health problems during that same summer. He was emotionally drained after his spring revival meeting, and the stressful episode with Sister Morbek occurred shortly thereafter. As she was recovering, Andrew was slipping into depression and ill health. He began complaining about one physical problem after another, from headaches to loss of vigor. At the same time, the rumors he heard about his relationship with Sister Morbek upset him and intensified the emotional pressure he felt.

He also heard rumors that someone had sent a letter to Bethlehem requesting an investigation into his recent behavior. Much later he learned that Zacharias and Tobias Morbek sent such a letter in September of 1862. During that same month Andrew wrote a letter to Bethlehem describing his physical and mental state, and then in December he wrote another letter in which he surprised church officials by requesting to be transferred away from Ephraim.

Early the next year Tobias Morbek became ill, apparently with pneumonia, and Andrew devoted a great deal of time ministering to his spiritual needs. He returned from a trip to Sturgeon Bay to find Morbek slipping toward death. "Deeply moved I fell on my knees at his bedside and sent praise and thanks to the dear Savior for the wonderful support and the glorious hope so abundantly bestowed upon this poor disciple on his journey homeward." After his prayer Andrew sang several "going-home" hymns. The next morning, as Morbek lay dying, Andrew held a simple service at the bedside and sang a few verses softly. Tobias Morbek drew his last breath with Andrew holding his hand and singing "Salighed i Evighed er hist de Guds Udvalgtes Lod." When he finished, Morbek exclaimed "Gloria!" in a strong voice, and died. Andrew burst into tears.

****

Throughout the difficult year of 1862, Andrew was sustained and renewed by his affection for Anna Munda, his "beloved and spiritual child." Ever since she had given herself to Jesus at the Christmas eve service of 1861, Andrew had seen her in a new light. Always fond of his little daughter, he now saw in her a spirituality and calmness that was unusual for one so young. "She was a child of prayer and no one needed to prompt her to read her bible, for that was her favorite treasure and how often did we not see her bowed down over her bible, quiet as a lamb, lost in concentration over what she was reading ...." "Moreover, she possessed an unusual sweet voice and with her remarkable memory she could repeat a great many songs and hymns, both Norwegian and English." He was proud that she was an excellent student and a favorite of her teacher, Pauline Johnson. Although he was often away from Ephraim and frequently preoccupied with church and community business, Anna Munda remained in his thoughts, and when he was home he found ways to spend time with her. He loved all his children, to be sure, but Anna Munda was special.

As 1862 drew to a close, "an epidemic of whooping cough gripped the settlement, nearly all the children in the neighborhood being stricken." Each of Andrew's four children "suffered a good deal on account of this severe cough, especially our precious nine year old daughter Anna Munda ...." There was no quick cure for this debilitating illness and a vaccine was more than 40 years away. Little could be done to relieve the symptoms, which included coughs of increasing intensity followed by a loud gasping for breath that sounded like a rasping whoop. The children's faces often turned blue during these frightening and exhausting spasms, and pneumonia, also untreatable, was a dangerous and common complication. Anna Munda "in the course of many weeks, became so weak that we expected her dear Savior would remove her while in this illness and take her home in eternal glory. Nevertheless this severe cough in her case came to an end early in March and we parents were very thankful and happy over the outcome."

Andrew and Laura were tremendously relieved to see Anna Munda on her feet again and not coughing. As they thought back over the course of her long illness they remarked on her unusual and wonderful patience—she had never complained and "Between her coughing spells her face was radiant with the most charming smile." During her illness she had not been able to talk much, but they noticed that she spent her time reading her Bible and praying. There was a spiritual serenity about her that seemed far beyond her years.

After a week, Anna Munda was forced to return to her bed again, and the optimism Andrew and Laura had allowed themselves to feel turned to dread. "Although the whooping cough had ceased, our dear Munda had become so weak that she was unable to walk and as day after day passed her strength did not return." Andrew was puzzled and greatly apprehensive. "She did not cough now and she seemed to have no fever; nor did she have much pain and she was always fully conscious, but her body faded away as a withered flower." With dismay he realized that "From the very beginning, when she first took sick, she had a firm belief that she would never arise from her sick bed physically well, but that she would be privileged 'to go home to her dear Savior,' and this assurance filled her heart with intense joy and happiness."

Andrew was torn. His life had been devoted to helping souls find eternal salvation, and as he looked upon his daughter he was fully aware that she "was born again and filled with the holy spirit!" "She ... burned with a longing for heaven and a desire to see her Savior face to face." How could he reconcile his reluctance to lose his beloved child with the joy he should feel at her ardently desired ascension to her "heavenly home"?

The following three weeks were a time of poignant agony for Andrew. He and the community knew that Anna Munda lay dying, yet her quiet joy reached out and profoundly touched all around her. Many visitors came to the white house on the hill, and "She spoke frankly to each and every one about her rich blessing, about her burning love for her precious Savior and about her intense longing 'to go home to the Lord.'" Departing callers often commented to Laura and Andrew, "Munda is already mature for heaven!" and Pauline Johnson, a frequent and favorite visitor, confided to Andrew that "I have received far more encouragement from precious Anna Munda than I can give her."

Her strength continued to diminish as March drew to an end, but her faith seemed to increase, and "Her longing to go home and see her Savior's countenance and forever be with him became more and more intense, although she loved her parents and brothers." At times she would awaken to see her parents weeping beside her bed and would comfort them gently. "Dear mama and papa! do not grieve and weep for soon we will meet again in heaven with Jesus and there we shall never, never be separated."

The last three days of Anna Munda's life made an intense and indelible impression on Andrew. With the help of church members, he and Laura maintained a constant vigil at her bedside. On the last Sunday of her life "her body was very weak; throughout the day she said very little but her face radiated a great inward joy and peace. Towards evening—the sympathizing sister P. Johnson was with us—an increased bodily strength manifested itself in our dear child. With a strong, enthusiastic voice she exclaimed: 'Today it's Sunday; Oh, I'm so happy! Very, very soon I'll be home in heaven with my dear Jesus!' Immediately she commenced to sing with a very fascinating voice: 'I want to be an angel and with the angels stand'... She sang the three verses very clearly and plainly...." "The impression which this inspiring song produced on us who were present was most wonderful. The presence of the Lord seemed to permeate the whole room where we were and our good sister Johnson, as if completely overcome, declared that she never before had experienced any thing so touching. But we parents were to be witnesses a few days later to something incomparably more remarkable."

Anna Munda's struggle cast a veil of sadness over the entire village. In such a small community, hardship that came to one family was shared by all, and Anna Munda's illness was of special concern. Although her spirituality was bewildering to some, everyone acknowledged that she was an exceptional child who "possessed unusual talents." Whenever small groups gathered, the conversation was subdued and inevitably turned to the sad event taking place at the Iverson house.

On the last day of March, it became "all too evident that the departure of our heaven-minded child was near ..." and an older woman of the congregation came to be with the family during the night. The vigil had taken its toll on Laura, who was heavily pregnant and completely exhausted. "My dear wife, never strong, was so worn out by vigilance and grief that it was absolutely impossible for her to remain with us. I pleaded with her to retire and try to get a good night's sleep." She agreed but only on the condition that "if it appears that the Lord comes tonight to take our dear child home, please awaken me as I wish to be present. This I promised her."

While her mother slept in another room Anna Munda also slept peacefully, but around midnight Andrew noticed that her breathing was becoming shallow and her pulse could scarcely be detected. Taking one of her hands in his, he felt how cold it was and realized that he should probably awaken Laura. Something held him back, however, and as midnight passed Anna Munda appeared to rally and her peaceful sleep resumed. Andrew spent the long hours of the night praying unceasingly "for my dear little daughter, whom I knew all too well we would soon have to surrender ...." As dawn approached Anna Munda began to slip away. "Her emaciated little body became colder and still colder; her breathing became weaker and weaker and irregular and, at dawn, when we could no longer feel her pulse, I hastened to the bedside of my sleeping wife and awakened her. She knew immediately what the call meant and as she had lain down fully dressed, she was immediately on her feet and we hastened to our loving little favorite's bed ...."

Upon seeing her child, and noticing that "signs of death were unmistakably present," Laura broke down. Sobbing, she said to Andrew, "Oh that our dear Munda would only open her eyes so that she might recognize us and so that we could take our last painful leave with her!" Just as Andrew was assuring her that even if their daughter were to open her eyes, she was too near death to recognize them, something extraordinary occurred. Anna Munda, who moments before had been cold and nearly lifeless, opened her eyes and said in a loud, clear voice, "Oh, the precious Lord Jesus! Oh, the dear Savior! How happy I am! How happy I am!" "Soon, very soon, I'll be in heaven and there I'll be an angel!" She then began to sing the family's favorite hymn. But although the song was very familiar to all who were present, there was a striking difference. "[The] melody was not natural—it was heavenly." Andrew was overwhelmed. "Never, never will I ever be permitted to listen to such a melody until by the grace of the lamb I shall pass saved into the glory of heaven ...." Showing no signs of pain, Anna Munda sang all four verses as tears streamed down her parents' faces.

When the "supernatural song" ended, she began to speak in a clear, strong voice, saying "I belong to my dear Savior and soon, yes, very soon, I'll be with him in heaven and there I'll be an angel." She described heaven so movingly and vividly that it occurred to Andrew to ask, "My dear Munda! Have you already been permitted a view of heaven and has your soul been there?" "No, dear papa! I have not yet seen heaven, but soon, very soon, I'll be there and oh! how blessed it will be!" She spoke at length about heaven and the joy that would follow when all were reunited there, mentioning her parents, H.A. Schultz, and his daughter, and other devout members of the church. "She very earnestly expressed her burning wish that she might be permitted to meet all the members of the congregation in heaven." She spoke in this manner for an hour and a quarter, and "During this time no sickness of any kind was visible to my eyes on our beloved Munda ...." Moved and overwhelmed, Andrew almost allowed himself to hope that the miraculous had happened, that she had been healed.

"Finally—tenderly smiling—she said slowly, 'Dear papa! would it be a sin for me if I now went to sleep—I feel so sleepy?'—'My precious child,' I answered, 'it is no sin at all; it is a necessity. Just lay your tired little head down tenderly as if in the arms and lap of Jesus and sleep sweetly!' Everything in the room became quiet and soon our precious little daughter fell into a peaceful sleep...." She slept quietly throughout the morning, under the watchful gaze of Andrew and one or more members of the congregation. That day was the first of April—spring was coming—but none of the people in the sick room noticed or cared.

A little after noon, Anna Munda awakened and said, "I see that I am still among you here below; don't you think, dear papa, that the Savior will soon come and take me home?" She awakened several times throughout the afternoon, with the same question, and each time Andrew attempted to reassure her. It was very difficult for him. It was clear that she yearned to be with Jesus, but at the same time he was deeply grieved at the prospect of saying goodbye to his beloved daughter.

Toward evening, her question to him became a little more direct. "Dear papa! are you also praying that my dear Lord Jesus will soon come and take me in His arms home to heaven?" Through his tears he answered, "Although it is very painful to us, your parents, to separate from you whom we love so tenderly; nevertheless, to see your intense longing to meet your dear Savior face to face in heaven, I would not keep you here, even though I could, and for that reason I can sincerely pray the Lord that He soon will come and take you home." His words seemed to strengthen her and she smiled at him and "spoke tender and sympathizing words" to her mother.

As the emotionally draining day gave way to night, Andrew marveled at his ability to get along with almost no sleep. His love for his daughter sustained him "as if with silken cords." She continued to awaken periodically, to look at the mantel clock, and to ask her father to pray that the Lord would come soon. Each time, he knelt at her bedside and prayed aloud in Norwegian. As midnight approached, she lay quietly awake, watching the clock and asked, "Dear papa! won't you please pray for me in English that the Lord will come and take me home?" This he did "with a burning earnestness, while bathed in a stream of tears." The end was near.

At four o'clock in the morning, just before the first hint of dawn began to lighten the sky, Andrew sensed that a great change was about to take place. "I immediately called my weak, grieving wife and three sons from their sleep and soon we were all standing weeping, around the bedside of this so dearly beloved wanderer to heaven who lay there continually gazing at all of us." As they all knelt beside her bed to pray, they heard her say, "'When I lay me down to sleep, I pray the Lord my soul to keep'—and then not a word, not a sound, any more."

An hour later, on April 2, 1863, Anna Munda Eleonora Iverson died. She went "to sleep so quietly and so sweetly—like a babe in its mother's arms—while everyone noticed a very wonderful peaceful smile on her lips ...." Her parents and brothers knelt at her bedside and Andrew prayed. "I poured out my soul in praise and gratitude to the great Friend of Children, the Savior, for our beloved Munda's triumphant departure ...." "We had scarcely risen from our knees when the church bell in Ephraim announced in mournful tones to all in the settlement that she who was such a highly praised disciple of Jesus, Anna Munda, had 'gone home', and more than one tear was shed."

Andrew's grief was nearly unbearable, yet it was mixed with the knowledge that something remarkable had happened. He realized that even if he had the power to recall the child he loved so much, he would not do so. He could not deny her the privilege of looking "upon her Savior's glorious countenance, which had been her heart's desire so long." Nevertheless it was terribly difficult for him to accept her loss, and he was almost overcome "with a burning and intense longing to follow after our precious daughter to the heavenly home, there to be liberated forever from the dark, sinful world full of tears."

The community gathered around the Iverson family to extend heartfelt sympathy and to assist with funeral arrangements. Andrew felt a tremendous amount of anxiety when he realized he would have to preside at the funeral service. "I almost trembled like a leaf when I thought of this heart-rending ceremony, for I knew that I myself would have to officiate; but I prayed without ceasing and out of the depths of my grieving heart that the Lord would comfort, strengthen, and help me and these prayers were graciously heard."

The whole congregation and almost everyone else in the settlement attended Anna Munda's funeral. Young men from the neighborhood carried her body, in its beautiful coffin, from her home on the hill down to the church where Andrew, sustained by the Lord, was able to conduct the service. After the ceremony, the coffin was carried up the hill to the cemetery, with the mourners following slowly behind, mud clinging to their shoes. Although the sky was clear and blue, deep under the large cedar trees a few patches of snow still lingered. "We gently lowered the tired little body of our blessed daughter, to rest until the resurrection morn—while we read the beautiful liturgy of our church ...."

Returning home was a sorrowful occasion for Laura and Andrew. "I will not refer to the painful emptiness which now seemed to stalk everywhere in our home, when we returned home from the never-to-be-forgotten burial and bereavement—bereavement such as the soul can seldom experience seemed to permeate the atmosphere of the whole house and we pressed to our sorrowing bosoms our dear sons, Alfred 11 years old, John 6 years old and little Joseph 2 years old." But Andrew knew they must carry on. "We mourning parents had to understand that it was necessary for us to walk in faith. No complaining was heard, but in our soul's deepest chamber there was a whisper: 'The Lord gave and the Lord hath taken away; blessed be the name of the Lord.'"

Three weeks after Anna Munda's funeral, Laura gave birth to another daughter, who was given the name of her departed sister, Anna Munda Eleonora. This "sweet little rose" helped heal the vast emptiness Andrew and Laura felt, and they had high hopes that she might lead a long and healthy life.

8

A PREMONITION

Andrew had suspended all his usual duties and concerns during the month of Anna Munda's sickness and death, but following his daughter's funeral in early April he attempted to resume his routine. He found, however, that he was struggling to regain his equilibrium, and that one crisis seemed to follow another. He could no longer ignore the fact that he faced problems in Ephraim and problems elsewhere.

One of the first challenges to confront him involved church politics in Sturgeon Bay, where his attempts to establish a Moravian congregation were being undermined by a devious Quaker. Because of Anna Munda's illness, Andrew had missed the annual meeting of the trustees of this congregation at which the completion of their church building was to be discussed. At the previous year's meeting the members, which included several individuals of different faiths, had voted to have the new building dedicated as a Moravian Church. At this year's annual meeting a new trustee was to be elected, and since Andrew was not able to attend, he had sent a message indicating his hope that they would select someone of the Moravian faith. Unfortunately his advice was ignored and Ole Johnson, a Quaker who had actively sought the position, was elected. Furthermore, as soon as he was elected he offered to be secretary for the congregation, and his offer was accepted.

Andrew believed that Johnson was willing to do whatever was necessary to make sure the building they were constructing never became a Moravian Church, and in May he decided to travel to Sturgeon Bay to meet with the trustees and other members of the congregation. He borrowed a dilapidated old sailboat and invited his sons, Alfred and Johnnie, to sail down to Sturgeon Bay with him. Alfred was 10 and Johnnie was 6 years old, and if Andrew had known that their lives would be at risk on the return trip he certainly would have left them at home.

The trustees' meeting proceeded better than Andrew had anticipated, with secretary Johnson presenting a lengthy report on the status of both the congregation and the church building. Andrew listened carefully, making a few suggestions here and there, and the meeting was both amicable and productive. Johnson went out of his way to be friendly, but after the meeting was over Andrew was still left with a feeling of uneasiness, and he became more determined than ever to see that his Moravian congregation in Sturgeon Bay had their own church building.

Following the meeting, Andrew gathered up his two sons and left Sturgeon Bay, sailing northward toward home. He soon noticed dark storm clouds overtaking them from the south, and at that point he regretted he had chosen to sail far out from shore to catch the steady breeze. As the wind picked up, the groaning old boat began to wallow in waves that grew larger and larger, so Andrew quickly dropped the sail and began to look for shelter. The children became frightened as the storm grew in intensity, but their father was unable to leave his position at the rudder to reassure them. When white-capped waves rolled into the teetering boat Andrew shouted at Alfred to begin bailing, and he did so as if his life depended on it. And in fact it did. Meanwhile little Johnnie huddled near his father and shivered, his small hands hanging onto whatever was available.

Andrew "let the boat plow ahead with naked masts, while the storm howled, creating waves whose tops seemed everywhere to be so white as if they were enveloped in a snow-storm. It was fortunate that I had been so well trained from my childhood to manage a boat, even in a storm, but, truly speaking, it was really the hand of God that preserved us." Finally they managed to reach the shelter of one of the Strawberry Islands, where they waited out the storm and said a prayer of thankfulness. Later he learned that "sea-faring brethren in Sturgeon Bay who had heard the wild storm were in great fear that we were lost en route home."

Not long after Andrew's trip to Sturgeon Bay, a Reverend F. Hagen arrived in Ephraim to visit with Andrew and his congregation. Hagen was from the Moravian Church's P.E.C. (Provincial Elders' Conference) Board in Bethlehem. Andrew did not know exactly why he had been sent to Ephraim, but he found him to be "a wonderful and powerful minister." "He took a great deal of interest in all our affairs and corrected several irregularities among us. I gained his full confidence and thanked the Lord for having sent us such an experienced brother."

Andrew wondered if Hagen's visit might have something to do with discontent in the congregation, because he continued to hear rumors that several members had written to Bethlehem. He had no doubt there were disruptive forces in the community, and his thoughts sometimes turned to the likelihood that he might have to leave the village he founded. He decided he could confide in Hagen, and before his guest left Fish Creek on the steamer, Andrew took the opportunity to talk with him about his situation. He reminded his visitor that the previous fall he had sent a letter to Bethlehem requesting a transfer. He reiterated that it was time for him to seek a ministry elsewhere, and that he hoped Bethlehem might find another Scandinavian minister to replace him. Hagen listened carefully and told Andrew he would present the request to his superiors.

Andrew anticipated hearing from Bethlehem soon, but he wondered if they would understand his situation. He did not completely understand it himself, and he had not been altogether candid with Hagen. This was a very difficult period for Andrew, and he was anxious, depressed, and often felt ill. In truth, neither he nor anyone else knew everything that was going on.

A few weeks after Hagen's departure Andrew received a different type of communication from Bethlehem, suggesting that he should investigate the possibility of establishing a Moravian Church in the Chicago area. A man named M. Olsen had written to Bethlehem informing Church leaders that there were many people in the Chicago area interested in organizing themselves into a Moravian congregation. Although Andrew was somewhat pessimistic about this venture, he made his way to Chicago as soon as he could arrange it. Upon arriving, he visited individually with everyone interested in establishing a Scandinavian Moravian Church, including M. Olsen who Andrew found to be a very "odd and peculiar" person.

Andrew's next step was to set up a meeting with the entire group. After opening the meeting "with song, prayer, and scripture reading," he made a brief presentation and then set forth the rules and regulations of the Church, stressing that everyone who wished to become a member of the Church would have to accept and abide by all these rules. When he asked whether they were willing to be bound by such regulations a number of people enthusiastically accepted the tenets of the Church, but Olsen's response came as a surprise. He stated that although he could accept most of the Church's rules, there were some to which he could never consent. As Olsen continued his discourse on the unacceptability of many of the regulations, Andrew watched the faces of others in attendance begin to show questioning looks. By the time Olsen finished, many in the previously favorable audience had become less certain and seemed unwilling to make the sincere commitment required to establish a Moravian congregation. Andrew's heart sank. All his efforts were to no avail. He had lost another battle for souls.

Hoping for a much-needed respite from his recent tribulations, Andrew left Chicago for Leland, Illinois, where he planned to visit friends and preach. There he received an unusually friendly welcome that did much to lift his spirits. It turned out that a young Lutheran minister had begun preaching and organizing a Lutheran congregation in the community, but he was disliked by many people and "all the awakened Christians had resigned from the congregation and as they knew me from my previous visit, they were in great expectation to see me again."

Andrew was struck with the great spiritual need that existed in Leland. "Several of the more experienced believers, with whom I was obliged to visit in their homes, asked me with tear-stained eyes if it would not be possible for me to come and be their steady minister ...." "I answered that while I should very much like to do so, it was a matter over which I had no control and that such a change would have to come from the [administration] in Bethlehem."

From Leland, Andrew continued his travels, journeying 15 miles to nearby Mission Point, where he was also greeted with warmth and friendliness. As in Leland, a Lutheran minister had established a congregation and he too was disliked by many of his constituents, who said he conducted himself more like a military leader than a man of God. No wonder everyone was glad to see Andrew. Many of his friends in Mission Point implored him to find a way to move to the area and serve the two communities, and they assured him they could provide housing and financial support. Andrew was flattered. He gave them considerable encouragement and told them that if they were serious, the two settlements should make a written petition to Bethlehem.

On the way back to Ephraim, Andrew was the happiest he had been in a long time. He felt wanted again. If it became necessary to say goodbye to Ephraim, it would at least be on his terms. And if things worked out, his new mission would be to serve the deserving Illinois communities of Leland and Mission Point.

Although 1863 had been stressful, and although he derived less and less pleasure from returning home to Ephraim, two events occurred that helped Andrew deal with his increasingly depressed mood. First of all, "the young ladies in the Academy at Bethlehem" sent him $100 that he used to obtain "a beautiful and speedy horse and a new saddle." Now his frequent trips to Sturgeon Bay would be easier. He would no longer be "compelled to walk thirty miles in one day over the worst kind of roads, through swamps full of water and in the summer swarming with mosquitoes." He tired more easily than he once did and he often did not feel well. He looked forward to spending less time walking—it would be a pleasure to ride like "a gentleman ...."

The second event was the receipt of two communications on the same day, one from Leland and the other from Mission Point. These letters were in the form of petitions formally requesting that Andrew move to Illinois to assume responsibility for the two congregations. The letters also stated that a formal request had been sent to Bethlehem. Later Andrew received a notice from from Bethlehem saying "that they were favorable to my accepting the call in Illinois." It was likely that such a move could be made "if they could locate a suitable brother, either in Denmark or Norway, who could take up the work in my place in Ephraim and Sturgeon Bay." The news encouraged Andrew, and he began to feel more hopeful about the future.

"The approaching Christmas, 1863, and New Year 1864, were not celebrated with the joy and encouragement which had prevailed in past years in Ephraim, as it seemed that grief tinged our thoughts and actions. I had a premonition, and truly so, that this Christmas and New Year were to be my last in dear Ephraim."

****

Near the end of January 1864 Andrew received a letter from H. Hanson, a fellow Moravian and confidante in Sturgeon Bay, stating that their church building was nearing completion. The letter also contained the distressing news that Ole Johnson, the congregation's secretary, had talked with each member of the group and declared "that the newly constructed building would never belong to the Moravian Church." In defense of his statements Johnson offered distorted and self-serving reasons, and he vigorously and persuasively argued for another meeting to once again vote on which religious group should have control of the building.

Andrew was furious when he heard the news from Sturgeon Bay. Didn't he have enough problems in Ephraim? He was tiring of the constant battle to maintain his mental equilibrium in the face of one crisis after another. Nevertheless, he traveled to Sturgeon Bay the next day and prayed he would have the strength to do what needed to be done. He was exhausted by the time he arrived at H. Hanson's home, where he spent the night. Hanson brought Andrew up-to-date on the situation. Later that evening after a much-needed period of rest, Andrew laid out his plans "to counteract and overcome the evil which had been done."

Since Ole Johnson lived on the other side of Sturgeon Bay, it was several days before he learned that Andrew was in town. This gave Andrew time to spend quiet, reassuring visits with members of the congregation committed to the Moravian faith—and time to put his plan into action. He carefully prepared a legal document of incorporation for the Scandinavian Moravian Church in Sturgeon Bay and called together seven male members of the congregation to serve as Directors: Niels Thorstensen, Anthoni Thompson, Capt. N.P. Nelson, Hans Hanson, Christian Knudsen, Hans J. Hansen and Ambrosius Knudson. The group, led by Andrew, went to a Justice of the Peace where they signed the document and had it notarized, thereafter receiving an affidavit. They then visited the Register of Deeds to have the document recorded and properly registered. The document was dated January 30, 1864.

The next step was to transfer title of the property to the newly incorporated congregation. The church building had been erected on an acre of land donated by Anthoni Thompson, now a Director in the corporation set up in behalf of the congregation. After leaving the Register of Deeds office, the group went directly to Thompson's house to transfer ownership of the acre of land. Using information provided by Thompson, Andrew sat down and prepared a description and deed for the tract. When completed, it was signed by Anthoni Thompson and his wife, Maren, in the presence of two witnesses. The group then set out again for the Register of Deeds office where the deed, showing transfer of ownership of the property to the Scandinavian Moravian Congregation of Sturgeon Bay, was duly registered. It was a moment of triumph for Andrew and his fellow Moravians.

That Sunday Andrew held two services at the Thompson house, and during each service he announced that there would be a meeting of the trustees of the congregation the next afternoon. He said the meeting would be held at the newly completed church building.

Andrew opened the meeting with a prayer and then permitted Ole Johnson, who had made so much trouble for the congregation but who was still secretary, to give his report. Andrew sat quietly and listened to the presentation. When Johnson concluded, Andrew indicated that all was satisfactory so far. He then fixed Johnson with an intent look and informed him that upon his arrival in Sturgeon Bay he was surprised and chagrined to learn that Johnson had been actively fomenting unrest in the congregation. With his jaw set and his piercing stare fixed on Johnson, he declared that Johnson "had been the cause of great confusion and unrest, because of his desire to take this building away from the Moravian Church and have it voted into another denomination ...." Johnson was stunned. He sat silent and grim-faced as Andrew continued to address him. "You know very well to whom the building was voted and if you had not been satisfied with that decision, you could have declined to participate in all further construction work ...."

Andrew also reminded his antagonist that when he accepted the trusteeship he was obliged to serve the interests of the Moravian Church congregation. At that time he could have refused the office, without dishonor, "but you accepted the office willingly and even offered yourself to act as the secretary for the congregation." "Now, just as this church building is almost completed, you have commenced to destroy all the order and law which have prevailed and you cannot deny that you have caused confusion and unrest. Is not such action on your part not only very unjust and unchristianlike, but even cunning, unfriendly and full of enmity?" Rather than let the matter lie, Andrew continued to press his case until Johnson "broke down into violent weeping." When he finally regained his composure, Johnson promised he would withdraw his participation in the congregation and would not create any further dissension.

After the meeting broke up and Johnson departed, members of the group congratulated each other on not divulging that the congregation had been incorporated and that they now had in hand a legally binding deed to the property on which the church building was constructed. Andrew "joyfully" returned to Ephraim feeling that the conflict in Sturgeon Bay had been finally resolved. He was wrong.

Two weeks later Andrew learned that Johnson had spent a great deal of time talking with members of the Scandinavian population in Sturgeon Bay, including members of the Moravian congregation. He was clever, and he played up his position in the group of workers involved in construction of the new church building. A smooth talker, he artfully planted seeds of discontent in the minds of his listeners. He argued that there should be a special meeting to decide, once and for all, the building's fate, and he even took it upon himself to set a day and place for this unusual assembly. He knew what he wanted and he would stop at nothing to achieve his goal, which was to determine the religious affiliation of the building.

Johnson reinforced his position by packing the special meeting with Lutherans who had "done nothing at all to assist in the building of the church." "Through his flattering remarks, it was a simple matter for Johnson to be chosen as the chairman of the meeting and he himself appointed himself as the secretary of the meeting." The meeting quickly degenerated into a confused and stormy confrontation. "When Johnson discovered that he could neither get the church building voted in favor of the Quakers denomination nor for the 'Evangelical Church,' he spoke in favor of the Lutheran Church and at last the votes were cast ...." Members of the Moravian congregation refused to vote, while all the Lutherans in attendance voted in support of the motion. Johnson was overjoyed—at last he had revenge for his recent humiliation by Andrew. Quickly and with great flourish, he prepared a document indicating that on that date at a "General Assembly" meeting, the newly erected church building was accepted as belonging to the Lutheran denomination. He and several of his co-conspirators confidently signed the document and the meeting was adjourned.

As soon as possible Johnson and his entourage took the document to a Notary Public to obtain an affidavit to the veracity of the agreement. The Notary turned out to be well-acquainted with the affairs of the Moravian congregation. "When this Notary Public had hastily scanned the document, he burst out into loud laughter and said as he handed the paper back to Johnson that he could just as well throw it in the stove and burn it, as it was of absolutely no use. He told him further that this church building had been voted on at the first Regular meeting as belonging to the Scandinavian Moravian Church in Sturgeon Bay with over two-thirds majority and that the minutes of said meeting had been recorded. He also stated further that the above-mentioned congregation had been legally incorporated with trustees and that Mr. Anthoni Thompson and his wife had deeded to the congregation the lot on which the building was erected—everything recorded—and that no power could invalidate these rights, etc."

The smug smiles worn by Johnson and his friends when they entered the Notary's office faded into disbelieving expressions as they came to realize the futility of their efforts. With Johnson, the feeling of disbelief was quickly replaced by anger and bitterness. He hated Andrew—and for years thereafter he vehemently claimed that, thanks to Andrew, the Moravians had "stolen" the church building.

****

Andrew had triumphed in Sturgeon Bay. In early February he returned to Ephraim in an optimistic and hopeful frame of mind, but his happiness was short-lived. Almost immediately he had to contend with the unceasing rumors about his behavior that continued to circulate in the village, and while he was worrying about this situation, his only surviving daughter became ill. Laura and Andrew's third Anna Munda died, apparently of pneumonia, on February 22, 1864, dealing the family another crushing blow.

At the funeral service for his ten-month-old child, Andrew managed to read a poem he had composed the previous day. The first verse read:

Og Ilbud kom atter igjen.
Min Gud! hvem faar Budskab at gaa?
Erdet dig, lille Engel! maa dudrage hen
Gjennem Jordanens Morkvand, hvor kommer du frem
I det Dybe med Fodder saa smaa?

And the messenger comes again
My God, who receives your command to go?
Is it you, little angel? Must you drag her
Through earth's dark trials, how can she come forth
From that deep sleep with a body so frail?

When he tried to speak further he was so overcome with grief that he was unable to continue the service. Pauline Johnson, the Iversons' faithful friend, "sang solemnly and softly a suitable 'going-home' song in English and after a brief prayer and the blessing, we left the church, walking slowly with bowed heads past my house, in which again this bereavement was felt most painfully, to the 'Lord's Acre,' where we tenderly deposited our departed little treasure by the side of her blessed sister, bearing the same name, Anna Munda Eleonora ...."

Back at the church Andrew faced another painful responsibility—recording his daughter's death in the Church Book. Turning to the Döde (Deaths) section, he inscribed the name Anna Munda Eleonora in his beautiful handwriting, noting sorrowfully that it was directly beneath the same name he had written only 10 months previously. The death of his third Anna Munda was another tragedy to be endured by Andrew, whose life was continuing to swing back and forth between tragedy and triumph.

****

Compounding Andrew's problems in the village was his realization that the Lutherans, with Peter Peterson as their leader, were attempting to expand into Moravian territory. For several years after Peterson arrived in Ephraim, Andrew enjoyed his support but lately the relationship had become strained. Although Peterson was a devout Lutheran, his wife Mary attended services at the Moravian church. In fact, she had been "truly converted" during Andrew's second big revival meeting in Ephraim and soon began attending Moravian prayer meetings regularly. Eventually she decided that she would like to become an official member of the Moravian congregation, but her husband refused to allow her to do so, and thereafter he went out of his way to tease his wife about her interest in the Moravian Church. When Andrew heard about this he began to see Peterson more as an enemy than a friend.

Andrew was well aware of the growing number of Lutherans in the area and felt threatened by them. He believed his Moravian colony was being undermined by dilution with other faiths, and Peterson seemed to have emerged as the leader of the "stiff Lutherans, who could neither accept the true word of God nor the simple rules and ordinances of the Moravian Church." Andrew found that many Lutherans were "continually unfriendly towards us and very seldom came to our meetings, but in the course of time found a friend and leader in Mr. Peterson, whose store they often frequented."

Early in 1864, "these enemies finally persuaded Mr. Peterson, without difficulty, to write to a certain Pastor Bjorn (a very prominent Lutheran), asking him to visit Ephraim as there were so many Lutherans in the vicinity who were not served by any pastor, etc." Bjorn agreed to come, and two of Ephraim's leading Lutherans asked permission to use the Moravian Church for the visiting minister's services.

Andrew was angry about the possibility of having to allow the enemy's advocate the privilege of preaching in his own church, but he kept quiet and duly met with church trustees and elders to make a decision. To keep peace in the community, they decided to allow the Lutherans to use the church building, but Andrew advised some of the elders to be present to "pay particular attention to any attempt to speak unkindly or make derogatory statements against the Moravian Church ...."

Although the Lutherans were very enthusiastic about Bjorn's preaching, their enthusiasm was diminished "when they were requested to 'dig up' to cover the pastor's demand ... for his visit." They considered his fee to be altogether too high, and "Later Mr. Peterson expressed himself sarcastically in his store in the presence of a group of countrymen: 'The Lutheran preachers are smart people for they demand ten cents for each word in their sermons!' This statement created a hearty laugh. However, from this visit was sown the seed for the later bitter opposition of the Lutherans to the Moravian Church in Ephraim ...." Andrew fails to mention that the converse was also true—namely that he and most of his fellow Moravians just as bitterly opposed the existence of a Lutheran Church in the village.

9

"A TRAIL OF TEARS"

Spring of 1864 was a time of reckoning for Andrew. He realized he had lost the support of influential members of his congregation and it was difficult for him to know what to do or how to behave. He was becoming resigned to the fact that he must now leave the little village that meant so much to him.

In March he walked the familiar trail to Sturgeon Bay. He had been forced to sell his "beautiful and speedy" horse because he could no longer afford to feed it. In Sturgeon Bay he visited with members of the congregation in their homes, and he was relieved to learn that his nemesis, Ole Johnson, had finally given up his efforts to wrest the new church building from the Moravians. The congregation decided that the church should be dedicated the next Sunday, and Andrew was there to officiate at the first Holy Communion. In spite of his depressed mood, Andrew preached a powerful sermon, for he knew there would not be many more visits to Sturgeon Bay. "Not a few consciences became awakened and I remember especially one of them, a young daughter [of a Quaker]—at that time about 15 years old—who became deeply touched and a believer in the Lord Jesus. Very often under a stream of tears she had told me how earnestly she desired that her sin-stained soul might be saved, receive religious instruction and be baptized, and she added with deep regret that it was not likely that her father would permit her to be baptized." The young lady's name was Martine Bakke.

Andrew later asked Bakke's father if he would grant his daughter's wish to be baptized. Although the father's response to Andrew was ambiguous, he later told his daughter she could not be baptized a Moravian as long as she lived in his house. Andrew "comforted her and pleaded with her to just cling to the Savior when her wish would surely be realized ...." It would take three years for her wish to become reality—and Andrew himself would perform the baptism.

During the spring Andrew received several letters from his friend, H. Thompson in Leland, Illinois, who said everyone was eagerly awaiting word on whether or not he would be joining them as their pastor. This was a welcome message, for Andrew was weary of the rejection he felt in Ephraim and ready for a fresh start. In May Andrew received word from Bethlehem that the Church had located someone to replace him. His replacement, from Christiansfeld, Denmark, was J.J. Groenfeldt, who agreed to serve both the Ephraim and Sturgeon Bay congregations. Andrew was told he need not await Groenfeldt's arrival before departing for Leland. This news meant the waiting was over for Andrew, and that it was time to accept the reality that his life in Ephraim was over. In the back of his mind there had been a vague hope that somehow his congregation would rally behind him and Bethlehem would send a last-minute plea for him to remain in place. The news that his replacement was en route to America dashed any such hope.

With sadness, Andrew and Laura discussed the matter and decided to leave Ephraim near the end of June. Andrew contacted the congregation in Illinois to let them know that he and his family would be joining them. As he faced his inevitable departure from Ephraim, Andrew began making preparations. "I now advised the congregation in Ephraim that it was my intention soon to remove to Illinois. Some brethren listened to this news with deep regret; others were perhaps well satisfied with this change. For sometime I was very busy, arranging my temporal affairs."

Early in June, Andrew made a last trip to Sturgeon Bay to participate in two farewell meetings at the new church and say goodbye to his friends. In many respects he now felt more welcome in Sturgeon Bay than in Ephraim. The "goodbye" services on Sunday were moving affairs. "Nearly everyone was bathed in tears; I had never previously experienced anything so tinged with sadness in Sturgeon Bay."

Andrew missed the presence of the H. Hanson family at the church services, for they were special friends and he had always been a welcome guest in their home during his stays in Sturgeon Bay. He learned that a timber fire had been burning in the Sturgeon Bay area and was threatening the Hanson homestead. This explained the unusually strong smell of wood smoke Andrew had noticed as he neared Sturgeon Bay. He decided to visit the Hanson family as soon as possible, for he was concerned about their welfare.

On Monday Andrew made his way on foot toward the Hanson farm a mile or so outside Sturgeon Bay. When he had walked to within a quarter of a mile of their home, he discovered the fire was still raging on both sides of the road, but he found a break in the fire line and managed to slip through it and reach the Hanson homestead. As Andrew approached he saw Hanson and his family sitting in a field, their clothes blackened with soot and ash, "watching the fire which was still burning in the stumps and in the foundation of the barn, now destroyed." The family had not slept at all the previous night as they "worked desperately carrying water to save their home." Andrew consoled them as best he could, but when he mentioned that he was moving to Illinois and had come to tell them goodbye, "brother Hanson broke out weeping and could not say a word."

"Leaving the children to watch the fire, we went into the house which had always been to me a very sacred home. Here we fell on our knees and while the tears flowed copiously, we prayed as if our hearts would melt. It was almost impossible for me to tear myself away from this faithful brother and sister and the final painful separation I will not describe." It was part of the Moravian tradition that members of the faith were considered to be brothers and sisters, not in a literal way, but in a way that implied the kind of bonding that can exist between real siblings. Andrew loved the Hanson family, and he would always remember that they provided him with "another good home and where I had so often received sweet rest and excellent entertainment and refreshments after my weary thirty miles on foot in past years."

As Andrew began the trip back to Ephraim he realized he felt very much a part of many families in the area. He had loved them and prayed for them. He had always tried to be there when they were sick or in need of spiritual guidance. And they would always be a part of him. "As I proceeded home the long, weary way, old memories held my attention and tears came to my eyes again and again, so that this became a 'trail of tears,' although I could plainly see my gain in my removal and separation."

On a Sunday early in July Andrew preached his last sermon in Ephraim—it was his farewell address to the church and community he had founded. "With tearful eyes I begged all my brethren and friends to forgive me for all my shortcomings through all the years which we had been together, just as from the depths of my heart I forgave all who had in any way wronged me and that in this separation it was my firm hope and belief that we could part with reconciled hearts as true brethren and friends. It is impossible for me to describe the emotion and the weeping prevalent in this gathering nor can I say much about the many sincere farewell handclasps which followed. I draw the curtain over the scene."

"When our household goods were boxed, I sent it [sic] by boat to Fish Creek, with orders to hold it there until our arrival. But when the time for our departure from Ephraim arrived, our oldest son, Alfred, became ill with the measles. This illness delayed us several days. We had previously promised brother and sister [Pauline] Johnson to visit them in their cozy home (two miles from Ephraim) and to remain with them for a few days before our departure.

"At last, on the morning of the 6th of July, our Alfred had so far recovered that my wife and children could proceed via boat over to brother and sister Johnson. I remained behind for a few days in the dear home as if lost in deep sorrow of reminiscences. I was completely alone there with my God and Savior, but it will never be possible for me to interpret my feelings in these my last hours in my home, now being surrendered forever. When finally I stepped out and closed the door, it was as if I was about to lose my breath and that my heart would break, but I finally managed to exclaim 'Farewell dear home; farewell, dear Ephraim!'

"With sad and slow steps I took the road but for over a half mile around the bay simple Ephraim (to me seemingly the most precious spot in the world) was visible and many, many times in that short distance I turned around ... to get just one more view of the dear home which now disappeared behind me in the distance. Just where the road turned into the woods and where I viewed for the last time my favorite spot, I broke into violent weeping, crying out my last farewell. The tears ceased perhaps as I walked on but my bleeding heart sighed deeply again and again."

****

Of the thousands of miles Andrew had walked in his lifetime, the two miles from Ephraim to the home of Martin and Pauline Johnson were the most difficult of all. Upon arriving at the Johnson house and being greeted by Pauline, Andrew stood silently for moment. Then he said in a quiet, sad voice: "I have now said my last, painful farewell to my never-to-be-forgotten home in Ephraim ...." Tears flowed again from his eyes as the weeping Laura greeted him, and "Our faithful and sympathizing sister [Pauline] wept with us and felt just as sad ...."

The Iverson family remained with the Johnsons for several days, after which they traveled by boat to Fish Creek, accompanied by Pauline. "In Fish Creek, where we enjoyed the hospitality with our friends, Mr. and Mrs. A. Thorp, we remained until the 11th of July before our steamer came. When our household goods were on board, the painful separation and touching farewells followed with our faithful and most sympathizing friend, sister P. Johnson, as well as leave-taking with other friends, and our sad journey had commenced."

Andrew was 41 years old when he said goodbye to his beloved Ephraim. His dream had come to an end. There is no evidence that he ever visited Ephraim again.

After Ephraim

1864 - 1907

10

A NEW BEGINNING, AND AN END

With both sadness and anticipation, Andrew shepherded his family onto the steamship that would begin the long journey to their new home in Leland, Illinois. They planned to take the ship from Fish Creek to Fort Howard and then transfer to a train for the remainder of the trip to Leland, the small, prairie village about 50 miles southwest of Chicago. After boarding the ship, Laura, Andrew, Alfred, Johnnie, and little Joseph stood at the rail watching as Door County faded from view. Andrew was nearly overcome with emotion as he realized that the community he had created was slipping away from him as surely as the high, green bluffs were slipping away behind the steamer. It was July 11, 1864, only 11 years from the time he had brought his small flock up to the "beautiful bay" with such high hopes. How quickly the years had passed.

The trip was scarcely under way when both he and Laura noticed that something was amiss with Johnnie. "En route on this sad trip ... we noticed that our dear son, Johnnie, did not feel well and we feared that he would be stricken with measles, which proved to be the case ...." Just as they had been forced to delay their departure from Ephraim because of Alfred's measles, this time they had to stay with friends in Fort Howard for several days, waiting until Johnnie became well enough to continue the trip by train.

Johnnie continued to improve but three-year-old Joseph fell ill on the train. It seemed to his distressed parents that the family could not escape sickness. The midsummer heat, combined with their worry about Joseph, made the two-day train trip seem much longer, but at last the weary family arrived in Leland. As they emerged from the train, carrying Joseph, they saw that many friends were gathered at the depot to greet them, including their good friend H. Thompson who was "awaiting us with his comfortable carriage and horses and who brought us to his beautiful home, where kind Mrs. Thompson received us with great cordiality. Two rooms were placed at our disposal and our sick little son received excellent care."

The following day was Johnnie's seventh birthday, but there was little time or inclination for celebration. It was Sunday, and despite his fatigue and emotional turmoil, Andrew decided to preach his first sermon as a member of the community. "The news of my arrival spread like wildfire over the whole settlement and also the announcement that I was willing to give my inaugural sermon the following day ...." Preaching in a school house, he felt reassured as he watched the room fill with a large and appreciative gathering. "My poor heart was touched and I was able to preach the true word of God in all earnestness ...." "After the benediction, nearly everyone came forward and wished me welcome, pressing my hand eagerly." The warm response and the worshipers' obvious delight in having him with them went a long way toward easing the pain he felt when he recalled his last months in Ephraim.

When Andrew accepted the Leland pastorship, he consented to preach every other Sunday at Mission Point, a tiny village 15 miles over the prairie and across the river. Friends agreed to provide transportation, and shortly after he arrived he traveled to Mission Point, as promised, and delivered a sermon to a responsive and welcoming group. He had little time to enjoy this reception, because as soon as he got back to the Thompsons' house in Leland, he discovered "that Johnnie and Joseph were very ill with a burning fever which had seized them the previous night. Immediately upon my return, I prepared my homeopathic fever remedy, prescribing it carefully. The following morning the fever had left Johnnie and he was able to sit up, but our dear Joseph, although a little better, was still ill with fever; he also had a bad cough and pains in his little lungs." Although the boys had been diagnosed originally with measles, the disease had evidently so weakened them that they had been stricken with secondary infections.

Caring for the two boys and their lively older brother while living in the Thompsons' guest quarters proved to be a trying experience. Fortunately a rented house soon became available and the family moved in, "taking our sick little son along with us tenderly." Johnnie began to improve rapidly but when Joseph failed to respond to his father's treatments, Andrew sought help. Two doctors practiced in town and he consulted the older one first. His efforts were of no value, although he prescribed "certain strong medicines from the drug store ...." When he was unable to diagnose Joseph's illness, Andrew next called in the younger doctor, who was also mystified by the disease.

A third doctor from out of town saw Joseph when he had been sick nearly four weeks. This man was a homeopathic physician who diagnosed Joseph's illness as "Quick Consumption," saying it was so far advanced that "he feared a cure was impossible." Nevertheless he left "certain special medicines and careful instructions ...." "But this treatment did not have the desired result. Our dear little Joseph did not improve, but, on the contrary, grew worse day by day, and he suffered especially at night. It was impossible for him to lie in bed during these trying hours of the night, being most satisfied when he could be carried around in my arms." Anguished and weary, Andrew spent every night for the next two weeks walking the floor of his small rented house, carrying his son. As he walked slowly back and forth, he thought of Anna Munda who had died only six months previously, and of her sister who had died just 10 months before that. Tears sometimes filled his eyes—was he about to lose another child? Grief often threatened to overwhelm him, and he asked God to give him the strength to carry on and to endure the prolonged vigil and lack of sleep.

In the early hours of August 26, Joseph appeared so emaciated and weak that Andrew and Laura believed he would not live through the night. To their surprise, by morning he had improved and asked to come to the breakfast table and sit in his father's lap. Andrew and Laura were overjoyed, but it was the last time he would share breakfast with his family. By noon he was in such pain that once again Andrew began pacing the floor. While he paced, cradling his dying son in his arms, Reverend J.J. Groenfeldt and his wife appeared unexpectedly at the door. They were on their way to Ephraim and on instruction from Bethlehem had stopped by to obtain information about the churches in Ephraim and Sturgeon Bay. Although Laura and Andrew were griefstricken and nearing exhaustion, they managed to offer the Groenfeldts simple refreshments, and Andrew even found time to spend a few moments talking with Groenfeldt about the Ephraim and Sturgeon Bay congregations.

An hour or so after the Groenfeldts arrived, Joseph died. "The Savior came and took our precious child home, releasing him from all suffering." Andrew was devastated by the loss of his son, but he had little time to mourn because the Groenfeldts were leaving that same evening and he felt obliged to tell them good-bye and make sure they had directions on the correct route to Ephraim.

Two days later Laura and Andrew buried their fourth child. "The solemn burial of our dearly beloved Joseph ... took place with many sympathizing friends in attendance." Because there was no Moravian minister in the area other than Andrew, a Swedish Methodist minister officiated, using the Moravian liturgy. The long trip to the cemetery in the oppressively hot and humid weather became "a trial of pain, and when we returned, how empty and void our home seemed ...." "Andrew took comfort in the presence of his surviving sons, Alfred and Johnnie, but he regretted that he could not record Joseph's death in the Church Book, where his baptism was recorded. The book remained at the church in Ephraim.

****

During the rest of the year and throughout the following spring (1865), Andrew diligently preached the word of God to his followers in Leland and Mission Point. The winter trips across the prairie to Mission Point were taxing for him, because "The terrible and bitterly cold storms of the prairies were much harder for me to endure than the intense cold of northern Wisconsin." His meetings were well-attended and worshipers were quick to tell him how much they benefited from his sermons. They made sure the Iverson family did not want for "the temporal necessities," and Andrew considered himself fortunate to be among his many friends in Leland. Nevertheless, there was something that bothered him greatly: it was becoming increasingly clear that despite his followers' delight in his presence, they had no real interest in establishing a Moravian church in the area. He had known when he arrived that most were Lutherans who had fallen out with their former pastor, but ever the evangelist, he was hopeful he would be able to convert them. But as time went by he grew frustrated by his inability to effect any conversions.

In the spring of 1865, the entire community was shaken by the news of President Lincoln's assassination, and Scandinavians throughout the area conducted services of mourning and remembrance. The shock of this traumatic event had scarcely subsided when Andrew received a visit from Reverend S. Wolle, who had been sent by Bethlehem to investigate conditions in Leland and Mission Point.

Andrew talked with Wolle at length and told him frankly that the chance of establishing a Moravian church in the area was remote. He explained that although the Lutherans "loved the creed and the cult ..." of the Moravian Church, they did not want to affiliate with it. They preferred to remain Lutherans. After visiting with congregations in each village, and even preaching a brief sermon in Mission Point, Wolle told Andrew that he agreed completely with his assessment of the situation. Both men believed that the people of the area were sincere and honest Christians, and both deeply regretted that they were not willing to become Moravians.

As Andrew's second winter in Leland approached, his health seemed to deteriorate along with the weather. The regular trips to Mission Point were an increasing burden, and at one point he became snowbound in that community for three weeks. It continued to surprise him that he suffered far more from the intense cold in Leland than he ever had during his years in northern Wisconsin. He believed that the cold, damp air he encountered on his trips over the prairie caused him to contract erysipelas, a painful inflammation of the skin. This disease can cause the sufferer to feel quite ill with fever, chills, headache, and nausea, but Andrew faithfully continued his missions of outreach. And no matter how busy he was or how sick he felt, he wrote regularly to Bethlehem informing them of his activities and of conditions in the area. In many of these letters he expressed his dissatisfaction with his assignment in Leland and requested a change. With time his requests for a transfer became more urgent.

After a year and a half in Leland, Andrew was even more dissatisfied and depressed. He felt increasingly ineffectual in his efforts to establish a Moravian church in the area and his physical condition had not improved. In addition Laura had contracted pneumonia, forcing Andrew to nurse her back to health with homeopathic remedies. As if this were not enough, the local Scandinavian Methodists decided to hold a series of big revival meetings that he took as a challenge to his role as spiritual leader of the community.

Andrew found the Methodists intolerable, "partly because of their great noise and outcry in their revival meetings which became unseemly disorderly, and also partly because of their peculiar teachings." He found it impossible to work with them. When their well-advertised revival meetings began in the winter of 1865-66, many Lutherans attended, curious about reports of fanaticism and visions. A number of the more moderate Lutherans came to Andrew and requested that he hold his own meetings as a kind of competition with the Methodists. They explained that these meetings would be "for the purpose of leading souls in the right way to Christ and by means of this work attempt to hinder precious souls from going astray because of flaming and fanatical emotions of the senses, etc." Ever the proselytizer, Andrew agreed.

Because he so often felt sick, Andrew enlisted the assistance of a local merchant who was also an ordained Lutheran minister. The two men decided to hold a number of meetings, beginning in the large Lutheran church in town and then spreading out to homes in Leland and the surrounding area. They began when the weather warmed up in the spring, and their plan was to continue into the summer. In some respects, revival meetings could be considered spiritual entertainment, and good preachers and good weather usually meant large crowds. Andrew's revival meetings in the spring of 1866 were well-attended and quite successful, with a number of people openly dedicating their lives to Christ. Even after several weeks, the meetings still drew large crowds, but Andrew felt too weak and ill to continue, and he was obliged to abandon the effort. His competitive spirit took satisfaction, however, in the knowledge that he probably dampened the efforts of the opposition. "As far as I know, no great success crowned the efforts of the Methodists in their stormy meetings, but perhaps it suffices to say no more."

Andrew was not the only one writing to Bethlehem in early 1866. Because he had remained in contact with his old friends in Fort Howard, he knew that an increasing number of Scandinavians were settling there and he also heard that several families from Ephraim had moved back to the area. They were without a church or minister, so Andrew prevailed upon them to write to Bethlehem, petitioning for his transfer to Fort Howard. He was ready and eager to leave the plains of Illinois.

After the exchange of a number of letters, Bethlehem granted their request and in the middle of August notified Andrew of his new assignment. "I received a call from them to go to Fort Howard, there to organize that band of countrymen as a little H.M. Moravian Church, serve them with the word of God and the holy sacraments and at the same time investigate if it would be possible to find other new fields for the work, etc."

Although this was the outcome Andrew had earnestly desired, he prayed about the matter very seriously before accepting the call. He then faced the prospect of informing his friends in Leland. These people had shown him kindness and love, and he was well aware that he had never "been privileged to work among better people ...." It was painful for him to tell them he was leaving. "This piece of news I can truthfully say struck my Illinois friends like a thunder-bolt, for none of them could have imagined that I might be called away so soon and it filled them with deep regret."

"I had no sooner announced my departure before they asked me the reason for leaving and it was not difficult to answer their question." Andrew told them honestly that the climate did not agree with him or his wife but more important, the fact that most of them "clung so tenaciously to the Lutheran name ..." was a great disappointment to him. Their immediate response was to insist that if only he would continue to serve them, "they would be willing to be received into the Moravian Church..." in both Leland and Mission Point. "I answered them that I was very sorry that this declaration from them came too late, as I had now accepted the call to remove to Fort Howard to organize a small brethrens congregation there and it was impossible for me to cancel the acceptance of that call."

Andrew began preparations for his departure. "On Sunday the 26th of August (1866) I delivered my farewell sermon in the church at Mission Point.

I'm not going to say much about the tears and the weeping, nor about the very painful separation, but I was requested to visit them as often as possible, the expenses of my trips ... they were willing to bear ...." "With a sorrowing heart I went back to Leland. Here it was my painful duty to deliver my farewell sermon one week later, the 2nd of September, for a very good audience. I'm not going to say much about this service, if I could, for in truth it was very sad."

With mixed emotions the Iversons packed up their household belongings and prepared to leave Leland, which had been their home for almost two years. They would be taking the train to Fort Howard, via Chicago. As he anticipated his new assignment Andrew felt a renewed sense of hope, but he realized that taking leave of his many good friends in Leland would be difficult. Most difficult of all would be leaving Joseph. Several days before their departure, Andrew, Laura, Alfred, and Johnnie made the long trip out to the cemetery, and "with great emotion said farewell to Joseph's grave—one son less than when we came." Next came the parting from their friends. "A large circle of sympathizing and sorrowing friends accompanied us to the depot and at the hour of departure we said good-bye with much weeping. I can never forget it."

The train trip afforded Andrew plenty of time for reflection. He had come to Leland in a state of shock and grief, sorrowing for the loss of Ephraim and wondering how much of the loss was his fault. He had felt unappreciated and rejected. The people of Leland had welcomed him warmly and many became his good friends. They had extended him every courtesy and he once again felt needed. He now felt remorseful that it had not worked out better, but he could never have foreseen the terrible disappointments that would befall him in Leland. Losing his youngest son only a few weeks after arriving had been a crushing blow—one of many in the recent past. Nearly as demoralizing was the realization that the people of Leland and Mission Point, who had so vocally urged him to come and serve their spiritual needs, seemed determined to cling to their Lutheranism. His lack of success in convincing them to accept Moravianism shook his faith in his ability as an evangelist. His persistent illnesses and his dislike of the climate merely added to his unhappiness. Yet he would never forget the kindness and love he felt from the people of Leland and Mission Point. The feeling that he had let them down nagged him, and he was genuinely grieved about leaving behind his friends on the prairie.

****

On September 23, 1866, Andrew delivered his inaugural sermon in Fort Howard. As usual, he spoke in his native Norwegian. He and his family had arrived three days earlier and had been received with joy by their many friends. Unaccountably, this happy reception did not move Andrew, who felt quite depressed. Nevertheless he immediately launched into the task of formally organizing his followers into a Moravian congregation. It would be the third Scandinavian Moravian Church in Wisconsin—all founded by Andrew Iverson.

Although it was necessary to hold church services in a schoolhouse, conditions were far better for Andrew in Fort Howard than they had been in Leland. Here he found worshipers eager to embrace the Moravian creed and he expanded his services to include two on Sunday, a prayer service on Thursday evening, and a Sunday school for children. His health improved and to his surprise he discovered that one of his converts from Door County, Martine (Bakke) Solway, wished to become a member of his congregation. Three years earlier when she was a 15-year-old living in Sturgeon Bay, she had begged to be baptized in the Moravian Church, but her Quaker father had forbidden it as long as she lived in his house. She had since moved to Fort Howard, and when she discovered that Andrew was her new minister, she quickly expressed her desire that he baptize her. He looked forward to doing so but "told her that she would need a somewhat extended period of religious instruction ...." Andrew recommended that this instruction continue weekly until Christmastime.

Before the year ended Andrew finally made the last payment to H.A. Schultz for the money he had borrowed to buy the land on which Ephraim was established. Closing the transaction was a poignant moment for Andrew, for his thoughts were drawn back to Ephraim. In spite of the way things turned out, he would always cherish Schultz's kindness and support. "He had waited with great patience a long time past the due date for this payment and we were deeply grateful to him for this consideration."

Andrew felt encouraged with his achievements in Fort Howard and was not surprised when various members of the congregation approached him with the idea of raising money to build a church. He began soliciting contributions immediately and soon obtained pledges and outright gifts of several hundred dollars. News of this success reached members of the Lutheran community and motivated them to see whether they could raise more money than the Moravians in order to build their own church. The competition was lopsided, as there were far more Lutherans in the Green Bay–Fort Howard area than there were Moravians, so Andrew counseled his congregation not to be discouraged but "just remain quiet and faithful."

Meantime, as the Christmas season of 1866 approached, the number of people joining the Moravian church grew. Andrew had developed a warm friendship with a Congregational minister, Reverend David Curtiss, who offered to let the Moravian congregation use his church on Christmas Day. The opportunity to hold this important service in a real church, combined with news that a baptism would take place, drew so many worshipers that the church was filled to capacity. "Naturally on this occasion the hostile-minded Lutherans were present," but Andrew was otherwise filled with the Christmas spirit. Rising to the occasion, he preached an inspired sermon.

The climax of the Christmas service was the baptism of Martine Solway. "Our young sister, supported most wonderfully by the Lord's power of grace, rendered meekly but firmly a living, clear faith (not something committed to memory) for the great gathering. Many of those present broke out into audible weeping and, after a burning prayer, this young soul, born again, was baptized in the death of Jesus and in the name of the Holy Trinity and received the blessing by the laying on of hands—then it was practically impossible for my voice to be heard because of the loud weeping in the great gathering and the bigoted Lutherans who were present were compelled to weep with the rest of them."

His first Christmas service in Fort Howard and an important baptism were very satisfying achievements for Andrew, who had labored diligently but unsuccessfully to obtain converts in Leland. He remembered the 1866 Christmas season as "one of the most precious I have ever experienced." For Martine Solway also it was a season of fulfillment. She was deeply moved by her baptism and "told us frankly on that day that she never before had experienced so blessed a season ... and it seemed to her to be a fore-taste of heaven itself."

****

The effort to raise money for the new church building gained momentum in the spring of 1867. Andrew and members of the congregation worked steadily to obtain the needed funds, encouraging church members and local Moravians to contribute as much as possible. Mrs. Otto Tank, whose husband had died almost three years previously, aided the cause greatly. She donated two building lots to the congregation, promising to deed them over to the church as soon as construction began. Andrew seemed to take perverse delight in the Lutherans' lack of success in persuading her to do the same for them.

Bethlehem advised Andrew to begin building as quickly as possible, even though he might not have sufficient funds with which to complete the church. Administrators promised that when funds ran out, they would place a notice in *The Moravian* about Fort Howard's need and would permit him to expand his solicitations to Moravian churches throughout Wisconsin and Minnesota. With that directive in mind he redoubled his efforts, and by fall he had raised enough money to buy materials and begin construction. Andrew served as architect, and construction began on November 19, 1867. "The work progressed rapidly for a few weeks, so that when winter set in, the timber frame and its tower were covered. This was a good beginning but after that work had to be suspended for several weeks, partly because of intensely cold weather and partly for the lack of funds."

While awaiting warmer weather, Andrew continued to hold Sunday services in the schoolhouse, although it had become inadequate for their needs. He conducted evening services in the homes of congregation members or in his own home that he had purchased in September with the help of friends. When 1868 arrived, Andrew departed on a trip of several weeks duration to solicit funds from all the Moravian congregations in Wisconsin and Minnesota. Heartened by their generosity and sacrifice, he returned with sufficient money to resume building. Fund-raising was taking more time than he liked or had anticipated, but he was determined to see the church built. Construction continued throughout the spring and summer, and by fall real headway had been made. "It was with great encouragement that we beheld the progress of the work on our beautiful new church and I myself did everything I could as much as my time permitted on the interior of the church. During the fall, without any assistance, I personally constructed the pulpit, etc."

In the late fall, Andrew interrupted his own construction efforts on the church to undertake a three-week journey to Bethlehem. Although the principal reason for the trip was to give Andrew an opportunity to attend the Provincial Synod as a delegate, there were two other equally important objectives. One was to seek donations from Moravian churches in the east, and the other was to take John along and enroll him as a student at *Nazareth Hall*, a Moravian school in Nazareth, Pennsylvania, near Bethlehem.

Although he had traveled widely over the past 18 years, Andrew had not been back to Bethlehem since his ordination, and he looked forward to returning—memories of his previous visit were still vivid in his mind. He and John were accompanied on the trip by J.J. Groenfeldt of Ephraim. After arriving in Bethlehem, John remained with his father during the impressive 10-day synod and then the two of them traveled to his new school in nearby Nazareth. John was only 11 years old and it was very difficult for Andrew to contemplate leaving him, but he was grateful his son would have the opportunity to attend this fine school. He was privileged to do so because he was the son of a Moravian minister.

After a "sad leave-taking" from John, Andrew began his disagreeable rounds of solicitation, starting with the church in Nazareth. "This business, which was not at all to my liking, I had also finished in Bethlehem during my stay there." He continued to travel westward toward home, stopping at Moravian churches along the way, always asking for funds to complete the church building at Fort Howard. He was on the road for three weeks. During his final stop in Hope, Indiana, he became so ill and hoarse that he could scarcely speak, and he was in that condition when he arrived home on December 22, 1868, "where I was received with the greatest joy by my family and the congregation." While his rigorous trip had been fairly successful, it did not meet his fund-raising expectations. "The collection received for our church on this journey was considerable ... but it was not sufficient to cover the full balance." Regardless, work on the church building continued.

As 1869 began, Andrew had been in Fort Howard for nearly two and a half years and felt a real sense of satisfaction in what he had accomplished. His health had been restored, membership in the congregation was increasing, his sermons were reaching a wide variety of worshipers, and dedication of the new church building was scheduled for February 14, 1869.

The dedication of the Fort Howard Moravian Church was an impressive day-long event. J.J. Groenfeldt of Ephraim conducted the morning service. Speaking in Norwegian, he preached a powerful inaugural sermon to a nearly packed sanctuary. The afternoon service was a special event that featured seven preachers representing six nationalities. Also present was Mrs. Otto Tank, who had donated the land. Each of the ministers gave an inspiring talk, and when the Baptist preacher's turn came he eloquently implored the audience to contribute enough money to meet the church's remaining debt, which was around $250. "The old gentleman was a gifted speaker and made a deep impression upon his hearers." But when the money was counted during the service there was sufficient cash to meet only one-third of the debt. The preacher mounted the rostrum again, and in language even more persuasive than before, he thundered out an appeal for pledges. This time enough was collected to pay off the balance of the debt. Andrew was overwhelmed. "In three languages I endeavored to express thanks to brethren and friends who were present for their self-sacrifice. In doing this, I was deeply moved and my Master and Lord made the task easy for me. This remarkable gathering—so richly blessed—closed with a heartfelt prayer of thanks and the Lord's blessing."

The dedication continued into the evening. "At 7:30 P.M., another large gathering of countrymen took place in our newly dedicated church and ... Groenfeldt delivered again another powerful sermon to the great edification of our faithful brethren. A deep solemnity prevailed and the beautiful chandeliers spread their soft radiance over the audience, symbolical of the light from above, Christ the true light, and we prayed as if in distress at that meeting that the Shepherd of the Flock might be revealed in all His glory in this His dedicated house." Andrew was content. He had been successful in founding another church. It was a belated birthday present for him, since he had turned 46 in December.

****

During the remainder of 1869 the congregation flourished and increased in size. It was a time of great satisfaction for Andrew. In Leland he had been forced to question his effectiveness as a preacher and as a missionary, but now he was the respected leader of a growing congregation that worshipped in a beautiful new church. He felt vindicated, and late in the year he was easily persuaded to commence a series of revival meetings that were highly successful. They prompted an unusual event.

The conversion of a 20-year-old member of his Bible class made a powerful and lasting impression on Andrew. He had noticed the young woman for some time and had become concerned about her as she "seemed to be carrying a heavy load of sin, although her life seemingly was always correct." During one of the classes, she "suddenly arose, trembling like a leaf ... and amidst a stream of tears made an outcry of distress in the following words: 'Oh, as a poor sinner I feel that I am absolutely lost, after God's judgment—a big sinner! Oh, I'm so unhappy, so unhappy!'—after which, in a sobbing voice, she directed her cry to me, begging that I would pray for her." In response to her anguish, Andrew exhorted everyone present to kneel and pray, and he begged God to give him the grace to help this lost soul find her Savior. "When I had finally finished my burning prayer like a beggar, the young soul had found peace, believing in the blood of Jesus."

"This change of heart ... was the beginning of a real revival among many of our listeners." At their request Andrew embarked upon a taxing series of revival meetings which were held every night for seven weeks. The success of the revival exceeded his expectations. "The work of salvation went deeper and deeper ... and the audiences increased. Even old women came to our meetings in terrible snowstorms, evening after evening, and even the Lutheran minister's wife was now and then present." He calculated that during the seven weeks, 25 or more people "had experienced a true awakening and conversion ...."

It was an invigorating time for Andrew—but trouble was not far away. As the decade of 1870 got under way, competition for church members increased. The Lutherans, who were frequent participants in this contest, were now joined by the Methodists. Trouble with the Methodists began during one of Andrew's last revival meetings. "A strange Swedish man," apparently a member of a Methodist congregation in Chicago, began attending church services and visiting Andrew in his home. His presence seemed innocuous at first, although Andrew did caution "him not to preach any methodism in our meetings and he had positively and definitely promised me that he would not do so." In spite of Andrew's admonition, "this Methodist arose one evening in one of our meetings toward its close (the church was crowded and the Lutheran Minister's wife was also present) and, contrary to his promise to me, he began to address the newly awakened as the one who could show them a better way to salvation, which the Methodist church held out ...." Andrew was dumbfounded—and angry.

"Most of those present were amazed to hear such an address and their hearts were filled with grief. I felt it necessary to interrupt him in his sectarian address and openly declare to the audience that he had broken his promise to me that he would not recommend methodism, etc. I also made it known that I felt obliged to close the weekly evening gatherings. More than one heart was grieved over this announcement."

It was the end of the revival meetings but it was not the end of the Methodists. The strange Swede who had boldly proselytized during Andrew's church service was a spy from the Scandinavian Methodist Church in Chicago. Shortly thereafter two Danish Methodist preachers appeared in Fort Howard and told Andrew very frankly that their purpose was to convert all Scandinavians in the area. They "appeared on the scene as courageous fighters," and their activities caused quite a bit of excitement. Suddenly they disappeared and were replaced by the Swede who had started it all—it turned out that he too was a Methodist minister. He proceeded to bring his family to the community, rent a large hall, and hold daily revival meetings. Services were said to be noisy, exciting, and attended by fanatically enthusiastic crowds. Soon he was proclaiming he had converted 31 people, including four that Andrew had recently worked hard to convert. At first Andrew was furious, but his fury turned to satisfaction when he learned that "thirty persons, his whole converted flock, could now be found only in saloons, at dances, and at card parties—totally fallen—and that only one remained faithful." In spite of this set-back, the Methodist preacher persevered and succeeded in establishing a congregation that lasted for eight years.

Relationships with the Lutherans were reasonably harmonious for a number of years. Andrew did chafe at the thought of their attempting to build a church faster than he could, but aside from that incident there was mutual respect. Their pastor, P. Dahl, was "a gentle and real friendly personality" who became one of Andrew's trusted friends. Toward the end of the 1870s, Dahl was replaced by a minister who Andrew called "a stiff, yes, bigotted [sic], Lutheran—truly a dangerous man." When he began proselytizing in the Moravian congregation, especially among the younger members, he brought out all Andrew's old enmity toward Lutherans. After a few years, this preacher became embroiled in arguments with members of his own church, but to Andrew's way of thinking he had already "showed his colors."

Attendance at Andrew's church declined slowly but steadily during the 1870s, and the challenge of keeping his congregation intact became a strain. Andrew wondered if people were tiring of his preaching. Nevertheless he continued to travel, carrying the word of God to people in locations outside Fort Howard. Although his trips were fewer and less arduous than in the past, he established a very successful preaching place at Ashwaubenon (four miles south of Fort Howard) and others at Little Suamico and Shawano. Perhaps at heart he was still a missionary.

Contributing to the erosion of his congregation during the 1870s were the deaths of many older church members and an inability to find young people to fill the pews. There were two deaths he remembered in amazing detail when he wrote his recollections. In a situation eerily reminiscent of Elizabeth Morbek's illness in Ephraim, he presided at the bedside of 23-year-old Dora Aga for about a week. Her death from tuberculosis while in an exalted state of mind affected him greatly. He was also in sad attendance at the deathbed of Martine Solway, his first convert in Fort Howard. She too died in a state of grace. "It seemed to me that her face radiated as if from a light above, as she lay there smiling but it also seemed that she was already crossing the river. She was still able to say that she had felt the Savior's handclasp and was very happy."

As 1879 drew to a close, attendance at Andrew's church had decreased by almost 50 percent. The Lutherans and Methodists had managed to win over some of his converts and the depression of the 1870s forced a number of the remaining men and their families to leave Fort Howard to look for work elsewhere. By 1880 Andrew had been at Fort Howard for 14 years—longer than he had served any church, but for many reasons he was dissatisfied with his situation. Although he derived some pleasure from trips to nearby preaching places and from his work with young children in his church, he was restless and unhappy and he wrote repeatedly to Bethlehem asking for a transfer. Unfortunately, his request was not granted.

Andrew's ministry at Fort Howard, and indeed his life as a minister, ended in January of 1883, shortly after his 60th birthday. "This imperfect service terminated in deep gloom and intense sorrow in the beginning of the year 1883, after I had served there sixteen years. I had written the management of the church in Bethlehem more than once, requesting them to transfer me to another field of labor and if they had acceded to this important and serious demand, it would have been incomparably better for me and equally as well for the Master's service—but they didn't act in time." Andrew's memories of the events associated with his disgrace were so painful that he did not discuss them in his recollections. In truth, he was deposed from the Church and told to leave Fort Howard after having confessed to living in adultery with a seventeen-year-old member of his congregation.

It was a sad and humbling end to the ministry of an intense and dedicated man. He knew that his ignominious fall was likely to diminish his remarkable record of achievements as a pioneer missionary in the Moravian Church, and he asked forgiveness of his congregation as well as that of his superiors in Bethlehem. He was not sure whether either forgave him, but he did know "that the great faithful Friend of Sinners and Savior Himself, out of His unspeakable mercy, forgave me for all my shortcomings and sins and washed me white in the blood of the Lamb, after my repeated prayers."

Andrew chose to end his recollections with the conclusion of his ministry at Fort Howard. He began writing these memoirs more than 10 years later, and he was 76 years old when he completed recounting the activity of the Scandinavian Moravian Church in Wisconsin. Although he was not a minister for the last 16 years of his life, he remained a devout Moravian. He was confident of his place in history and viewed his achievements with a mixture of humility and pride. "What has been done by me only will pass away and be forgotten but what in reality Christ has done through me and by means of me as a tool, that will remain through all Eternities' Eternity, to His glorious honor and praise!" In a touching last sentence he reveals the part of his life's work that was dearest to his heart when he writes, "Thus may the odd Moravian Church of dear Ephraim, Sturgeon Bay, and Fort Howard continue to live! AMEN."

So End The Recollections Of Andrew Michael Iverson

APPENDIX

Figure 4. **CHRONOLOGY**

1823 (December 27) — Andreas (Andrew) Michael Iverson is born.
1824 (March 24) — Laurenze (Laura) Hansen (Iverson) is born.
1848 (May 29) — Wisconsin is admitted to statehood.
1849 (March 5) — Zachary Taylor is inaugurated as President of the U.S.
1849 (March 23) — Andrew Iverson and Laura Hansen marry.
1849 (April 26) — Andrew and Laura Iverson depart Stavanger, Norway, on the schooner *Ebenezer*, bound for America (date from ship's manifest).
1849 (June 19) — The *Ebenezer* arrives in New York (date from ship's manifest).
1849 (June 29) — Andrew and Laura Iverson arrive in Milwaukee.
1849 (December 31) — Anna Munda Laurenze Iverson is born to Laura and Andrew in Milwaukee.
1850 (May 6) — Iverson is ordained at Bethlehem, Pennsylvania.
1850 (mid-May) — Iverson meets Otto Tank in New York and they depart together for Milwaukee.
1850 (July 9) — Millard Fillmore becomes President of the United States.
1850 (August 1) — Iverson and his congregation depart Milwaukee for Green Bay.
1850 (August 2) — Anna Munda Iverson dies on ship en route to Green Bay.
1850 (August) — Iverson and his congregation begin establishing a Moravian community on land owned by Otto Tank in Green Bay.
1851 (March) — Iverson's congregation severs ties with Otto Tank.
1852 (spring) — Ole Larsen purchases Eagle Island.
1852 (July 4) — Alfred Martin Iverson is born to Laura and Andrew in Green Bay.
1853 (February) — Iverson and his companions walk from Green Bay to Eagle Island. Guided by Ole Larsen, they select land along the shore of Eagle Harbor as a new home for the Moravian congregation.
1853 (spring) — Iverson and his parishioners begin the move to Ephraim and the slow task of carving a settlement (Ephraim) out of the wilderness.
1853 (November) — Iverson's house in Ephraim is completed.
1854 (October) — Iverson family departs for New Denmark/Cooperstown, Wisconsin, where they will spend the winter.
1854 (November 5) — Anna Munda Eleonora Iverson is born to Laura and Andrew in Cooperstown.
1856 (summer) — A severe drought in Ephraim results in a serious food shortage the following winter.

1856 (autumn) — Peter Peterson moves to Ephraim from Cooperstown and starts a freight and trading service. He later builds a general store.
1856 (autumn) — German immigrants establish settlement east of Ephraim.
1857 — Iverson is elected Superintendent of Schools for Gibraltar area.
1857 (July 16) — John Huss Iverson is born to Laura and Andrew in Ephraim.
1858 (May) — Reverend H.A. Schultz, of Bethlehem, Pennsylvania, visits Ephraim.
1858–59 — Aslag Anderson builds dock and store in Ephraim.
1859 — Charles Darwin publishes *On The Origin of the Species.*
1859 (June) — The first Ephraim schoolhouse is completed.
1859 (December 18) — The Ephraim Moravian Church is completed and dedicated.
1861 (February 20) — Lauritz Joseph Andreas Iverson is born to Laura and Andrew in Ephraim.
1861 (March) — Abraham Lincoln is inaugurated as President.
1861 (April) — The Civil War begins.
1863 (January 1) — The Emancipation Proclamation takes effect.
1863 (April 2) — Anna Munda Eleonora Iverson dies in Ephraim (she is Laura and Andrew's second Anna Munda).
1863 (April 26) — Anna Munda Eleonora Iverson is born to Laura and Andrew in Ephraim (she is their third Anna Munda).
1864 (February 22) — Anna Munda Eleonora Iverson dies in Ephraim.
1864 (early July) — Iverson and his family leave Ephraim forever.
1864 (July 15) — The Iverson family arrives in Leland, Illinois.
1864 (August 26) — Lauritz Joseph Iverson dies in Leland, Illinois.
1866 (early September) — The Iverson family leaves Leland for Fort Howard.
1868 (late fall) — Iverson travels to Bethlehem, Pennsylvania, to attend the Provincial Synod, enroll his son, John, at Nazareth Hall, and collect funds for the Moravian Church under construction in Fort Howard.
1869 (February 14) — The Fort Howard Moravian Church is dedicated.
1871 (October) — The great Chicago fire occurs. Forest and brush fires also occur in northeastern Wisconsin due to hot, dry, summer.
1876 (June) — General Custer is defeated at the Battle of Little Big Horn.
1882 — Robert Koch discovers the bacterium responsible for tuberculosis.
1883 (January) — Iverson is deposed from the ministry of the Moravian Church.
1893 (July 21) — Laura Iverson dies.
1902 (February 22) — John Huss Iverson dies in New York City.
1902 (October 18) — Alfred Martin Iverson dies in Sturgeon Bay.
1907 (January 16) — Andrew Michael Iverson dies in Sturgeon Bay.

Figure 5 – Iverson family tree beginning with Andrew and Laura.

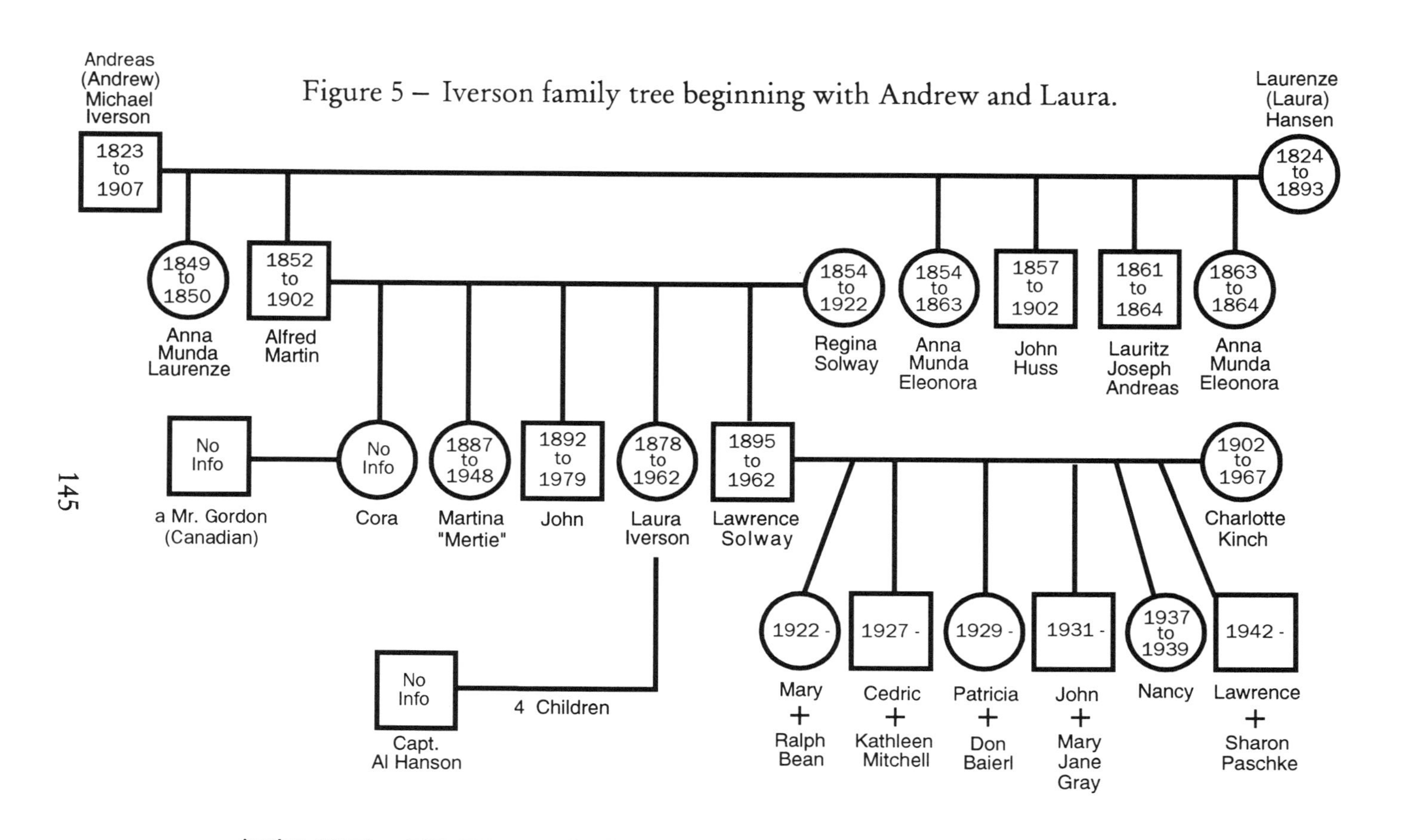

SOURCES

1. Anderson, Harry H., and Frederick I. Olson, 1981. *Milwaukee, At the Gathering of the Waters*, Continental Heritage Press, Tulsa, OK, 266 pp.

2. Beck, Siegfried, 1928. *Aus dem Leben von Niels Otto Tank* (The Life Story of Niels Otto Tank). Handwritten manuscript (unpublished) in German from materials of the Moravian Mission at Paramaribo, Surinam, as communicated by Bishop Karl A. Mueller (copy provided by Eva Groenfeldt, Sturgeon Bay, WI, 1994 - translation by Alexander Pivovarov), 25 pp. Copies available in the archives of the Ephraim Foundation (P.O. Box 165, Ephraim, WI 54211), the Ephraim Public Library, and in the Laurie Room of the Sturgeon Bay Library.

3. Byfield, A.F., 1953. *Ephraim, 1853–1953*, Booklet underwritten by the Men's Club of Ephraim, George Banta Publishing Co., Menasha, WI, 85 pp.

4. Combs, William K. (date of publication unknown). *Midwestern, Rural Clothing of the 1840s*, Lincoln Log Cabin, State Historic Site, Lerna, IL (copy provided by Heritage Hill, Green Bay, WI).

5. Conzen, Kathleen N., 1976. *Immigrant Milwaukee, 1836–1860*, Harvard University Press, Cambridge, MA, 300 pp.

6. Current, Richard N., 1976. *The History of Wisconsin, Vol. II, The Civil War Era, 1848-1873*, State Historical Society of Wisconsin, Madison, 659 pp.

7. Dana, Richard Henry, 1869. *Two Years Before the Mast*, Signet Classic, Penguin Books, NY, 371 pp.

8. De Schweinitz, Edmund, 1885. *The History of the Church Known as The Unitas Fratrum or The Unity Of The Brethren*, Moravian Publication Office, Bethlehem, PA, 693 pp.

9. Field, James A., 1982. *Brief Notes on Parson Andrew (Andreas) M. Iverson's Memoirs*. Unpublished manuscript summarizing Iverson's recollections (ref. 21) and making use of unpublished notes provided by John Kahlert, 14 pp. A copy is available in the archives of the Ephraim Foundation (P.O. Box 165, Ephraim, WI 54211), the Ephraim Public Library, and in the Laurie Room of the Sturgeon Bay Public Library. Information used with permission.

10. Fieve, Ronald R., 1975. *Moodswing*, William Morrow & Company, Inc. (Bantam Book edition, 1976), New York, NY, 244 pp.

11. Graf, Paul A., 1964. *A Shorter History of the Sister Bay Moravian Church.* Unpublished manuscript, 23 pp. At the time this book was written, Graf was the minister of the Sturgeon Bay Moravian Church. A copy of the manuscript is available in the archives of the Ephraim Foundation (P.O. Box 165, Ephraim, WI 54211), the Ephraim Public Library, and in the Laurie Room of the Sturgeon Bay Public Library.

12. Henderson, Margerate G., and Ethel Dewey Speerschneider, 1949. *It Happened Here*, State Historical Society of Wisconsin, Madison, 266 pp.

13. Hirth, Walter M. and Mary Kay Hirth, 1986. *Schooner Days in Door County*, Voyageur Press, Minneapolis, MN, 147 pp.

14. *History of Northern Wisconsin*, 1881. *An account of its settlement, growth, development and resources; an extensive sketch of its counties, cities, towns and villages - their improvements, industries, manufactories; biographical sketches of prominent men and early settlers, etc.*, The Western Historical Co. (A.T. Andreas, proprietor), Chicago, IL, 1,218 pp.

15. Holand, Hjalmar R., 1917. *History of Door County, Wisconsin*, Vol. 1, S.J. Clarke Publishing Co., Chicago, 459 pp.

16. Holand, Hjalmar R., 1943. *Old Peninsula Days* (6th ed.), Pioneer Publishing Co., Ephraim, WI, 295 pp.

17. Holand, Hjalmar R., 1957. *My First Eighty Years*, Twayne Publishers, Inc., New York, NY, 256 pp.

18. Holand, Hjalmar R., 1978. *Norwegians in America: The Last Migration.* Translated by Helmer M. Blegen. Original title: (*Den Siste Folkevandring Sagastubber Fra Nybyggerlivit I America*), The Center For Western Studies, Augustana College, Sioux Falls, SD, 240 pp.

19. Hoyler, Clement, 1919. *Ephraim in the Making*, In: "Early Days in Ephraim" (H.R. Holand, ed.), Peninsula Historical Review, Door County Historical Society, Sturgeon Bay, WI, pp. 4–21.

20. *Inventory of the Church Archives of Wisconsin, Moravian Church*, 1938. Prepared by The Historical Records Survey, Division of Women's and Professional Projects Works Progress Administration, Madison, WI, 53 pp.

21. Iverson, Andreas M., 1897. *A Brief Account of the Activity of the Evangelical Moravian Church Among the Scandinavians in Wisconsin*, Translated from the Norwegian in 1929 by John Boler. Original Manuscript (in Norwegian) held by the Moravian Church in Ephraim, WI. The Boler translation was obtained from the State Historical Society of Wisconsin as a photocopy having a length of 203 pages. An identical copy is in the archives of the Ephraim Foundation (P.O. Box 165, Ephraim, WI 54211). A copy is also available at the Sturgeon Bay Public Library. In the present narrative, references to Iverson's "recollections" indicate information garnered from the Boler translation of Iverson's "*A Brief Account....*" All quotations in the present narrative are from Iverson's recollections unless otherwise indicated.

22. Jamison, Kay R., 1993. *Touched With Fire: Manic-Depressive Illness and the Artistic Temperament*, Free Press/Macmillan, New York, NY, 370 pp.

23. Johansen, John H., 1978. *Through These Many Years. Commemorating the 125th Anniversary of the Ephraim Moravian Congregation, 1853-1978*, Pamphlet from the Ephraim Moravian Church, 39 pp.

24. Kahlert, John, with Photographs by Albert Quinlan, 1978. *Early Door County Buildings*, Second Edition, Meadow Lane Publishers, Baileys Harbor, WI, 53 pp.

25. Kahlert, John, with Photographs by Albert Quinlan, 1981. *Pioneer Cemeteries, Door County Wisconsin*, Meadow Lane Publishers, Baileys Harbor, WI, 205 pp.

26. Lewis, Ruth E., 1931. *Ephraim — A Replica of a Seacoast Village in Far Off Norway*, Wisconsin Magazine of History, Sept.–Oct. issue, p. 3–4.

27. Lotz, M. Marvin, 1994. *Discovering Door County's Past*, Volume One, Holly House Press, Fish Creek, WI, 458 pp.

28. Martin, Charles I., 1881. *History of Door County*, Expositor Job Print, Sturgeon Bay, WI, p. 51.

29. Maddocks, Melvin, 1981. *The Atlantic Crossing*, Time-Life Books, Alexandria, VA, 176 pp.

30. Melville, Herman, 1849. *Redburn, His First Voyage*, Doubleday Anchor Books, Doubleday and Co., Inc., Garden City, NY, 301 pp.

31. Naess, Harald S., 1984. *Introduction to A.M. Iverson's "A Brief Account of the Activity — Its Commencement and Continuation Since 1849 — of the Evangelical Moravian Church Among the Scandinavians in Wisconsin,"* unpublished sections from a larger manuscript on Niels Otto Tank and Andreas Michael Iverson. The two sections number 64 pages in length and a copy is in the archives of the Ephraim Foundation (P.O. Box 165, Ephraim, WI 54211), the Ephraim Public Library, and in the Laurie Room of the Sturgeon Bay Public Library. Information from this manuscript used with permission.

32. Naess, Harald S., 1993. *Nils Otto Tank: All in All, a Man of Good Will*, Wisconsin Academy Review, Vol. 39, No. 4, pp. 27–31.

33. Nelson, Carl, 1929. *Reminiscences of a Pioneer*, In: "Early Days in Ephraim (H.R. Holand, ed.), Peninsula Historical Review, Door County Historical Society, Sturgeon Bay, WI, pp. 33–40.

34. *New Grolier Multimedia Encyclopedia*, 1989–1993, The Software Toolworks, Novato, CA.

35. Oneson, Irvin, 1985. *The Moravian Community at Ephraim. Its Beginnings*. Unpublished manuscript written by the great grandson of Abraham Oneson (Aanesen), a member of the original colony of settlers, 56 pp. Copy of this manuscript is in the archives of the Ephraim Foundation (P.O. Box 165, Ephraim, WI 54211), the Ephraim Public Library, and in the Laurie Room of the Sturgeon Bay Public Library. Information from this manuscript used with permission.

36. Petterson, Lucille (translator), 1986. *Ephraim is My Home Now: Letters of Anna and Anders Petterson, 1884–1889*. Wisconsin Magazine of History (State Historical Society of Wisconsin). In four parts: *Part I*, Vol. 69, No. 3, pp. 187–210, *Part II*, Vol. 69, No. 4, pp. 285–304, *Part III*, Vol. 70, No. 1, pp. 32-56, and *Part IV*, Vol. 70, No. 2, pp. 107-131.

37. *Record of School District Number Four in the Town of Gibraltar (New District No. 2)*, 1858 to 1883. Original Minutes of the School District Meetings, Archives of the Ephraim Foundation (Box 165, Ephraim, WI 54211).

38. *Register* for the Moravian Church congregations served by Andrew Iverson from 1850–1870. This register, in Iverson's handwriting, lists baptisms, deaths, marriages, and other information about Moravians in Iverson's ministry. It is written in Norwegian. Access to the book was kindly provided by Dr. Gary Kinkel, then pastor of the Moravian Church in Ephraim, where it is preserved in the church archives.

39. Rosenshield, Jill, 1993. *The Tank Library: Caroline Tank's Memorial to Her Husband*, Wisconsin Academy Review, Vol. 39, No. 4, pp. 32–37.

40. Schaefer, Joseph, 1940. *Scandinavian Moravians in Wisconsin*, The Wisconsin Magazine of History, Vol. 24, No. 1, pp. 25–38.

41. Stevens, David H., 1959. *Ole Larsen of Door County*, in: "The Peninsula," a periodical of the Door County Historical Society, May, No. 4, pp. 1–5.

42. Stafford, Kate, and Harald Naess, 1984. *On Both Sides of the Ocean, A Part of Per Hagen's Journey* (translation by Stafford and Naess of a manuscript written by Peter Peterson, with accompanying notes), The Norwegian-American Historical Association, Northfield, MN, 70 pp.

43. Stocker, Harry E., 1924. *A Home Mission History of the Moravian Church in the United States and Canada*, Special Publication Committee of the Moravian Church, Bethlehem, PA, 256 pp.

44. *The Moravian Church Miscellany*, 1850, p. 22. Published by the Moravian Church, Bethlehem, PA.

45. *The Moravian*, 1856, p. 410. Published by the Moravian Church, Bethlehem, PA.

46. *The Moravian*, 1857, p. 66.

47. *The Moravian*, 1857, p. 79.

48. *The Moravian*, 1857, p. 90.

49. *The Moravian*, 1857, p. 218.

50. *The Moravian*, 1859, p. 89.

51. *The Moravian*, 1860, p. 69.

52. *The Moravian*, 1860, p. 73.

53. *The Moravian*, 1860, p. 369.

54. Timmons, Helen Torgerson, 1993. *Anderson Memoirs*, an account of the Anderson family written by Aslag Anderson's granddaughter (whose mother was Agnes Anderson Torgerson). Unpublished manuscript in the archives of the Ephraim Foundation (P.O. Box 165, Ephraim, WI 54211), 35 pp.

55. Westphal, George, 1929. *A Brief Account of the Ephraim Moravian Church*, In: "Early Days in Ephraim" (H.R. Holand, ed.), Peninsula Historical Review, Door County Historical Society, Sturgeon Bay, WI, pp. 21–33.

56. *World Book Encyclopedia*, 1969. Field Enterprises Educational Corporation, Chicago.

57. Zeitlin, Richard H., 1977. *Germans in Wisconsin*, The State Historical Society of Wisconsin, pp. 1–30.

INDEX OF NOTES

Chapter One

Chapter Two

Chapter Three

Chapter Four

CHAPTER ONE

Note 1 (p. 9): Iverson's Early Years — Andreas Michael Iverson was born December 27, 1823, in Oddernes, Norway, which is now part of the coastal city of Kristiansand about 150 miles southwest of Oslo. His father, Johannes Iverson, was a successful farmer who was 57 years old when Andrew was born; the father died when his son was 11 years old. Iverson's mother was named Marte Marie. Little more is known about Iverson's childhood, although it is clear that he had artistic skill and early on he must have learned woodworking and carpentry. Also, there is no information about how he made his way to the mission school in Stavanger. Naess (31) observes that Iverson seemed to have some of the predisposing characteristics often associated with 19th century Norwegian missionaries, including being from the southern or western part of Norway and being a younger son who had lost his parent(s) at an early age.

Note 2 (p. 9): A Brief History of the Moravian Church — The seeds of Moravianism were sown in the early 1400s in Bohemia, now part of what became Czechoslovakia, by John Huss (1369–1415). Huss, who was on the faculty of Prague University and became its Rector in 1402, supported the writings of English theologian John Wycliffe, known for his attacks on the excesses of the Roman Catholic Church and its influence in politics.

A tall man "with a thin, pale, sad face (8)," Huss was a rationalist, thinker, and masterful speaker. His sermons and writings rang with clarity and truth. During a period when the Catholic Church shamelessly sold forgiveness, Huss took a stand against these "papal indulgences." He also remained steadfast in his support of Wycliffe, and in his writings and sermons he argued eloquently against the abuse of church power. Although Huss expounded his arguments against church excesses with patience, care, and reason, Catholic Church leaders felt threatened by his logic and collectively viewed him as a heretic. As a result of their efforts he was pressured into voluntary exile, although he continued his scholarly writing.

After a year and seven months in exile, Huss agreed to plead his case at a General Council called by the Catholic Church, with safe conduct supposedly guaranteed by both King Sigismund of Poland and Pope John the Twenty-third. During the Council the attending Bishops repeatedly asked Huss to admit his errors and recant his writings. He refused unflinchingly and presented his case with restrained eloquence and a forgiving demeanor. It was to no avail; the six Bishops assuming responsibility for the ceremony of degradation condemned him for heresy saying "Thus we deliver your soul to the devil!" They formally announced Huss's excommunication and sentenced him to be burned at the stake. The King and the Pope failed to intervene with the protection they had promised—they betrayed Huss—they wanted him dead.

After being bound to the stake with seven wet thongs and a heavy chain around his neck, Huss exclaimed "Willingly do I suffer myself to be bound with this chain for the sake of the holy name of my Lord Jesus Christ, who, for my sake, was far more cruelly bound (8)." He began to sing a hymn as the torch was applied. As the wind drove flames into his face, onlookers could see that his lips continued to move even after no sound could be heard. Fortunately, his agony was brief.

Huss's martyrdom in 1415 touched off the bloody "Hussite Wars" between the Catholic Church, whose empire dominated all of Europe, and those who wished to practice a less dogmatic religion based on the belief that the teachings of the Bible were more important than the edicts of the Pope. His martyrdom also launched the "Hussite Movement," the forerunner of the modern Moravian Church. According to De Schweinitz (8), "A peculiar feature of the Hussite movement was the preaching of itinerant evangelists, in private houses or open fields (where) they attracted large congregations ...." Andrew Iverson, some 400 years later, would serve well the evangelistic spirit of the Hussite Movement, from which many of his beliefs evolved.

After the conflicts ended in an uneasy truce, a group of Huss's reformers settled in Lititz, a town near Prague, where in 1457 they established themselves as "The Unitas Fratrum," or the Unity of the Brethren. Their movement, which antedated the coming Reformation of the 1500s, spread to the nearby province of Moravia and later to Poland. The doctrine of The Unitas Fratrum, with its emphasis on the Bible, evangelism, hymn singing, and church schools, was still spreading when Martin Luther defied the Roman Catholic Church in 1517 and triggered the religious Reformation movement throughout Europe. Religious revolutions occurred in one European province after another as more and more groups sought a simpler religion that preached the infallibility of the Bible rather than that of the Pope. As a result of these bloody conflicts, Protestant religions, from Anabaptists to Lutherans to Waldenses, gained legitimacy and followers during the 1500s.

The Unitas Fratrum, which shared many beliefs with Lutherans and other new Protestant groups, emerged from the Reformation intact. By the early 1700s several sects had evolved from The Unitas Fratrum movement, and in parts of Europe there was intermittent persecution of these sects. In 1722, Christian David, leader of The Unitas Fratrum group that had remained in Moravia, led his followers to Saxony (now part of Germany).

In Saxony, Count Nikolaus Ludwig von Zinzendorf (1700-1760) offered David and his followers sanctuary on his large estate. He shared and nurtured the group's beliefs and helped them establish the village of Herrnhut on his land. In 1727 the movement was renamed the Moravian Church because so many of its adherents had come from Moravia. Thus The Unitas Fratrum movement became the Moravian Church, which was also called The Renewed Church of the Brethren. Although the movement spread to Scandinavian countries, its followers there were, and are, few in number. In Norway, the Evangelical Lutheran Church is the nation's official church.

The Moravian Church liturgy is less formal than that of the Lutheran Church, and it has been said that Moravian services are more emotional than intellectual. From its inception, Moravianism provided a powerful, easily understood message that appealed to many unsophisticated people, such as farmers and fishermen. Further, evangelism and missionary work have always been part of the Moravian Church, and Andrew Iverson became one of the church's most effective evangelists in America in the 1800s.

Note 3 (p. 9): The Mission School at Stavanger, Norway — The Norwegian Missionary Society's school in Stavanger served the interests of several religious groups. Although only the Lutheran Church, as the country's official religion, could administer the sacraments and certificates of graduation, some of the individuals involved in establishing the school were Moravians. As a result, a number of its early graduates were sympathetic to Moravian beliefs.

Shortly after the school was established, friction arose among students and faculty members over religious inclinations. In spite of the fact that they were all Protestants, rumors abounded that a Moravian influence was beginning to undermine Lutheran doctrine. Among the students who were preoccupied with Moravian beliefs that challenged Lutheran control of the school was Andrew Iverson.

Iverson and two other students with Moravian leanings were singled out and forced to answer written questions about their beliefs. They received pointed reminders about the school's rules and regulations, and they were asked to reaffirm their dedication to the Lutheran Church as the official national religion of Norway. As a result, Iverson and the others felt persecuted.

Naess (31) suggests that Iverson was not an ideal student. For example, Iverson claimed he had difficulty studying more than two hours a day because of poor eyesight. There is also no question that he preferred the Moravian to the Lutheran Church, and that his goal was to become an evangelist in some far-away land. Even as a young man he undoubtedly showed the stubbornness and strong beliefs that characterized him after he began his work in America.

One of the rules of the Missionary School was that no student could marry or even become engaged without obtaining approval from the Board of the Norwegian Missionary Society. According to Naess (31), Iverson sought exemption from the no-marriage rule, and about six months before he left school he wrote the following letter to the Board. The letter was written on April 18, 1848.

> "Because I have been experiencing for quite some time—and in a severe way—that I do not thrive outside the married station, and as I am fully convinced that I do not possess the gift of grace mentioned by the Apostle in 1st Cor. 7.7., and since after these experiences, which have not been superficial—that I can declare before God—I consider it almost impossible for me to travel as an unmarried man to a warmer climate, where marriage, according to the testimony of respected men is highly necessary for those who do not possess the gift of abstinence, which Mr. Thommesen has also assured me of orally, I feel obliged, since it is for me a matter of utmost importance, to place before the Board my serious request for its kind permission to leave this place as a married man. Truly I can confess that I would not have come forward with such a request had I not been forced to do so, because I have always held the view, since I gave myself up to missionary service, to be as unassuming as possible; however, a real necessity is and remains a necessity, and what is truly necessary I hope no feeling Christian will refuse any one. Thus it cannot be the intention of the Society to place on any one of its emissaries a yoke, under which for a whole lifetime they would have to cower and sigh, and which will be too heavy to carry—and the refusal of my request would become such an oppressive yoke, that I can assure you under my hand and seal, for thus I have come to know myself in this regard. I would like to add, that the travel expenses from Norway to Africa I would be able to cover for myself and a spouse, if I were to receive one, and if the journey materializes. In turning to the honored Board with my supplication and asking its members kindly to do what is possible for its realization, I hope our merciful Lord will direct matters so that I get my heartfelt wish fulfilled."

The letter was signed "Respectfully, A.M. Iverson." What his rambling and wordy narrative fails to mention is that he was in love and had become engaged to be married. At the time the letter was written, Iverson expected to be sent to Africa like all the other recent graduates. But shortly thereafter he heard rumors that officials were planning to send him to a strict Lutheran missionary institute in Germany for further indoctrination.

In response to the news that he might be sent to Germany to exorcise some of his Moravian leanings, Iverson wrote another letter to the Board asking to leave the Norwegian Missionary Society (31). He said that he planned to travel to America and work as a missionary among the Indians, and if the Society wanted to keep him in its service, he would abide by all its teachings in his mission work. The Board responded that they would waive reimbursement for his educational expenses and would sanction his mission work in America among Scandinavian immigrants.

In January of 1849 Iverson left the Norwegian Missionary Society School, and on March 23 he married Laurenze (Laura) Hansen. The family tree resulting from this marriage is shown in Fig. 5 (p. 145).

Note 4 (p. 10): The Date on Which Andrew and Laura Sailed for America — According to Iverson's recollections, he and Laura left Stavanger on April 28, 1849. However, Captain H.C. Clausen of the schooner *Ebenezer*, the emigrant ship on which they traveled to New York, indicates on the manifest that they departed April 26, 1849. Also, although Iverson recalls that they arrived in New York on June 13, 1849, the manifest shows an arrival date of June 19. These discrepancies are not particularly significant, but they should be noted. A copy of the ship's arrival manifest, including a list of passengers, is available at the Wisconsin State Historical Society in Madison.

Note 5 (p. 10): Another Schooner Named *Ebenezer* — Fordel Hogenson, born in Norway in 1849, was 24 years old when he immigrated to Door County with his family. After settling first in Sister Bay, Hogenson later moved to Ephraim and earned a living by farming and hiring out as a carpenter. By the late 1800s, Hogenson had acquired some capital and decided to construct a schooner along the shore bordering his property, which is now the site of the Evergreen Beach Motel. He and his sons built a three-masted scow schooner measuring 57 feet long by about 15 feet in width. It was launched in June of 1890 and christened the *Ebenezer*. The sturdy schooner "became the workhorse of Ephraim, transporting food and other necessities to the people on the west side of northern Door County (13)." Whether Hogenson named his schooner after the one that brought Iverson to America is unclear, although it would seem appropriate. Later Hogenson began to take tourists into his home and around 1897 he built the Evergreen Beach Hotel, the main structure of which was renovated as the Evergreen Beach Motel (still in operation near the corner of Highway 42 and German Road).

Note 6 (p. 11): Further Comment about Emigrant Ships — The Iversons traveled in relative luxury in their deck-level cabin, and it is noteworthy that Andrew never mentions venturing below—his services for emigrants traveling in steerage were always held on deck as weather permitted. Today it is difficult to imagine the wretched conditions endured by emigrants traveling below decks in steerage. Herman Melville (30), who worked as a crewman aboard an emigrant ship in the early 1800s, recalled a voyage where "We had not been at sea one week, when to hold your head down the fore hatchway was like holding it down a suddenly opened cess-pool." Beyond the discomfort associated with crowded conditions and rough seas, disease took a terrible toll among emigrants on board ship. On one English ship, 24 passengers died of cholera in a single day, and by the time the captain turned back about 10 days into the voyage, 83 passengers had died; the remaining passengers left the ship to spread the disease to those ashore. Another English ship sailing from Liverpool lost 107 of its 475 steerage passengers to typhus during its Atlantic crossing (29).

Note 7 (p. 16, 20): Iverson's Preaching Style and Appearance — Joseph Schaefer, Editor of the *Wisconsin Magazine of History* in the 1940s, made the following comments about Iverson's preaching (40): "As a preacher, judging from his own account in the book written by him, he was tremendously vital. Speaking always without notes, and 'in a loud voice,' he strove to make his hearers conscious of sin, of repentance, and atonement through Jesus Christ. While he severely criticized the Methodists for their ranting, and the Lutherans for their cold, stiff attitude toward religion, he was certainly in his practice nearer the former than the latter. Indeed, the measure of success in his meetings would seem to have been the dearth or abundance of tears shed both by himself and by the congregation. No move, secular or religious, was undertaken without previous resort to 'burning prayer.'" Iverson delivered most of his sermons in Norwegian but he could preach in German or English when appropriate.

There are only three known photographs of Iverson. The most familiar one, taken when he was about 30 years old (Fig. 6), clearly shows his piercing eyes and square jaw. Naess (31) says the following about Iverson's appearance: "He cannot have been a man of imposing build, since he speaks repeatedly of his

FIGURE 6 — Photograph of Iverson probably taken when he was around 30 years old (photo source: Ephraim Foundation). Piercing eyes and a square jaw were among his most prominent facial features.

frail constitution and of feeling dwarfed by the powerful frame of Otto Tank." "An almost fanatical determination also speaks out of his eyes ...." Although Iverson did speak often of his "frail constitution," the evidence suggests that he was hardly frail in terms of physical prowess. Considering the long distances he walked regularly and the many adventures that tested his endurance, it is likely that he was wiry and possessed great physical stamina.

Note 8 (p. 17): Iverson's Certification as a Moravian Minister — The certification document (Fig. 7) reads: "This is to certify That the Bearer, the Revd. Andrew Michael Iversen, a native of Norway, is a regularly ordained

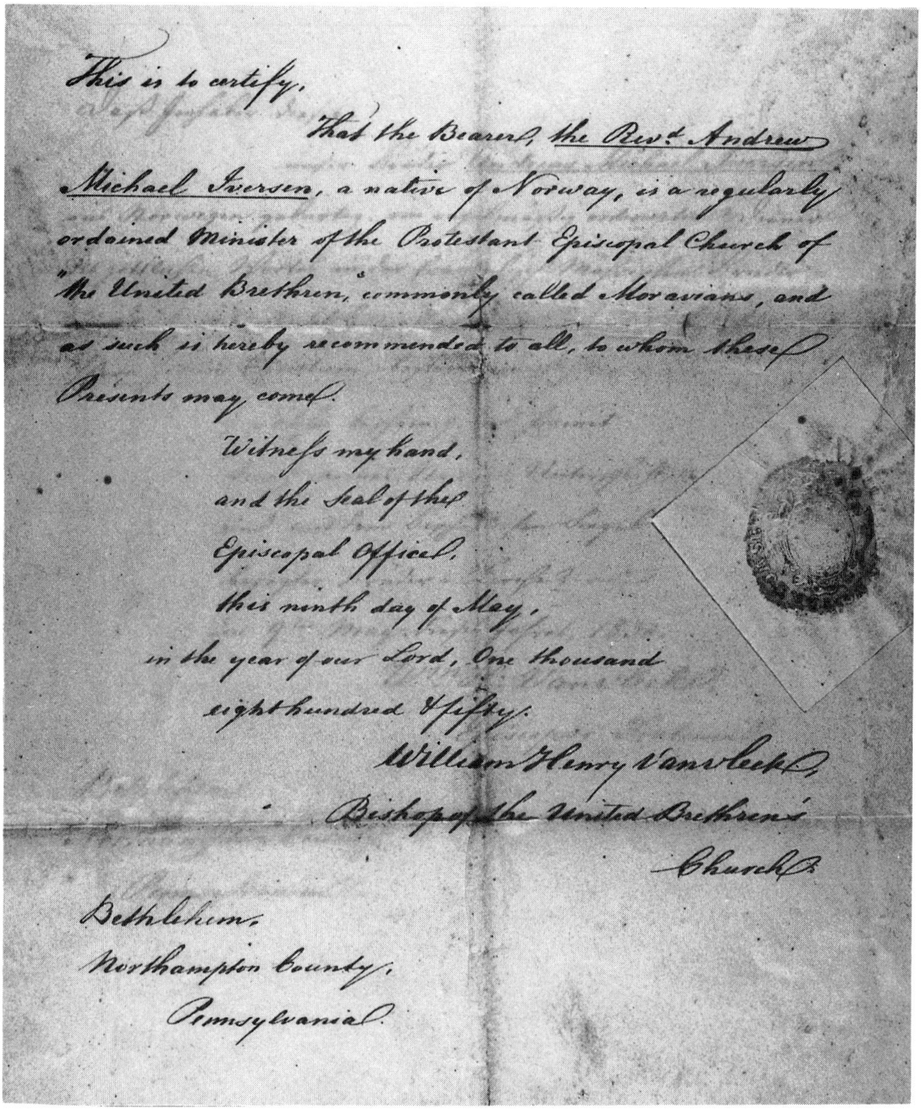

This is to certify,

That the Bearer, the Revd Andrew Michael Iversen, a native of Norway, is a regularly ordained Minister of the Protestant Episcopal Church of "the United Brethren," commonly called Moravians, and as such is hereby recommended to all, to whom these Presents may come.

Witness my hand,
and the Seal of the
Episcopal Office,
this ninth day of May,
in the year of our Lord, One thousand
eight hundred & fifty.

William Henry Vanvleek,
Bishop of the United Brethren's
Church.

Bethlehem,
Northampton County,
Pennsylvania.

FIGURE 7 — English version of Iverson's certificate letter as an ordained Moravian minister, issued May 9, 1850 (source: Cedric Iverson).

minister of the Protestant Episcopal Church of 'The United Brethren,' commonly called Moravians, and as such is hereby recommended to all, to whom these Presents may come." It is dated May 9, 1850, and signed in Bethlehem, Pennsylvania, by William Henry Vanvleek, Bishop of the United

Brethren's Church, and the Church seal is affixed. One side of the document is in English, and the other is in Norwegian. Iverson is referred to as "Andrew" in the English version, and his last name is spelled "Iversen," although he actually used "Iverson" in America. While most Americans place considerable emphasis on the spelling of their last names, Scandinavians of the time were less concerned about the use of the "-son" and "-sen" suffixes. In fact, in the Church Register (38) Iverson kept, he spelled his own name "Iversen" and "Iverson" at various times.

Note 9 (p. 18): Moravians of the Time Referred to Each Other as Brother and Sister — The Moravian religion holds that members of the faith should interact as brothers and sisters, sharing in and united by the blood of Christ. From its beginnings in the 15th century through the 1800s, Moravians addressed each other as brothers and sisters. In his writings, Iverson always refers to fellow Moravians by using the appellation Brother or Sister before their last name.

Note 10 (p. 18): Iverson's Letters to the Moravian Administrative Office in Bethlehem, Pennsylvania — As soon as Iverson arrived in America he began to write regularly to church leaders in Bethlehem. He was eager to please his superiors and he went out of his way to provide them with a lively account of his efforts in behalf of the Church. The letters were usually addressed to Reverend Henry A. Schultz, editor of several of the Church's publications, who was supportive of the young immigrant preacher and who later became a financial benefactor to Iverson and his followers. There can be no doubt that Schultz first came to know Iverson through his letters. These letters reveal Iverson's passion for his mission in America and provide details of his adventures in the Wisconsin wilderness. Schultz saw to it that many of them were published in *The Moravian Church Miscellany* or *The Moravian*, which eventually replaced the *Miscellany*. These monthly periodicals were circulated among Moravians throughout America, although distribution to the midwestern and western frontiers was spotty compared to that of the eastern United States. Iverson's writings added excitement and adventure to publications that often made for sedate and repetitious reading.

One of Iverson's first letters to Bethlehem was published in the first issue of the first volume of *The Moravian Church Miscellany* (44). Iverson wrote the letter in German and dated it September 15, 1849, about three months after his arrival in Milwaukee. Schultz, as editor, provided a brief introduction to the letter: "We give Mr. Iwersen's [sic] letter with very slight alterations in the

the peculiarities of his style, believing that the spirit of childlike faith and love to Jesus, which breathes in this letter, will deeply interest and touch the heart of every christian [sic] reader." The letter is presented below in its entirety, exactly as printed in *The Moravian Church Miscellany* (44).

> DEAR AND VENERABLE BRETHREN IN THE PROV. H. CONFERENCE! — In the faith, that we are closely united in the cross of our praiseworthy Savior, I address myself to you in confidence that you will take care of me and my brethren and sisters here in Milwaukee. A few souls have from time to time gathered here. These souls, who have more or less stood in unity with the dear United Brethren, have felt an increased necessity to be formed into a Moravian congregation, and this they have laid before the feet of our Redeemer in that faith, that he would accept them in grace and mercy, and fulfil their wish, when his hour is coming.—
>
> Our beloved Br. Bigler gave us the hope, that you, in Jesus Christ and in his grace intimately beloved brethren, will take hearty care of us here in Milwaukee. Oh brethren! would you help a little flock, which is one spirit with you? Can you bear in your hearts, that we must be hungry for the sacrament, and we can not be sated?—We are few, yet we are more than them in Matth. 18, 20. We have not much of earthly goods; but the Lord possess [sic] the silver and the gold in the land. Oh! that He would open the hearts for us! our prayer to you, dear and respectable brethren is the same, as that of the man of Macedonia, "Come over and help us!"—Oh! come over dear brethren! We have no orderings (regulations) as you in your Bethlehem, where you cradle the child Jesus, and kneel around his manger; yea, we have no Bethlehem as you! We have no holy sacraments as you! Oh! brethren *reflect upon this*!!—In the time I have lived here, Jesus has not permitted me to stand inactive. I have by his grace, preached, prayed, visited the sick, spoken with them, and told them, that one thing is needful, assisted them as physician; and I have had happy results; but in all I am "an unprofitable servant." The Savior, however, has, in much grace and mercy confessed himself to us; He has won four souls for himself, and added them to our little flock.—Here, in Milwaukee, our brethren and sisters live in a narrow condition, and it will be difficult for them to contribute to the support of a minister *here*. But they have honestly assisted me, and at this time I have had a needy sustenance, and no more I desire of this world; yea! I would rather bear hardship with the men of God, than to have all things in abundance with the children of the world.—I must add, that the divine service must be kept among us in the Danish and Norwegian language, because most of our brethren and sisters do not understand English.—As a desire of all our brethren and sisters, I must yet add, that they all humbly demand of your, brethren in the P.H.C., that I might be appointed and by the Moravian church ordained to be their minister, because they believe, that Jesus has sent me for this service, and because they love me much in the Lord. I also feel my whole heart fastened to them, and we are so heartily united, that the one brother or sister gladly divided the last

> mouthful of bread with the other. Dear brethren, I wish to come to Bethlehem, and my dear wife and I desire to be admitted as members of the Moravian church. If I come for a short time to Bethlehem, I will bring with me a declaration from my brethren and sisters here. At last, brethren! brethren! as true as you pray, that the little cross-congregation must be increased, that the kingdom of Jesus must come, as true (if you can) must you help us, that Jesus Christ also may be glorified by us! Think on Matth. 10, 42! The Lord Jesus Christ, our only true Savior, bless you and all your undertakings! In the love of Christ, our little flock and I salute you all, dear and beloved brethren. Your brother.
>
> A.M. Iwersen [sic]

From the beginning, Iverson's letters to Bethlehem contained grandiloquent pleas for recognition and requests for help for him and "his little flock." The above letter is typical of his use of emotional language threaded with Biblical references. As time went by, however, his letters became more substantive and consequently more interesting. Although his style remained quaintly effusive, later accounts of his adventures on the frontier were far more readable than his early letters. In 1857, Schultz made the following editorial comment about Iverson's letters. "It is true [they are] served in a style characteristic of the writer, and rich in idiomatic phrases, for, let us remind our readers, Br. I. is a native of Norway, who, since his appointment as our Missionary in the year 1849, has had to struggle with numberless trials and labours in his domestic relations; and, therefore, he had very little time left, in addition to his self-denying labours as a Missionary, among his Scandinavian countrymen in Wisconsin and Illinois, to devote himself to the study of the German and English languages. And yet, he has learned to speak and write both languages with admirable success, and to a greater degree than probably most of us would have been able to accomplish (49)."

Many of Iverson's letters reveal the isolation and loneliness of mission work on the frontier. He missed collegial relationships with other missionaries and often had doubts as to whether his arduous mission work was recognized and appreciated. Iverson was expected to be a source of spiritual support and guidance for settlers in a wide area; in Ephraim he was obliged to lead the way in establishing the community. But from whom could he draw emotional support and encouragement? His God was always there, to be sure, but he also needed support from his fellow man. It must have been comforting to know that in Shultz he had a steadfast friend in Bethlehem, and that thousands of church members were made aware of his isolation when they read his letters in Church periodicals. At the end of one of his letters to Bethlehem, he made the following plea. "I hear from you very seldom, and I frequently consider myself as standing in a desert. My soul thirsts for encouragement. I have often felt a great desire to see you in person, that I might speak with you about matters of which I cannot write. My whole heart is with you. May I fancy that your hearts are with mine? Sympathy I need, for I am frequently distressed. Now, the Savior bless you and all who love His glorious appearing! Your brother in Christ, A.M. Iverson (48)."

CHAPTER TWO

Note 1 (p. 19): Background on Nils Otto Tank — Although there has been a considerable amount written about Otto Tank, he remains a puzzling and tragic figure. The known facts about his early life are so interesting that writers such as Holand (15,16,17,18) have been tempted to add colorful speculation to a life already filled with drama. Harald Naess (31,32), however, provides information that is more accurate and no less engrossing. His writings contain information gleaned from books and articles published in Norway. He also had access to the Archives of the Moravian Church in Bethlehem, Pennsylvania, where he translated documents from the original Norwegian and German. His careful scholarship provides valuable information about Otto Tank, as well as some understanding of Tank's enigmatic relationship with Iverson. Another intriguing resource is an unpublished manuscript entitled *Aus dem Leben Niels Otto Tank* (The Life Story of Nils Otto Tank), by Siegfried Beck (2). Existing only in German, the hand-written document contains many details about Tank's youth as well as his years in Surinam.

Nils Otto Tank was born on March 11, 1800, near Halden, Norway. His father, Carsten Tank, was one of the richest men in Norway, owning large tracts of land and more than 100 farms, as well as sawmills, ships, and a tobacco factory. He counted both Norwegian and Swedish royalty as his friends, and as a powerful industrialist he wielded substantial influence in political matters. Kings, crown princes, and foreign dignitaries were frequent visitors at his home. He was a man of pride who was not above behaving in an ostentatious manner—he wore fancy clothes and drove expensive coaches.

Otto grew up in an elegant home called Rød Manor. Standing amidst many acres of fertile fields, the large house was surrounded by magnificent terraced gardens and was furnished with fine paintings and an excellent library that reflected Carsten's interest in science. A great sense of European and family history pervaded the estate: in its cemetery a famous political leader and a soldier lay buried not far from the bones of three of the family's favorite horses.

Legend had it that the name "Tank" dated from 1660, when King Friedrich III officially thanked the family for wartime financial assistance by telling them that from this time on their name would be Thank (2).

"Nils Otto Tank was certainly raised under extraordinary circumstances. Living in a beautiful home where royal visitors were not uncommon, he knew from an early age that he was heir to one of Norway's largest fortunes. Tank grew up to be a towering man, powerfully built, with his father's prominent nose and jaw, handsome, intelligent and well-mannered (31)." His father made sure that his son received the finest education available. Following a period of tutoring at home, he continued his schooling abroad, where he studied mining and engineering at various universities and traveled extensively in Germany and France. He became acquainted with the methods of international trade in London and actively pursued his interest in geology by joining a group of scientists on a trip across the continent.

Otto's father planned an illustrious future for his intelligent and ambitious son, and Holand (15,16) goes so far as to claim that Otto was close to becoming King of Norway. Naess (32), however, says there is no basis for that assertion, since the Tanks had no Norwegian royal blood. If such an idea existed, he states, it was probably based on the egotism of Carsten Tank. Beck (2) corroborates this idea, speculating that Carsten's wealth and political connections gave him grandiose ideas, perhaps leading him to believe that marriage to a princess might make it possible for Otto to become king.

During his childhood, Otto's two best friends were Kaja Jorgensen and Carl Wulff, "orphans" who had been brought up with him at Rød Manor. When Otto became a young man, he fell in love with Kaja and wanted to marry her. He was told that it would be impossible—she was his half-sister, his father's illegitimate daughter. He also learned that Carl Wulff was probably his half-brother. This devastating knowledge distanced him from his father and brought him closer to his mother.

Catherine von Cappelan, Otto's mother, was a deeply religious woman. She had been a member of the Moravian Society since her childhood, and in the years following her marriage she continued to find great comfort in her faith. Otto inherited his deep sense of religion from his mother and was converted to Moravianism around 1825. He quickly became interested in the Moravians' involvement with missionary work and actively collected money to support these efforts. In 1834 his dedication to his beliefs led him to join the Moravian colony at Christiansfeld, Denmark. He was placed in charge of the colony's stores and workshops where he put his knowledge of business and his organizational skills to good use.

Naess (31,32) makes it clear that Otto's desire to join the Christiansfeld colony was a natural outgrowth of his devotion to Moravian beliefs. Other writers, however, have advanced a variety of unlikely but entertaining theories to explain his decision. For example, Beck (2) says that Otto fell in love with the daughter of a clergyman in Herrnhut, Germany, and when he brought his "plebeian" bride home, he was disinherited by his father and subsequently decided to join the Moravian Brotherhood. Holand repeats essentially the same story in his *History of Door County* (15), but later, in *Norwegians in America* (18), he claims that Otto was traveling in the mountains near Herrnhut when he injured himself in an accident and was rescued and cared for by Moravians, who converted him to their faith. And in *My First Eighty Years* (17) Holand says that Otto left home after breaking with his father over his desired marriage to Kaja Jorgensen and went to live with Moravians who were friends of his mother's. These stories are probably just that—stories. The idea that the elder Tank disinherited his son in retaliation for his marriage is clearly not true, because Carsten Tank lost his money in the late 1820s and Otto did not marry until 1838. Naess's thorough research and access to Norwegian and German documents (31,32) make his explanation far more plausible.

In 1838 Otto married Mariane Fruhauf, the daughter of a Moravian minister. According to Naess (32), Mariane was chosen for Otto by the Moravian custom of drawing lots (see Note p. 170). In Otto and Mariane's case the lottery surely was guided by the hand of God, because they were an ideal match. Well-educated and cosmopolitan, Mariane had lived in England for a year, had worked in Holland, and most recently had been the principal of a girls' school in Switzerland. Nevertheless, she adjusted readily to the simple life at Christiansfeld, where the couple lived until 1841.

Carsten Tank, meanwhile, suffered disastrous business losses during the 1820s and as a result his political influence came to an end. He was forced to declare bankruptcy, and in 1829 he applied to the government for a pension. His son-in-law took over most of his property, including Rød Manor, where Carsten was permitted to live until his death in 1832. Although no sources mention it, presumably any of the estate Otto might have inherited was gone. At this time, however, he was a Moravian living in a commune and he had little need of great wealth.

In 1841, Tank received a call to become manager of the Moravian mission in Paramaribo, Surinam (Dutch Guiana), South America. In preparation for this assignment, he and Mariane spent a year at the Moravian settlement in Herrnhut, Germany, where he was ordained as a missionary. They arrived in Surinam on April 24, 1842. The mission there consisted of 24 European missionaries and workers and a congregation of more than 4,000 blacks. The total black population of the area was around 65,000, including 40,000 slaves.

"The five years Tank spent in Paramaribo marked an exciting period in his life, and also a time of difficulty and great personal loss. He was intensely active, both as a missionary and as an explorer in the jungles of the back country, and his many colorful descriptions appeared in the Moravian mission's *Periodical Accounts*. His only child, Mary, was born there in January 1843. Tragically, six months later, his wife Mariane was stricken with tropical fever and died. During her illness he stayed home with her for the first time since their marriage, and he later confessed that his restless activity had taken too much of the time they should have spent together. He was never to overcome the loss of Mariane (32)."

Following Mariane's death, Tank asked to be relieved of his position as manager of the mission, but before a replacement could be sent the mission's superintendent died, and Tank took over that position for the next two years (1846–1848). Despite the suffocating heat, he was a dynamic worker. Under his guidance the mission's stores prospered as never before and he was instrumental in setting up a number of new ones. He even persuaded the government to donate 10,000 acres to the mission for the purpose of establishing a lumbering industry. He was indefatigable in visiting the sick and made many mission journeys to the interior of Surinam. It was during these expeditions that he was assumed to be on the lookout for gold, but if he found any he never mentioned it to anyone. Nevertheless, because of his mining background, the possibility that Tank actually found gold fascinated people for many years.

Tank was not popular with the other missionaries, many of whom were wary of his increasingly ambitious business schemes and adamant opposition to slavery. His attempts to free the slaves, they feared, would antagonize the Dutch plantation owners, who would then close the plantations to missionary activity. Nevertheless, Tank remained tireless in his efforts to improve conditions for the slaves. In 1847, he planned a trip to investigate how slaves were treated in the West Indies and the United States, as well as to gather information on the status of former slaves. The main purpose of his trip, however, was to travel on to Holland to negotiate with the government about improving the slaves' situation on the Dutch plantations back in Surinam. Four-year-old Mary Tank accompanied her father on the trip.

During his visits to the West Indies and the United States Tank learned a great deal about educational levels and social conditions among former slaves. When he arrived in Holland he circulated this information and at the same time criticized treatment of slaves on plantations in Surinam. He was pleased that his ideas were well-received by Dutch officials. However, when they contacted the

Moravian mission in Surinam for corroboration, the missionaries refused to substantiate Tank's assessment of conditions there and responded to questions in an evasive manner. Perhaps this was not surprising since the missionaries were afraid of angering the plantation owners, but it put Tank in an extremely awkward position. The mission's repudiation made it impossible for him to return to Surinam, and as a result the Moravian Church's "attitude to him was henceforth cool and cautious (31)."

Tank remained in Holland, and while visiting in Amsterdam he made the acquaintance of Caroline van der Meulen, who had been a friend of his first wife. A highly educated woman, she had lived for several years in Oberlin, Ohio (39). She was also extraordinarily rich and was the owner of a magnificent library she had inherited from her father. In 1849 she married Tank and became Mary's stepmother. Shortly after the wedding Caroline and Otto traveled to his old home, Rød Manor. During that visit he disclosed to friends his dream of founding a Norwegian community in America—one that would combine religious service with agriculture and education. "I will try to make a real society for Jesus, where all will be like brothers," he said (31). Thanks to his new wealth he was in a position to pursue that dream, and the Moravian Church once again looked on him with favor.

In May 1850, Tank and his family traveled to New York. While it is clear he came to the United States with the intention of founding a Moravian colony, that was not the only reason for his interest in America. As a man of enormous wealth and considerable international business experience, he was eager to discover what investment opportunities might be available to him in the New World. Wealthy friends in New York had apprised him of possibilities in Wisconsin, mentioning specifically Green Bay and projects involving navigation on the Fox River. While in New York, Tank also met with Iverson. Apparently what he heard about the little Norwegian congregation in Milwaukee appealed to him, because he agreed to help Iverson and to accompany him back to Milwaukee. With the ambivalent approval of Bethlehem, Tank and his family arrived in Milwaukee in late May 1850.

Note 2 (p. 21): The Practice of Drawing Lots — According to Dr. Gary Kinkel, former Pastor of the Ephraim Moravian Church, drawing lots was at one time a common practice in Moravian communities. It became less common in the United States after the Civil War, but it remained in use in Germany until about 1900. This method was intended to remove all politics and human planning from the decision-making process and to rely directly on God's will. It was used not only for the selection of marriage partners but for nearly all important decisions. The drawing of lots was a solemn occasion. Biblical quotations were written out on pieces of paper, each one indicating either yes or no. They were placed in a box during a worship service while the whole gathering prayed to God for guidance. The question was then asked, and the person affected reached into the box and withdrew an answer.

Note 3 (p. 26): Who Went on the First Ship From Milwaukee to Green Bay? — When he wrote his recollections almost 50 years after the move from Milwaukee to Green Bay, Iverson could still remember the names of all 27 adults who left with him. Some were members of his congregation at the time of their departure, and all but one of the others became members later. He thought it was important to preserve their names, and he listed each one in his recollections. According to Norwegian custom, he divided the names into separate groups or "choirs." He entitled the list: "The First Scandinavian Brethren Congregation from Milwaukee to Green Bay, August 1st, 1850."

> **Unmarried men**: Zacharias Morbek, Adolph Cedarholm, Gabriel Wathne, Ole Olsen, Mads Johannessen, A. Aagesen, Rasmus W. Hansen, Christoffer Wathne, and Hendrik (Henry) Wathne.
>
> **Unmarried women**: Stine Marcussen, Inger Olsen, Anne Thompson, and Malene Wathne.
>
> **Widowers**: Zacharias Wathne, Tobias Morbek, and Jens Hetland.
>
> **Widow**: Bergitte Behrensen.
>
> **Married people**: Tonnes Davidson, Tobine Davidson, Abraham Aanesen (later Oneson), Catherine Aanesen, Elias Rasmussen, Karen Rasmussen, Lars Klinkenberg, Dorothea Klinkenberg, Laurenze Iverson, and Andrew Iverson.

Note 4 (p. 29): The Tank Cottage in Green Bay — The Tank Cottage still stands today. It was located on the banks of the Fox River during the time the Tank family lived in it, but it was later moved to Tank Park on the west side of Green Bay. In 1975 it was moved to its present location at Heritage Hill State Park, 2640 South Webster, Green Bay. There the cottage was restored and furnished with a number of Mrs. Tank's possessions—it is open to the public from Memorial Day through mid-October.

Note 5 (p. 31): What Really Happened in Green Bay Between Tank and Iverson? — In his recollections, Iverson writes movingly about his break with Tank over the congregation's desire to own their own land. His eloquent description of the humble brothers calling on Tank in his fine house and his recounting of their despair when Tank crushed their hopes make fine reading; however, it is not the complete story—it is only Iverson's view of what happened. A more complete picture of the circumstances surrounding the break between Iverson and Tank can be drawn from the writings of the other people intimately involved in events leading to the confrontation: Otto Tank, Friedrich Fett, and Christian Linke (an employee in Tank's store). Each wrote letters to Moravian Church officials describing their differing views of the situation. Although not readily available to the public, this correspondence, in Norwegian and German, is preserved in the archives at Bethlehem. Naess (31) had access to these documents and his research provides an historically accurate record of the perspectives of all four participants. This information is particularly valuable because Tank's personal collection of writings was completely destroyed, at his request, after his death (32).

Individual ownership of land was certainly at the heart of the break between Iverson and Tank, but many other factors complicated the situation. One of the most disputed questions was whether the Norwegian immigrants were lazy. In this, as with most aspects of the conflict, Linke aligned himself with Tank and Fett with Iverson.

Christian Linke was a German missionary worker with a troubled past. After refusing an assignment to serve a Sheboygan church because he was "afraid to face the congregation (31)," he opened a private school in Milwaukee. When the school failed, he moved to Green Bay where he found employment with Tank. He and Tank got along well but his relationship with Fett was strained. There were rumors that Fett opened letters addressed to Linke and that he also attempted to read letters Linke wrote to Bethlehem. In these letters Linke claimed the Norwegian immigrants were not willing to work. In his opinion the Moravians came to the United States "hoping for worldly advantages and believing that joining the Moravian Church would insure them a pleasant life without exertion (31)." He recounted an incident in which one Norwegian told him that "if someone gives me two oxen and no wagon to go with them, I will not thank him (31)." Linke gave a number of other examples of the Moravians' disinclination to exert themselves. For instance, he said that the Moravians liked the mission house Tank bought, but they did not like it when he moved in with them. They also did not like it when he asked them to pay rent, each according his own means. Linke claimed the Moravians wanted the $25 worth of building materials Tank loaned them to build their houses to be a gift, and that they complained when they were expected to repay the loan. And although they readily accepted the offer of credit at Tank's store, they did not like paying him back.

Linke was quite favorable in his assessment of Tank's efforts to keep the settlement going. He described Tank as an extremely active leader who was up early working in the fields, while Iverson sat on the sofa and smoked his pipe. Tank, he said, was genuinely concerned with the welfare of the Norwegians and "looked after them like a good father (31)." He was tolerant and forgiving of those who worked to improve their condition, and he worried about the problems the settlement was encountering. "Tank had often wept bitter tears over the unreasonable lack of gratitude he had met on all sides, and yet he still had a great love for his countrymen and would forget all if he could expect better things for them in the future (31)." Linke blamed Fett for making matters worse by siding with Iverson. The evidence suggests that there was quite a bit of truth to this assertion.

Fett had taken a fatherly and protective attitude toward Iverson from the beginning of their association. As the first Moravian Home Missionary in America, he occupied a position of considerable importance in the Moravian community and had Bethlehem's confidence. In style, he was similar to Iverson—emotional, enthusiastic, and occasionally effusive. But at age 50 he was quite a bit older than Iverson (who was then 26) and he had more education and more experience. Iverson and his congregation grew to trust Fett and relied upon him for guidance in many aspects of their lives. It was natural that they consulted him regarding their dealings with Tank and often took his advice. "Fett did not support the old Moravian idea of a commune, and his objections were listened to by the Norwegians who had come to this country eager to acquire private property (32)." When Tank refused to grant them titles to their land, the congregation turned to Fett for counsel, and he no doubt supported them in their determination to press for land of their own.

Tank was wary of Fett for a variety of reasons. He did not appreciate his opposition to a commune, and he may have disliked Fett's ecclesiastical fervor. Conversely, Fett was probably somewhat intimidated by the wealthy, well-educated, and sophisticated Tank, who did not look up to him the way Iverson did. In addition, Tank may have unwittingly offended Fett by treating him as a subordinate. As the first Moravian home missionary, Fett was technically Tank's superior, but because Tank had organized the commune and was in charge of the finances, he functioned in the capacity of leader and may occasionally have given orders to Fett.

Given the distrustful nature of so many of the participants, it is no wonder that when the question of land ownership arose, compromise and understanding were difficult, if not impossible. In fact, the conflict between Iverson and Tank can be best understood as a series of misunderstandings and unclear expectations that were exacerbated by the suspicions of everyone concerned. From its inception, the idea of a Norwegian Moravian commune in Green Bay was resisted by church fathers in Bethlehem. Because of their own wariness, they planted seeds of doubt in Iverson's mind before he met Tank. These were doubts that stayed with him and likely shaded his perceptions of Tank's actions and motives. The young and inexperienced Iverson simply never had the opportunity to get to know Tank without prejudice, and as a result he did not have a firm conviction that Tank's intentions were good.

Tank also played a part in predisposing the experiment to failure when he did not explain his ideas sufficiently to Iverson's congregation. In their initial meeting, Tank apparently did not make it completely clear that the settlement he was proposing was to be a commune modeled after the one at Christiansfeld in Denmark. In turn, congregation members were so excited about the plans outlined by Tank that they heard only the parts they wanted to hear. Tank later compounded the problem when he purchased land for the settlement but did not provide written contracts for each congregation member. Although he verbally spelled out the terms very carefully, with no written contracts there was too much room for misunderstanding.

Beyond the fact that Tank did not make his intentions clear and members of the congregation heard only what pleased them, it is probable that the Norwegian immigrants were really not amenable to communal living on a long-term basis. They remembered the tenant farmer system which had been abused in Norway (15) and were wary of becoming "tenants" on Tank's land. Many of them were sailors and fishermen who had little interest in farming. Furthermore, they were caught up in the American spirit of independence and wanted the privilege of owning land in the New World. They were unwilling to accept the fact that Tank's refusal to grant titles grew out of his plans for a communistic way of living. His refusal to grant legal titles was not in harmony with their "desire for a free, independent American existence (40)," but Tank was unable or unwilling to understand their perspective.

A perceptive summary of this conflict, which ultimately led to Iverson and his congregation breaking with Tank, is provided by Naess (31). "Apart from the real issues in the struggle—communal living and/or private ownership—the conflict was one of personalities. Iverson, a young newcomer to the Moravian Church, naturally relied on the judgment of the older Friedrich Fett, while

Tank ... allied himself with Christian Linke. And Linke, clearly an introverted man with serious personality problems, had little understanding either of an extrovert like Fett, or of the naive Norwegian immigrants—to him they appeared lazy, dishonest, and ungrateful. Tank, who had his own problems working with other people, needed more than anything else the advice of an understanding arbiter and could hardly have found a more unfortunate ally than Linke (31)."

"The Norwegians may well have been slow to take up work. They came from a country with a very different pace and had been slow to learn the lesson —mentioned in hundreds of immigrant letters—that 'in this country people work.' If Tank, always active that he was, expressed his dissatisfaction, the Norwegians may well have answered that they did not wish to work for nothing on land they did not own, and demanded a title or written contract saying they were the rightful owners of their lot. But, Tank seeing their lack of enterprise compared to that of older immigrants, can hardly have been expected to issue titles without some form of payment ... (31)."

"It is easy to see that Tank lacked the leadership—including knowledge of human nature and a sense of compromise—needed for a successful colonization project. But he was a generous and noble spirit and rewarded those who deserved it (31)."

At the end of his life, in a conversation with Holand, Iverson reflected on his relationship with Tank. "I suppose I was much to blame. I was young and did not understand him. How different things might have been if we had not been so blind (17)."

Note 6 (p. 31): What Happened to Tank after Iverson and His Followers Left Green Bay? — After Iverson decided to establish a colony of his own, Tank remained in Green Bay, residing with his wife and daughter in the home they had come to love. Although still a missionary of the Moravian Church, Tank had lost the confidence of church leaders in Bethlehem and he was without a constituency. In a rather plaintive letter to Bethlehem he asked, "Am I, an ordained Brother, now supposed to be removed? Tell me the truth, and I shall not cause any more trouble (32)."

When he received no encouragement from church leaders, Tank turned away completely from religious interests and spent his time investing his substantial assets. A large portion of this wealth was his wife's inheritance. Caroline and Otto had a prenuptial agreement stipulating that her property and assets remained in her name, although the agreement specified that he could manage her business affairs (39). Tank made many investments, most of which were quite successful, but development of the Fox River and railroad construction both brought him heavy losses. When he died, his obituary stated that he was "one of the most extensive property holders and heaviest capitalists in North West Wisconsin (31)."

But according to Naess (32), Tank's heart was not in his many business enterprises. He became more and more reclusive, enjoying the company of his books, his wife, and his daughter more than that of business acquaintances and townspeople. As he grew older, his thoughts turned increasingly to his years in Surinam, as well as to his daughter, Mary, with whom he enjoyed a close relationship. She had inherited her father's business and organizational skills and she managed the family estate. In addition she shared her father's missionary spirit and was active in community work.

Tank died in 1864 at the age of 64. Mary died only eight years later after compromising her health with her selfless efforts to care for survivors of the 1871 Peshtigo fire. She was 29 years old. For the next 20 years, Tank's wife, Caroline, lived on in the Tank cottage, alone among her family treasures and memories of her husband and daughter. Caroline Tank died in 1891. Otto, Caroline, and Mary are all buried in Nisky Cemetery, Bethlehem, Pennsylvania.

Note 7 (p. 31): What Happened to Friedrich Fett after Iverson Left Green Bay? — The move to Door County and the establishment of Ephraim did not end the friendship between Iverson and Fett. Although distance prevented the Scandinavian congregation from relying on Fett as it had in the early days, Iverson and Fett continued to maintain a close collegial relationship. In a letter published in *The Moravian* (46), Iverson mentions that whenever he visited Green Bay one of the first things he did was visit Fett. He refers to him as "my intimate friend, Br. Fett" and goes on to say that "Br. Fett has indeed been of much worth to me. More than once have we sympathized with each other, in our hearts' distress, and the brotherly love that exists between us had never, to my knowledge, been interrupted."

CHAPTER THREE

Note 1 (p. 35): Iverson Originally Looked at a Sturgeon Bay Site for His Moravian Colony — In his recollections Iverson mentions briefly that he and other members of the Fort Howard congregation sailed to Sturgeon Bay in 1852 looking for land to settle. They were dissatisfied with what they found, especially the thick pine forests that grew on land they considered unsuitable for farming. Thereafter, thanks to information provided by Ole Larsen, they learned about land farther north near Eagle Island. This was the impetus for their trip in February of 1853 to see the land for themselves.

According to Naess (31), church records in Bethlehem show that Iverson's efforts to locate land for his congregation were more complex than indicated in his recollections. In 1851 Iverson saw Sturgeon Bay from a ship on which he was a passenger. When he returned to Fort Howard, he mentioned the area to members of the congregation, and thereafter 10 Norwegian families, one of them Moravian, moved to Sturgeon Bay. In January 1852 Iverson and several others walked from Fort Howard to visit their countrymen in Door County, and he held a most welcome church service. Later, in May, Iverson and a few others rowed from Fort Howard to Sturgeon Bay, where he discovered that the settlers had begun to construct a house for him.

On subsequent visits Iverson learned that there might be legal problems with land on which the settlers believed they had purchased rights. Melchior Jacobs, another Norwegian, had obtained the rights to purchase a piece of land, and he told Iverson that he would be willing to sell it to the congregation if the money could be raised—shortly thereafter, however, Jacobs lost his claim to the property.

In general, Iverson was not enthusiastic about any of the tracts in Sturgeon Bay. For one thing, the natural beauty of the area did not impress him as much as some of the other places he had seen. He was also concerned that the "more worldly and sophisticated settlers" already living there might have a negative influence on his congregation (31). When he finally received funds to purchase land for the colony, he took his time about making a decision. When he returned to Sturgeon Bay over the ice in January 1853, he learned that his followers there had obtained purchase rights, but someone else had managed to purchase the land in spite of the agreement. Apparently the time period for them to exercise their rights had expired. At that point the Sturgeon Bay settlers were unhappy with the situation and there were accusations between Iverson and members of the group as to who was at fault for losing the land.

Following the fiasco in Sturgeon Bay, Iverson and his congregation, now with $500 in hand from H.A. Schultz, resumed their search for land that would better meet their needs and expectations. Having heard about the Eagle Harbor area from Ole Larsen, they planned a trip over the ice for February 1853, and as a result of this trip Iverson purchased the 425 acres that subsequently became Ephraim. Because Melchior Jacobs had lost his rights to land in Sturgeon Bay, he decided to join Iverson, Gabriel Wathne, and Abraham Oneson as the three passed through on their way to investigate the Eagle Harbor area.

Note 2 (p. 36): Ole Larsen (Fig. 8) — Aside from Iverson, there were three settlers who played key roles in establishing Ephraim. Ole Larsen was one of them. The other two were Peter Peterson and Aslag Anderson (Peterson moved to Ephraim in 1856 and Anderson in 1858).

FIGURE 8 — This is the only known photo that shows Ole Larsen's features (photo source: Ephraim Foundation). The photo was apparently taken when he was nearing middle age. Larsen played a major role in establishing Ephraim; he was always ready to assist Iverson and his fellow Moravians and he was valued for his wise counsel.

Larsen was born near Oslo, Norway, in 1806. As a young man he emigrated to America, where for a time he ran a small shop and lodging house in Buffalo, New York. He next made his way to Fort Howard, where he established a store and trading post. When Indians told him about a beautiful island with an excellent harbor much further north along Green Bay, he decided to sell his business and purchase the island. He moved to Eagle Island in 1850, where he logged and established a cordwood trade for wood-fueled steamships traveling the area. When the timber ran out, he moved his house and family across the bay to the mainland, where he farmed near Nicolet Bay in what is now Peninsula State Park (Fig. 9). Larsen died in 1871 and is buried in the Ephraim

Moravian Cemetery.

FIGURE 9 — Ole Larsen and members of his family are shown on their farm near the shore of Nicolet Bay (photo source: Ephraim Foundation). Note the steep bluff in the background. The building to the right is the house he moved from Eagle Island.

According to Kahlert (24), Larsen married three times and was the father of 11 children. He was married twice in Norway. His first wife died unexpectedly shortly after the marriage; five children resulted from a second marriage but his second wife died shortly before he emigrated. He apparently brought several of his children with him to America. Larsen's third wife was a member of the group that emigrated with Iverson; in fact, Iverson performed the marriage ceremony in Buffalo. Later Larsen and Iverson renewed their friendship in Fort Howard before Larsen moved north, although one of his daughters, Pauline, remained in Fort Howard as a member of Iverson's Moravian colony. Larsen was a Moravian, and he and his family were always supportive of Iverson. As mentioned earlier, it was because of Larsen that Iversen learned about the government land available near Eagle Island.

Larsen, a friendly, hard-working Norwegian, was a steadying influence in

Iverson's life. Kahlert (24) notes that he was described as a "frugal and honest man with lofty ideals." He allowed the first settlers to set up temporary shelters on his island while they worked to clear land across Eagle Harbor, and he permitted the Iverson family to live in his own house. He had a pony he often used to assist the settlers in moving objects that could not be moved by manpower alone. Larsen was involved in building the Ephraim Moravian Church and was one of the first trustees of the congregation; his daughter, Pauline, was dedicated to teaching children of the settlers, and she remained a devoted friend of the Iverson family through good times and bad.

Larsen played an important role in the establishment of Ephraim, and his story is well-told by David Stevens in an article written in 1959 for the Door County Historical Society (41).

Note 3 (p.41): How Many People First Settled Ephraim? — Holand (15) claims that in the summer of 1853 the first settlers numbered 21: Iverson, Andrew Nelson, H.P. Jacobs, Zacharias Wathne, Tobias Morbek, Zacharias Morbek, Abraham Oneson, Thomas Davidson, Henry Johnson and Gotfried Matthes. All were married. An additional settler was Gabriel Wathne, who was unmarried. Contrary to Holand, Iverson (21) recollects that by late fall there were eighteen people living in Ephraim. Perhaps this inconsistency means that in the summer of 1853 more settlers were involved in clearing land than remained into the fall, and probably some of them spent the winter in Sturgeon Bay or Fort Howard.

Note 4 (p. 41): Hans Peter Jacobs — Hans P. Jacobs, who changed his last name from Jacobsen, was born in Denmark in 1817 and graduated from the Royal Academy of Navigation in Denmark. He came to America in 1844 after sailing the ocean, as a navigator, for many years (14). He then sailed the Great Lakes for a number of years before settling in Door County, first in Sturgeon Bay and then in Ephraim. In the fall of 1853, at the age of 36, Jacobs carefully marked the logs of his small house in Sturgeon Bay and completely dismantled the structure. He moved the logs to the shore and lashed them together to make a raft that he floated slowly along the shoreline to Ephraim, a distance of about 30 miles. There he had purchased and cleared a tract of land. When his raft arrived at Eagle Harbor, other settlers gladly helped him wrestle the logs ashore. As soon as they dried out, strong men carried the logs up the hill to Jacobs' land overlooking the harbor, where he carefully reassembled them into his house. The house remained on the site for many years, as a home, post office, and meeting place for village leaders. About fifty years later, Tillie Valentine bought the house and, with a few additions, it became the first tourist "hotel" in Ephraim. It was called Stonewall Cottage (26). Jacobs was an important person in early Ephraim, serving as Town Clerk, School District Clerk, and for many years as postmaster. Jacobs shared Iverson's interest in homeopathic medicine. He purchased a small case of medicine and books, studied homeopathy on his own, and was often called upon to minister to the ill (14), especially after Iverson left the community in 1864. In 1881 Jacobs was reported to have made the following comment about his coming to Door County (28). "I shall never again be the first to help make a new settlement. It sometimes makes me shudder, even now, when I think of those first days, and it is a wonder how we got through." Jacobs died in 1894 and is buried in the Ephraim Moravian Cemetery.

Note 5 (p. 42): The Construction of a Simple Log Cabin — Thanks to Peter Peterson (42), we have a detailed description of how log houses were constructed by Scandinavian settlers in the middle 1800s. "First, they cut the timber, maple or beech as it happened to be, and they took care to get the logs as straight as possible. The bark was left on, as they had no time to even think of debarking the lumber. It was then hauled over to the building site by oxen, and all the neighbors helped with constructing the house, which generally was accomplished in one day. The work proceeds in this way: four of the best axe-men are chosen to be corner men, so that one man is standing at each corner as long as the raising lasts. The others roll up logs as soon as the corner men have placed the first ones, and they work in the following manner: a sharp ridge called a saddle is cut on the lowest log, and it is notched so that the next log can lie securely. The corner men then stand on this log and chop it vertically from both sides so that it fits into the saddle. When both logs are finished, they turn the top one over and let it fall with its groove on top of the sharp saddle, and there it remains in place. If there is a space between, so that it doesn't fit together exactly, this is no cause for concern, for it has to be chinked anyway. One man splits linden wood into suitable sizes, drives it in between the logs and daubs it with clay. Such houses aren't exactly elegant, but they serve the purpose and are cozy and warm enough, even in the coldest wintertime."

Note 6 (p. 42): The Iverson House (Figs. 10, 11, 12, C3) — Kahlert (24) provides an excellent description of the Iverson house, which at the time it was built and for many years thereafter was considered to be the finest in the area. The house has a central hallway with two rooms on each side. Because of its beamed ceiling, Kahlert (24) assumed that the large room facing east was the parlor where services were held until a church was built. This room is now used as a bedroom. In the second story there is a room and a loft. The outside of the house features vertical siding with batten strips covering the joints ("board and batten"). During construction of the house a small hut was built in the woods where Iverson and his helpers could spend the night. They apparently did this several times a week rather than returning to Eagle Island or to Blossomburg near Fish Creek, where Iverson's two helpers lived (see Note 7 below).

According to Kahlert (24), the Iversons did not move into their house until

FIGURE 10 — East side of the Iverson house looking west. The original part of the house is at the right, with the middle part being added a few years later. The most recent part is at the left.

November 1854, but Iverson recalls that the move took place in November 1853. Iverson is probably correct, for there is no record that he and his family lived any place but their house during the winter of 1853-54; however, the next year he and his family moved to New Denmark/Cooperstown in November 1854 to spend the winter.

FIGURES 11 (LEFT) AND 12 (RIGHT) — The east end of the original house is shown at the left in Fig. 11, while Fig. 12, at the right, shows the unusual window beside the north door, which was used as the "front" door by the Iversons (it was later covered by a porch). Generally, settlers' houses had few windows, for they were expensive. Iverson's house was meant to be the finest in the village, and it featured many windows.

There are no fireplaces in the Iverson house, which means that the building was heated by wood stoves—an expensive household necessity for that time and place. An interesting sidelight concerns the construction of one of the two brick chimneys used to vent the stoves. During completion of the roof, a hole was left for the chimney on the west side. When the chimney was actually built, it was discovered that the hole was in the wrong place. Rather than disturb the completed roof, the chimney was slanted to meet the opening (24).

According to Kahlert (24) "A stable with two stalls was built under the first floor in the side of the hill." In Europe, especially in Scandinavia, houses with a stable underneath are common, but the Iverson house provides the only known example of this in Door County. Most of the stones from the excavation under the house ended up in the stone wall Iverson built below his house along Moravia Street (see p. 54 and Fig. 13).

FIGURE 13 — View of the Iverson house from Moravia Street showing the beautiful stone wall constructed by Iverson that is still standing almost 150 years later. The large black walnut tree in the yard was either a sapling when Iverson built the house or was planted by Iverson. The main part of the house looks much as it did when built in 1853, although two additions were made over the years.

Note 7 (p. 42): Even Nelson and Peter Weborg — Ole Larsen was not the only member of the Fort Howard colony who moved to Door County before Iverson did. When conflict began to arise in Fort Howard, Even Nelson and Peter Weborg decided to move north. They built log houses in what came to be called the Blossomburg (then called Blossomborg; also referred to as Blossomberg by some writers) settlement at the north end of Fish Creek. The settlement later became one of Iverson's preaching places. Nelson, a cooper and carpenter, and Weborg, a fisherman and carpenter, were friends and supporters of Iverson and they played key roles in the construction of his house.

Note 8 (p. 42): Furniture — Poor settlers who built simple log homes in frontier America did not have the luxury of purchasing furniture in stores. Their furniture was mostly made by hand and today we would consider such items crude, or at best, rustic. They made benches of split logs with holes drilled for legs that had been fashioned from sawed-off pieces of tree, with the bark removed. Their beds were often constructed with rough planks or straight tree branches trimmed to support bedding. Children slept on straw or leaf-filled "mattresses" placed on the floor, often in a loft area above the main room of the log cabin. Clothes were hung on pegs.

Peter Peterson (42) indicates that the first house in which he and his wife lived was 20 feet long and 16 feet wide; it was made of logs with the bark left on. "There was a door in the middle of the side and a window in each gable-end—just one room, with the stove in the middle of the floor and a stovepipe going through the roof. The furniture was also very plain."

The following is a description of how Peterson constructed some of the furniture for their first log house in Cooperstown in 1850 (42).

> "The chairs were constructed in the following manner: linden blocks were split about eighteen inches long and shaped a little with the axe, then three legs were bored and the chair was finished. The tables were made in the same way, but [I] felt that [I] would like to have things a bit nicer, so [I] got some pieces of board, planed them a little, placed a sturdy leg under them, and then [we] had a proper eating table. [He mentions that he and his wife] had brought along a bedstead and a clock from Michigan, so everything was now in the best of order."

Note 9 (p. 43): Fishing in the Old Days — Was fishing as good in the 1800s as we have been led to believe? Unfortunately, there are not many first person accounts of fish catches during that period, although Carl Nelson (33) recalls catching 102 trout while fishing through the ice near "Door Bluff," 15 miles from Ephraim. His two companions caught 85 and 63 fish each, with the largest trout weighing 28 pounds. After successful expeditions such as this, the fish were salted and packed in barrels in preparation for selling in Green Bay, where at the time fish brought $5.00 a barrel. The fishermen's net profit was only

$3.00, however, because the barrels themselves cost $2.00. Most fishermen in the area obtained their barrels from Peter Weborg of Blossomburg. An especially busy area for commercial fishing activity was Washington Island. Many fishermen lived there in the early and mid-1800s, and by the 1860s it was common for 20,000 barrels of fish to be shipped from the island in a single season (27). Needless to say, coopers (barrel makers) were in great demand.

Note 10 (p. 44): The Names of Places — In his recollections, Iverson mentions both Cooperstown and New Denmark. He gives Cooperstown's location as near Mishicot, which was called "Mishicott" in the 1800s. The Cooperstown to which he refers still exists. A few miles west of it lies New Denmark. It was settled during the 1850–55 period by 20–30 Danish families and a few Norwegians (42). Today New Denmark appears on maps along Interstate 43 as Denmark, an incorporated village of about 1,400, and Cooperstown is a nearby hamlet. Iverson often uses New Denmark and Cooperstown interchangeably, and at one point he indicates that Cooperstown had its name changed to New Denmark. This appears to be incorrect, but the situation is confusing. Because his recollections are sometimes unclear about whether he was visiting New Denmark or Cooperstown, or points in between, we have simply used his terminology in the body of this book. For the purposes of the notes, however, we use the term New Denmark/Cooperstown.

Fort Howard and Green Bay were distinct communities in the early 1800s, being separated by the Fox River. As the area grew the two populations merged, and what was once Fort Howard is now merely the west side of Green Bay. Fort Howard was originally established in the middle 1700s as a French military installation and was later occupied by the British, who completed an elaborate fortified stockade on the site in 1816 (27).

Note 11 (p. 46): Peter Peterson — Peterson was born in Tvedestrand, Norway, in 1821, the illegitimate son of poor farmers. He became a sailor at a young age and eventually returned home, became engaged, and settled on a farm. Finding it difficult to save enough money to get married, he decided to emigrate to the New World and send for his fiancée later. This he did. The couple was married in Milwaukee and left shortly thereafter for Michigan. They later moved to New Denmark/Cooperstown and built a house. Peterson told his story in a brief memoir, *On Both Sides of the Ocean* (42), in which he wrote about himself in the third person and used his Norwegian name, Per Hagen. The manuscript was translated and made into a highly readable book.

Peterson comes across as a thoughtful, rational thinker driven by the principle that a person's fate is in his own hands. In many respects he was just the opposite of Iverson, who was not always pragmatic, and who was guided by the belief that his fate was often in God's hands rather than his own. Peterson apparently was a keen businessman, yet at the same time he was kind and generous.

When Iverson and his family spent the winter of 1854-55 in New Denmark/Cooperstown, they stayed in the home of Peter Peterson. At that time Iverson and Peterson became good friends. In his recollections, Iverson did not make it clear why he moved his family to New Denmark/Cooperstown for the winter, but Peterson (42) indicates that because of the early frost and the inability of the settlers of Ephraim to obtain provisions for winter, Iverson "became worried and moved to the Danish settlement with his entire family, which consisted of a wife, two children, and a maid." It is certainly difficult to understand why Iverson was so willing to leave his new house, the finest in Ephraim, and abandon the friends who looked to him for leadership and support. No doubt his pregnant wife and active young son were a consideration, but it is also likely that he was physically and mentally exhausted after more than a year of tremendous stress and activity. Naess (31) indicates that Iverson wrote to Bethlehem that his move to New Denmark/Cooperstown was made "to avoid the severity of the winter and the trials he should have had to endure in an imperfect 'log cabin' situated in the midst of a dreary forest, the ground of which is wont to be deeply covered with snow, and the trees bending and howling beneath the freezing blasts of winter winds."

In his recollections Iverson spoke warmly about how well the congregation in New Denmark/Cooperstown received him, but Peter Peterson in *On Both Sides of the Ocean* (42) tells a somewhat different story. He wrote that Iverson was preaching to Danes who were mainly Lutherans and Baptists, so relations between the visiting minister and the congregation "were not what they ought to have been."

Iverson's evangelistic style was evidently not well received by many of the more orthodox members of the congregation. That winter, according to Peterson (42), the Danes were sufficiently dissatisfied that they "sent a message to the Norwegian Lutheran minister in Manitowoc about coming up to preach. He did in fact come several times during the course of the winter, but that only made matters worse, for the Norwegian Lutheran minister belonged to a contentious party, emphasizing what is called the pure doctrine and opposing every other church party which was not to their liking ...."

The arrival of a Norwegian Lutheran minister to preach to what Iverson considered to be "his" congregation undoubtedly infuriated him, especially when the visiting minister showed the kind of intolerance toward other faiths that Iverson himself exhibited frequently. In his recollections he often refers to the "stubborn" Lutherans as "enemies of the brethren-congregation" and speaks of his disdain for the "wailing" of the Methodists. Peterson's account of Iverson's ministry in New Denmark/Cooperstown in the winter of 1854-55 reads with validity.

During that winter Iverson spent a great deal of time convincing Peter Peterson that he should sell his property and move to Ephraim. Peterson was finally persuaded. In *On Both Sides of the Ocean* (42), he writes that he and his wife arrived in Ephraim in the autumn of 1856, where they bought a lot and built a house. After buying a small fishing boat, he started a freight service and traded merchandise from his boat. Within a few years, the energetic Peterson built a general store, followed by a substantial shallow-water dock across the road from the store. The dock was 250 feet long, 16 feet wide, and cost $2,500 to build. From this dock Peterson estimated that he annually shipped 3,000 cords of wood, up to 10,000 fence posts, 1,000 telegraph poles, 600–700 cords of bark, and about 2,000 railroad ties (42). Peterson ran his store, the second general store in Ephraim, for many years; he later sold it to his adopted son, James Hanson, who operated it as Hanson's Store. The building and facade of the store are now part of the Edgewater Resort.

In written histories of Ephraim, Peterson is usually overshadowed by Iverson and Aslag Anderson, but he was an influential person in his own right. He was elected to various positions of leadership within the community, and as a staunch Lutheran, he was the driving force behind the building of the Lutheran Church in Ephraim. The church was dedicated in August of 1880, and in 1881 Peterson sold his house to the congregation to use as a parsonage. In 1883 he and Mary moved back to Norway, where they bought a farm and lived out their lives. Peterson died January 10, 1900, and Mary died in 1904 (42).

Because Peterson was a devout Lutheran, Iverson eventually came to view him as an enemy whose beliefs conflicted with his own. During the middle and late 1800s, it was common practice for members of one faith to try to persuade members of another faith to join their congregation. Since the population of Door County was small and congregation size was an accepted indicator of church strength, the competition for souls was relentless. In this regard, Iverson found Peterson a vigorous competitor, and they became bitter adversaries.

Note 12 (p. 47): The Winter of 1854–55 — Iverson does not write much about the impact of the winter of 1854–55 on the handful of settlers remaining in Ephraim, which is not surprising since he spent that winter in New

Denmark/Cooperstown. He does note that in the summer of 1854 the gardens planted by the settlers were "consumed and destroyed by a certain kind of worm," but he fails to mention that additional problems were encountered during the fall in getting provisions from Green Bay to Ephraim by sailing ship. And he certainly does not suggest that his desire to move his family to New Denmark/Cooperstown for the winter had anything to do with his fear that remaining in Ephraim might mean great hardship for them.

In *Old Peninsula Days* Holand (16) mentions that the settlers waited day after day in the late fall and early winter (of 1854) for the boat that was supposed to bring provisions to the colony. He wrote that the settlers' clothing "was worn out and their children were in need of shoes and underwear." He also wrote that during the winter "many of the settlers had nothing on which to live but potatoes and fish. Fish for breakfast, fish for dinner, fish for supper." In a quaint but probably inaccurate passage he suggests that the settlers spent their spare time "contriving strange footgear out of birch bark and moss and in baiting clumsy traps with frozen fish, usually in vain. That winter an old gunny sack was treasured as a priceless fabric."

It should be noted that although Holand's numerous writings about Door County history are certainly significant, they need to be read with caution. The above statements, for example, are probably embellished for dramatic effect, because there is no independent corroboration that the settlers were in such desperate straits. Holand is prone to exaggeration at times, and his writings are occasionally flawed by careless research. Nevertheless, his prolific but often repetitious commentaries provide considerable insight into pioneer days in Door County, and he had the advantage of talking first-hand with many of the early settlers, including Iverson.

CHAPTER FOUR

Note 1 (p. 48): How Cold Were Door County Winters in the 1800s? — There is little mention of precise temperatures in first-person accounts describing the severity of Door County winters in the 1800s. Martin (28) indicates that the winter of 1862-63 may have been the "coldest ever experienced in this section" but provides no temperature readings. Rather he presents a powerful description indicating that the arrival of the cold snap was unexpected and "its 'claws' were as sharp as though they had been ground on an iceberg, and polished on a jagged rock ...." To translate this vivid word picture to degrees below zero would be futile. The temperature in Racine County on January 1, 1864, was recorded at 31 degrees below zero (6). According to Henderson and Speerschneider (12), recorded temperatures in Wisconsin have ranged from 54 degrees below zero fahrenheit on January 24, 1921, to 111 degrees above on July 4, 1901. Anna Petterson of Ephraim wrote (36) that during the last week of November of 1884 "Everything froze in the pantry: milk, potatoes, everything actually glittered with ice. It is too cold to stay in the kitchen; so we took the cookstove into the bedroom." In 1888 she wrote that "Several hundred people, from the youngest to an old man, have frozen to death recently here ...." "Here where we are it has been 30 degrees below 0."

Note 2 (p.54): Preaching Places — As part of the evangelical outreach of the Home Missionary Society of the Moravian Church, ministers in frontier America were expected to travel around and preach in a variety of places. In his lifetime of evangelism, Iverson preached thousands of sermons in many different places in Wisconsin, Michigan, Illinois, and even Iowa. He was instrumental in establishing many churches, preaching places, and missions. The table (Fig. 14) below sets forth those attributed to Iverson in the *Inventory of The Church Archives of Wisconsin* (20).

FIGURE 14 — Iverson's churches, preaching places, and missions in Wisconsin.

1. Green Bay West (formerly Ft. Howard), 1850 to present, church
2. Denmark (formerly New Denmark), 1850–61, mission
3. Mishicot, 1850–61, mission
4. Ephraim, 1853 to present, church
5. Sturgeon Bay, 1857 to present, church
6. Marinette, MI, 1857–59, mission
7. Minnekaune, MI (near Marinette), 1857–83, preaching place
8. Manasseh (near Ephraim), 1861–1911, preaching place
9. Blossomburg (near Fish Creek), 1864–95, preaching place
10. Sister Bay, 1866 to present, preaching place, then church
11. Ashwaubenon, 1870 to present, intermittent mission
12. Big Suamico, 1875–83, preaching place
13. Shawano, 1876–?, preaching place
14. Egg Harbor, 1877–1911, church

Because settlers were often widely scattered, ministers preached to small groups in homes, schoolhouses, or whatever gathering place was available. In this way, they established "preaching places" (sometimes referred to as preaching "stations") that they visited on an irregular basis. Although this practice resulted in many people in many isolated places being served, it was not particularly conducive to establishing a permanent and sustainable congregation devoted to a given faith. As Iverson eventually learned, a sustainable congregation required a critical mass of people, a building devoted to worship, and, probably most important, a resident minister who could nurture a congregation on a day-to-day basis.

Note 3 (p. 59): The German Settlement — Within a few years after Scandinavian settlers began to establish Ephraim, German immigrants started settling land a few miles east of Ephraim, much of which was available from the government at very low cost. The general area of the settlement was east of Ephraim's Townline Road, across Highway 57 toward Lake Michigan, south toward Baileys Harbor to about Meadow Road, and north to where Settlement and Old Stage Roads intersect with Highway 57. It included hundreds of acres. Today Ephraim's "German Road" follows the old wagon road east from Ephraim and through the northern end of the old German settlement. The road was an important link between the German community and the village of Ephraim.

Almost four million German immigrants arrived in America between 1845 and 1900 (57), and many of them came to Wisconsin. Ephraim's nearby German Settlement was made up of poor immigrant families, mainly farmers from the province of Pomerania in the northwestern part of today's Germany. These families emigrated primarily because of crop failures and overcrowded farms in their homeland; later, during the 1880–1900 period, many more fled Europe because of the oppressive dominance of the province of Prussia, whose rulers began seizing land from farmers (57).

Among the earliest German immigrants to settle east of Ephraim were William Dorn, Herman Langohr, and Augustus Stoewer (Staver). In letters to relatives and friends, these and other early German settlers described the available land, the opportunities, and the freedom in America and encouraged those remaining in Europe emigrate. By 1900 the German Settlement was made up of about 20 families numbering approximately 150 individuals. Iverson established a preaching place in the German Settlement in 1861. In 1875, the Manesseh (also written Menasa) Moravian Church was built on the corner of Highway 57 and German Road (20). Later the church was moved to Sister Bay, and around 1915 a school, called Liberty Grove School, was erected on the site. It served mainly the German Settlement and was the pride of the community; the school closed about 1970 and the building is now used as a residence. During his years in Ephraim Iverson was very supportive of his German neighbors and they in turn appreciated his efforts to serve their spiritual needs.

CHAPTER FIVE

Note 1 (p. 64): How Serious Was the Crop Failure of 1857? — In *Old Peninsula Days* Holand (16) describes the impact of crop failure in Ephraim in 1857 in the following way.

> "The fact was that the little settlement that fall was very near starvation. The crops in 1857 were a complete failure, due to excessive heat and drought, and in dismay the colonists looked forward to the winter with nothing to eat. The bank at Green Bay would not lend a dollar on their real estate. The mills of Sturgeon Bay and Cedar River were shut down on account of the hard times. They were almost without clothing and shoes. There was not an overcoat in the settlement. Their summer garments, made largely of worn out grain bags, were now in tatters. They thought of the hardships of the winter before when they were so near starvation. Now their potato bins and corn cribs and grain boxes were empty. What were they to live on?"

Iverson's recollections suggest that while the situation was serious in Ephraim, it never approached the level of desperation described by Holand (mainly due to supplies purchased in exchange for fence posts). Villagers began construction of their church during the summer of 1857, and the idea that starving settlers, wearing tattered garments made from worn out grain bags, would spend most of the summer building a church is beyond comprehension.

Note 2 (p. 64): Where to Build the Church — Although Iverson strongly believed the church should be built up on the hill just north of his house, he yielded to a vocal minority. The original location of the church was on the shore, across from where the Ephraim Village Hall is now located. There are no known photographs showing the church on this site although Iverson shows it on the shore in two of his paintings (Figs. C1 and C2). Much later the congregation, perhaps with the encouragement of J.J. Groenfeldt who was pastor at the time, realized that Iverson had been right after all, and that the church building should not be located so close to the water. In the summer of 1883, while Groenfeldt was visiting Denmark, the building was moved up the hill to near the site originally chosen by Iverson; the move cost $321 and required the use of log rollers, skids, winches, and both horse and manpower (23,55). Apparently the structure was moved up present County Road Q to Moravia Street, then down Moravia and up an incline to its present site (23). In 1896 the church was extensively remodeled, and in 1916 an addition was made to the east side of the church. In the early 1950s another addition included four Sunday School rooms, a kitchen, and an enlarged fellowship hall; provision was made to add a pastor's study and workroom at a later date. The architect for the

FIGURE 15 — View of Ephraim in a photograph taken around 1885 (photo source: Ephraim Foundation). The church building had been moved up the hill a few years earlier, in 1883.

1950 addition was Frank Shattuck, who provided plans free of charge and supervised construction. Cost of the project was $30,000 and men in the congregation worked on the addition to keep the cost within budget (23).

Figure 15 (p. 193) is a view of Ephraim around 1885 shortly after the church building had been moved up the hill; this is the earliest known photograph of the building. An enlarged portion of the photograph (Fig. 16) shows the front of the church before later alterations changed its appearance. There is a double door to the west, which was the main entrance, with decorative trim work over the door. The steps leading to the entrance are of the pyramid type and railings can be seen. The steeple is the one designed by Iverson that he thought too small for the building—it was later enlarged. Note the picket-type fence around the church yard.

FIGURE 16 — Enlargement of a portion of Fig. 15 showing details of the original church building. Also see Fig. C4.

Note 3 (p. 68): How a Sophisticated Outsider Might Have Viewed the Townspeople of Ephraim — The visit of H.A. Schultz and his daughter raises the question of how outsiders viewed early Ephraim and its rugged settlers. Unfortunately, as a church administrator Schultz was in no position to record his candid reactions to either the place or the people. But the third pastor of the Ephraim Moravian Church, Anders Petterson, and his wife were under no such constraints. Petterson arrived in Ephraim in 1884 with his wife, Anna, who was raised in Copenhagen and educated as a music teacher. Both Anders and Anna were fairly sophisticated Europeans whose letters to Anna's mother provide an outsider's view of the people of Ephraim in the late 1800s (36). This is how Anna first described the townspeople. "As far as the brothers and sisters here are concerned, they are very, very plain people, mostly farmers who own some land, a few cattle, and a little house. They have very little money ... [and] are mostly Norwegians." Townspeople "speak very indistinctly, mixing English words with their Norwegian so that it is a real hodgepodge."

Note 4 (p. 71): Aslag Anderson — Aslag Anderson was born near Arndal, Norway, on August 8, 1829, not far from the farm where Peter Peterson was born and raised. The Anderson brothers and Peterson met in Norway, and Aslag and his brother, Halvor, arrived in America in 1848 on board the same ship with Peterson's wife-to-be, Mary (42). After Peter and Mary were married, they traveled with the Anderson brothers to Michigan, where the men worked at a sawmill. Later the Petersons left for Milwaukee and New Denmark, but the Anderson brothers remained in Michigan and worked as millwrights for about seven years. They moved to Cedar River, Michigan, in 1855, and a few years later made their way to Ephraim to visit Peter Peterson, who convinced them to settle in the community. In 1858 Aslag and Peterson reached an agreement with Iverson regarding construction of a pier in Ephraim. In exchange for 110 acres of land at about $1.15 an acre (its original cost), Anderson and Peterson agreed to build a first-class deepwater pier to which villagers would have free access. In the bargain, Halvor Anderson received a tract of land (56 acres) at the same price. Although Aslag and Peterson were partners in acquiring the land and building the dock, Aslag later bought out Peterson.

After Aslag and Peterson completed the deepwater pier in 1859 (35), Aslag gradually established himself as a shrewd businessman. Although the community had free access to the pier, Aslag became the local agent for all the commercial shipping and cargo that utilized his dock. In addition he operated a successful general store, farmed with his brother, Halvor, and made wise investments. Through his efforts, the Anderson family became relatively affluent. In 1861 he married Anna Margaretha Hansen, also from Norway, and they had thirteen children, ten of whom lived to adulthood (54). All members of the family were active in the Moravian Church and each contributed something to the community. The original warehouse was a small structure (Fig. 17), and according to oral history it was blown down in a windstorm. The replacement warehouse, as well as part of the pier, were destroyed by fire in the fall of 1880.

FIGURE 17 — Anderson's pier and dock around 1860 showing the original warehouse; cordwood and shingles are stacked on the dock (photo source: Ephraim Foundation).

Merchandise lost was valued at $2,500, for a total estimated loss of $5,000 (14). The third warehouse is still standing and is used in the summertime as an art gallery.

According to the Door County Register of Deeds, when the Moravian congregation made a final payment to H.A. Schultz in 1867, Aslag Anderson received a clear warranty deed to four parcels of land totaling 110 acres, for which he had paid a total of $124.67. At the same time, Halvor Anderson received a clear deed to several parcels of land totaling 56 acres for the sum of $65.39.

Aslag Anderson died August 5, 1892. His wife died in 1890.

Note 5 (p. 72): Some Discrepancies in Dates in Iverson's Recollections (21) — In recalling events that happened several decades earlier, Iverson appears to make remarkably few errors in assigning dates. The more difficult problem is trying to establish a specific chronological sequence when he fails to mention key dates that could be used as reference points. In writing this book, we tried to be as accurate as possible with dates. When we discovered discrepancies, we cross-checked the questionable dates against those found in other reference sources. Iverson's letters published in *The Moravian* are particularly important sources of specific dates. For example, in his recollections (21) Iverson writes that he ruptured a blood vessel in his lung when preaching at a revival in November of 1859. On the other hand, in his letter published on p. 89 of the March 24, 1859, issue of *The Moravian*, he says the incident occurred on the 4th Sunday of Advent (50); since the periodical was issued in March of 1859, this means that the event actually occurred in December of 1858.

Note 6 (p. 74): Ephraim's First Schoolhouse (Fig. 18) — In his recollections (21), Iverson suggests that the school district was organized and the first school building constructed in 1857. This appears to be incorrect. The original minutes of the school district meetings (37) indicate that the district was organized in 1858 and the first schoolhouse was built in 1859.

Note 7 (p. 74): Length of School Terms — In 1857, the state required six months of school each year, although later the requirement was increased to seven months a year. Typically there would be winter and summer terms of three months each.

Note 8 (p. 74): Pauline Larsen — Ole Larsen's daughter, Pauline, was a devout Moravian and a person on whom Iverson depended. One of her many contributions to early Ephraim was her ongoing effort to see that the settlers' children received a basic education. As early as 1853, she was helping children of the colony learn reading, writing, and arithmetic, and when Ephraim built its first schoolhouse she finally had the opportunity to teach in a more formalized setting.

According to Iverson's recollections (21), in the spring of 1858 Pauline and her fiance', Martin Johnson, took the steamer to Buffalo, New York, where her

FIGURE 18 — Log house said to be Ephraim's first schoolhouse (24). An addition has been made to the building and it is now used as a summer residence.

sisters lived. There Pauline and Martin were married. After remaining in Buffalo for a while, they returned to Ephraim during the summer and lived temporarily with the Iversons. Johnson purchased a substantial tract of land on the west side of Eagle Harbor, near the bluff, where he built a small house. While they awaited completion of the house, they probably lived with Pauline's parents, who had moved from Eagle Island to Nicolet Bay and established a farm (Fig. 9). Pauline taught until the end of the 1860-61 school year, when she was still being paid $4.00 a week. At that time there were two school terms, one beginning December 1 and the other June 1 for a total of seven months. There were 31 male children and 22 female children in the district. Text books used included Spelling, Reading, Arithmetic, Geography, and Grammar. Peter Peterson was clerk of the School District and Tobias Morbek was treasurer (37). Since most of the settlers were Norwegian, this is the language they spoke at home; at school, however, the children used English.

Note 9 (p. 76): The Delicate Constitution of Laura Iverson — Little information, either anecdotal or written, exists about Laura Iverson. Except for a single unflattering photograph (Fig. 19), even her physical appearance is not

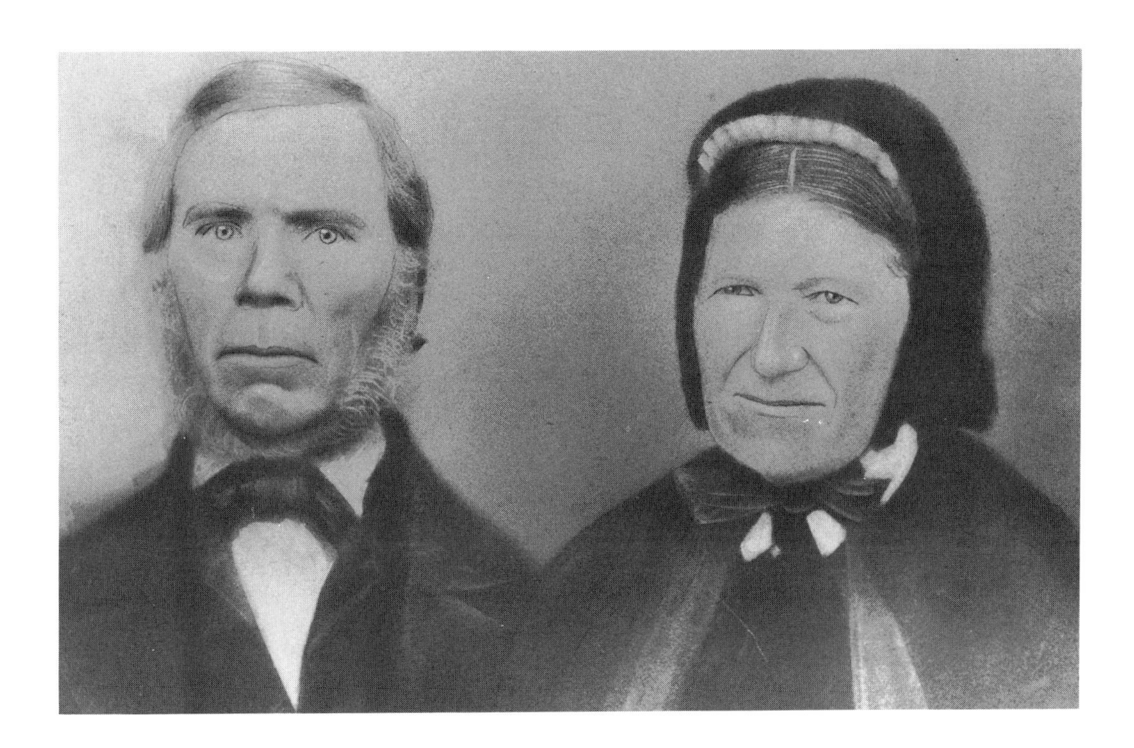

FIGURE 19 — Andrew and Laura Iverson (photo source: Ephraim Moravian Church). This is the only known photograph of Laura, which was probably taken when Andrew and Laura were between 35-40 years of age. The original print from which this copy was made has been rather crudely retouched, probably with a pencil, which detracts from the appearance of the subjects. Regardless, Andrew's eyes have the characteristic intense look, and Laura's expression could be interpreted as reflecting ill-health.

documented. Although Iverson (21) mentions his wife with some frequency in his recollections, it is often in connection with her ill health. "My dear wife, never strong (p. 147)," "My dear but weak wife (p. 147)," "My delicate wife (p. 81)," and "My poor Laura was terribly shaken up from the journey and very tired (p. 71)," are some of Iverson's written references to Laura, with the page numbers referring to Boler's translation (21). On at least one of these occasions she was eight months pregnant (p. 71). It is impossible to know just how frail she actually was, although a brief mention (31) in an 1849 report from the Board of the Norwegian Missionary Society in Stavanger states that Iverson had "become engaged to a girl, whose sickliness probably made her unsuitable for the mission." Certainly Laura had many reasons to be chronically unhappy, which could have contributed to her health problems. She was often pregnant during the early years, she suffered the loss of four young children, her peripatetic husband left home for long periods of time, and when he was in Ephraim he was involved primarily in ministering to the needs of others. Delicate though she may have been, she survived a harrowing ocean voyage, gave birth to six children, made a home under trying frontier conditions, endured the absences of her husband, suffered rumors about his relationship with other women, and lived to the age of 69. She was not living with Iverson at the time of her death, having chosen to remain alone in Green Bay after Iverson was asked to leave the pastorate in 1883. Nevertheless, she is buried in the family plot in Bay View Cemetery in Sturgeon Bay. The circumstances by which she came to be buried with her estranged husband are unknown, although the family in Sturgeon Bay, including Iverson himself, probably made the decision. No doubt the story of her difficult life on the frontier would be almost as interesting as her husband's.

Note 10 (p. 76): Leland, Mission Point, and Norway, Illinois — In the middle 1800s there were two settlements of Scandinavians in La Salle County, Illinois, which is located just southwest of Chicago in the middle of the state. Leland was, and is, located about 10 miles east of the Fox River, while Mission Point was established along the river about 15 miles to the southeast of Leland. During Iverson's time, this area was considered to be part of the great Midwestern prairie. Because of the large number of Norwegian immigrants settling Mission Point, the name of the place was eventually changed to Norway, Illinois. Today's maps show Norway as a very small hamlet.

Note 11 (p. 37, 40, 42, 77, 78): Iverson the Artist and Designer — The original Ephraim Moravian Church building was designed from drawings provided by Iverson, and he also designed his own house. In addition, he drew the original plat map for the village (Figs. 2 and 3), designed and built a substantial sailboat (p. 40), and constructed furniture (Fig. 20). When the church building was completed, he designed and built the pulpit, which is still in use (Fig. 21). He also designed the Fort Howard Moravian Church and built its pulpit. Iverson had a well-developed aesthetic sense and he was obviously skilled with his hands. Even his handwriting reflects his artistic ability (Fig. 22). He appreciated beauty wherever he found it, whether in his surroundings or in people. He was a surprisingly accomplished primitive watercolorist, as shown in Figs. C1 and C2. He wrote poetry and even composed music for many occasions, including dedication of the Ephraim Moravian Church (31; a copy of A.M. Iverson's Music Book is at Heritage Hill State Park in Green Bay). Based

FIGURE 20 — Table owned by Reverend John Groenfeldt and his wife Eva that is said to be an example of Iverson's skill as a woodworker.

on what is known of his sermons, he also had a flair for the dramatic. On one of his trips to Keokuk, Iowa, Iverson was taken to a high bluff overlooking the Mississippi River valley. His keen aesthetic sense is clearly evident in the way he recalled the scene he had enjoyed about 40 years earlier (21; p. 135):

"It is impossible for me to describe how these very impressive and remarkable views affected me, for they were very elevating and peculiar. I sat transfixed there for a long time, unable to say a word, for such wonderful views produced silence and amazement. However, the time came when we had to return, but it was with reluctance that I drove away." "But even now I seem to see in my mind's eye this very beautiful and magical panorama."

The above passage, his recollections, and his many letters to Bethlehem make it clear that Iverson was also a gifted, if untrained, writer. There is no doubt that Iverson had the kind of temperament often associated with artists and aesthetes, and Naess (31) describes him as showing "a naive optimism, also

FIGURE 21 — Pulpit constructed by Iverson in 1859 for the Ephraim Moravian Church.

enthusiasm and activity, and an ecstasy in which religion and sensuality coalesce." Of a girl about to be confirmed Iverson wrote: "I shall never forget the last preparation hour on the 29th of August (1854). Truly when Christ's beauties—I am so fond of this expression—appear in my mission in so visible a manner, I feel happy as a child ... With a look of sanctified mildness, and with a distinct but soft voice she answered my questions" (reported by Naess [31] as appearing in *The Moravian Church Miscellany*, 1855, p. 113).

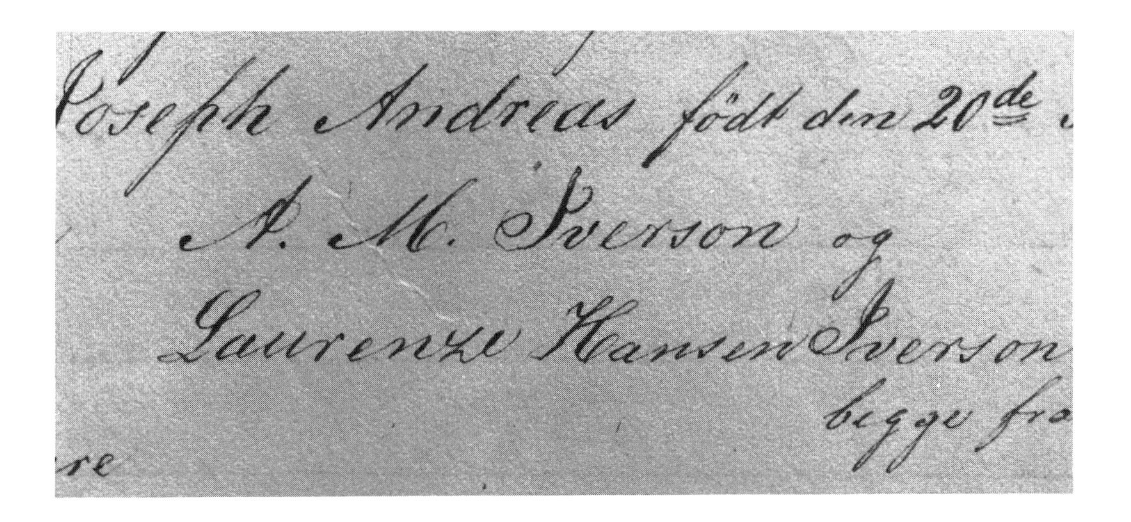

Joseph Andreas födt den 20de
A. M. Iverson og
Laurenze Hansen Iverson
begge fra
re

FIGURE 22 – Sample of Iverson's handwriting from the Church Register he kept. This is from the passage recording the birth of his son (Lauritz) Joseph Andreas.

Iverson apparently passed along his artistic talents, for in interviewing his descendants it became clear that this was a dominant family trait, although in several males artistic ability was expressed in skills related to engineering.

The mystique surrounding Iverson, the house he built, and the Moravian Church he established in Ephraim have inspired many modern artists to attempt to capture the spirit of Iverson and early Ephraim, and to convey in drawings and paintings the values the evangelist brought to a wilderness area. Two such paintings that relate to Iverson and early Ephraim are shown in Figs. C3 and C4.

ABOUT THE PAINTINGS

■ C1 — A watercolor painted around 1860 by Andrew Iverson. This painting hangs in the Ephraim Moravian Church. It depicts the church building at its original site along the shore, where it remained for 24 years until it was moved up the hill to its present site. Iverson has painted himself into the scene as the artist in the foreground.

■ C2 — A watercolor by Andrew Iverson bearing the inscription "Original Drawn From Nature In 1861 By A.M.I.". This painting is owned by Cedric Iverson, Andrew Iverson's great grandson. Although badly faded, it is reproduced here because it has never before been on public view. Note the pall of smoke that hangs over the cleared land in the distance, the site of the new village. With a hand lens, the church can be seen along the shoreline, with its steepled front apparently facing northwest. It appears that Iverson painted the scene from the vantage point of Eagle Island.

■ C3 — A Charles Peterson watercolor showing Iverson's image superimposed on his house, which he designed and helped build in 1853. Details of the house, as well as its two additions, are shown. The painting is used with permission of the artist and its owners.

■ C4 — Karsten Topelmann's gouache painting of the original Moravian Church located along the shore in Ephraim. Topelmann was commissioned to depict the church for the dust-jacket of this book. Before beginning the painting, he often visited the original site of the church and even waded out into the bay to watch the sunrise and its reflection on the water. Topelmann said of his painting: "To achieve an appropriate interpretation of the historic quality of this book, I painted a sunrise to signify the dawning of a new day, a new era, and the spirit of a new beginning filled with hope and anticipation." Details of the church are as seen in the earliest known photograph showing the structure (Fig. 16).

C1 - Watercolor by Andrew Iverson

C2 - Watercolor by Andrew Iverson

C3 - Watercolor by Charles Peterson

C4 - Gouache Painting by Karsten Topelmann

Chapter 6

Note 1 (p. 81; p. 208a–f): Clothing Worn by Midwestern Pioneers in the Middle 1800s (4) — The early settlers managed to survive very cold winters without the goosedown jackets, thermal underwear, and insulated boots we take for granted today. How did they manage? Or, for that matter, what did they wear during hot summer weather? And what kind of clothes did Iverson wear when he preached?

Protestant ministers, such as Iverson, generally wore black, knee-length frock coats with dark pants (p. 208a). Such coats were more tailored and formal than the looser, somewhat casual sack coats worn by laymen. The frock coat was worn with a white shirt buttoned to the top, a black single-breasted vest with a collar, and occasionally a dark cravat. One of Iverson's watercolor paintings (Fig. C1) shows a minister at an easel in the foreground, with a little girl standing nearby. The artist, presumably Iverson himself, is wearing a minister's standard outdoor attire: a black frock coat and a wide-brimmed hat.

The typical layman's outfit included straight-legged trousers, a long-sleeved shirt with buttons halfway down the front, and a vest (p. 208b). Winter clothing was made of wool, while summer shirts and vests were cotton or linen. A man never removed his shirt outside, even in very hot weather, because it was considered improper for him to expose his body in public. He might remove his vest while working, but he would keep it handy to slip on if anyone approached. In the winter he wore an overcoat constructed of heavy milled wool and cut very large to accommodate several layers of clothing underneath. Men's coats and overcoats were usually purchased, but most other items of clothing were made at home.

Men never went outside without hats. They wore hats with low crowns for work, and those who could afford them wore high-crowned hats (the Abe Lincoln "stove-pipe" hat) on more formal occasions. In colder weather most men wore hats with earflaps, but knit caps were also worn. They wore straw hats in the summertime.

Men's underwear consisted of full-length cotton britches (necessary to protect against itchy wool or canvas pants) and long-sleeved collarless undershirts. For cold weather, the undershirts might be made of wool flannel. In winter, men also wore hand-knit wool mittens, gloves (p. 208e), and scarves—all essential for warmth. Men's work shoes were made of sturdy leather, ankle high or boot length, and were kept well-greased.

Women had a rather standard everyday uniform (p. 208c). As they went about their indoor chores, they always wore day dresses, aprons, and day caps.

Rev. Iversen and his daughter

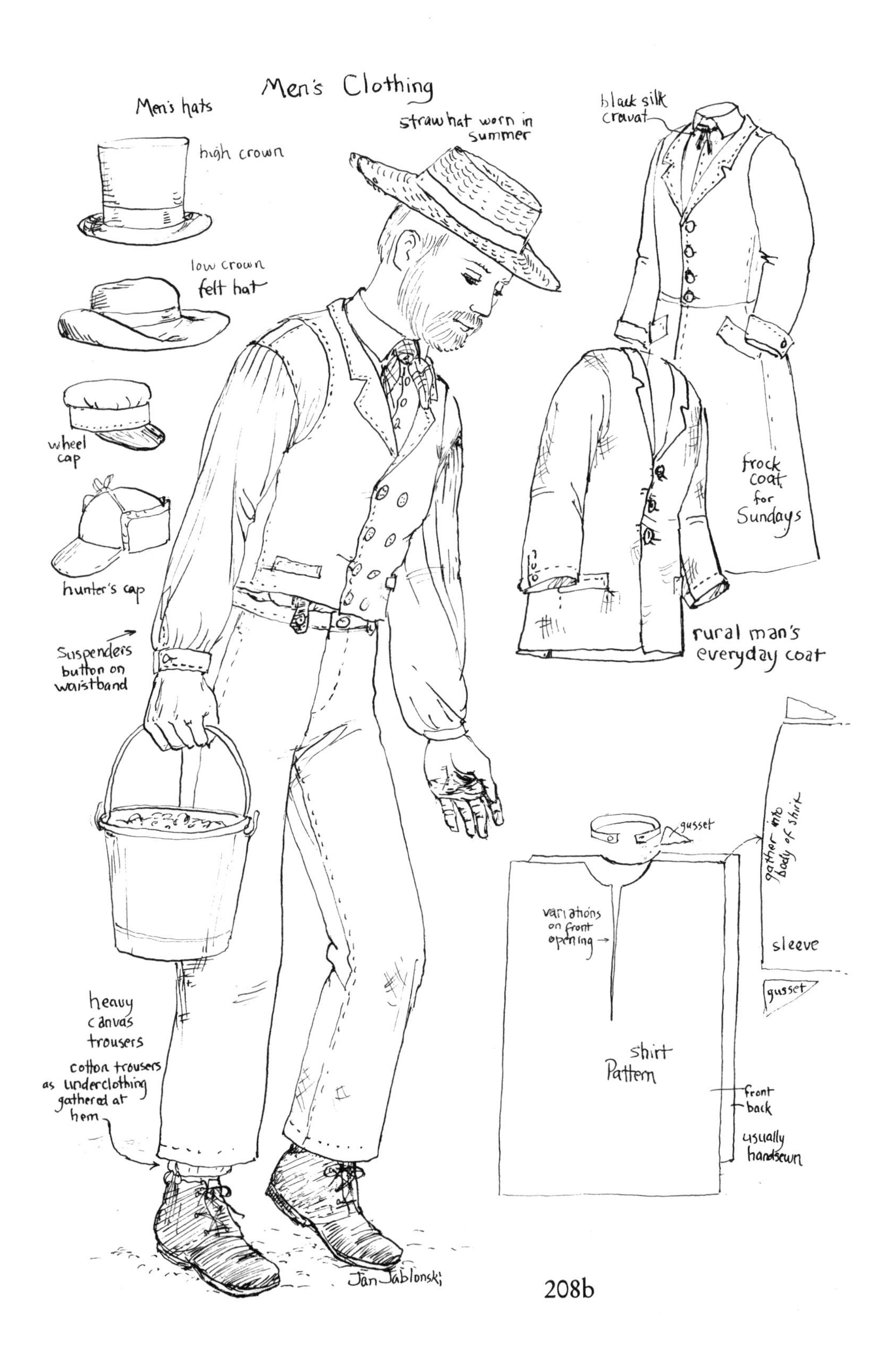
Men's Clothing
Men's hats
high crown
low crown
felt hat
wheel cap
hunter's cap
Suspenders button on waistband
straw hat worn in summer
black silk cravat
frock coat for Sundays
rural man's everyday coat
heavy canvas trousers
cotton trousers as underclothing gathered at hem
gusset
gather into body of shirt
variations on front opening
sleeve
gusset
shirt Pattern
front
back
usually handsewn
Jan Jablonski

Women's Clothing
Dress Pattern
gather here
sleeve
Bodice
gusset
gather into Bodice
skirt
day cap
shawl
sunbonnet
Spencer
chemise
drawstring in waistband
Pantaloons
hoop skirt
Petticoat
linen or cotton apron
Jan Jablonski
rural everyday dress
handmade buttonholes
Jan Jablonski
work boots for everyday
(leather slippers for dress-up)
similar to men's style

Jan
Jablonski

glove knitting
lesson
Jan M.
Jablonski

The collarless day dresses were ankle-length and had fitted bodices, long sleeves, and buttons down the front. They were handsewn of simple materials such as cotton, linen, wool, or linsey woolsey in plain, printed, striped, checked, or plaid patterns. They usually had a pocket on the right side. Aprons, which were always worn around the house, had no pockets and were made of plain, striped, or checked material—but never prints. All married women wore white cotton day caps when they were inside. These simple caps tied under the chin and often had a small ruffle around the face. When working outside, women wore sunbonnets to protect their skin from the sun. It was important to show as little skin as possible, and the only reason a woman rolled up her sleeves was to keep them clean and dry. Women's everyday shoes were usually made of strong leather and were quite similar to men's work shoes. Underwear for women consisted of several layers of petticoats (even while doing chores), a chemise, and long pantaloons. If it was very cold, they sometimes wore quilted petticoats for added warmth.

For church-going and special occasions, women set aside nicer or newer versions of their usual dresses and wore cloth or leather slippers instead of heavy work shoes. In the winter they wore bonnets with scarves to hold them on and protect their ears and necks. Women did not wear winter coats—they wore woolen shawls. Shawls were easy to make at home and were the most economical and practical type of outer garment. Usually plaid or checked, they could be worn over as many layers of clothes as desired.

Children's clothing (p. 208d–f) was invariably homemade and often handed down. For the first few years boys and girls were dressed alike in "frocks," which were knee-length, full-skirted dresses. Sometimes the only way to distinguish the sexes, particularly in photographs, was to notice where the hair was parted—if on the side, the child was a boy, if in the middle, the youngster was a girl. After the age of four or five, children wore small versions of adult clothes. In most instances these garments were made from salvageable portions of their parents' worn-out clothing. The early settlers did not waste a single piece of fabric. After making and remaking garments for themselves and their children, they used any remaining scraps for quilts.

Note 2 (p. 82): Early Moravian Evangelism — According to Dr. Gary Kinkel, former Pastor of the Ephraim Moravian Church, when the Moravian movement was established in Europe, emphasis was placed on mission work and evangelism with no regard for establishing fixed churches. Moravian doctrine was meant to supplement the message provided by other denominations of the day. The emphasis was not on converting people to the Moravian Church, but on providing a brotherhood of spiritual intimacy and study not practiced by other denominations. "The Moravian movement was one that spanned denominational barriers," Kinkel stated. Thus there were members of the Lutheran and other reformed denominations, and even some members of the Catholic faith, who considered themselves also to be Moravians. "To be a Moravian didn't mean to be part of a church denomination," according to Kinkel, and Moravian missionaries in Africa, for example, would establish a mission station, recruit followers, and later turn the station over to some other denomination to sustain the congregation.

When the Moravian movement began to establish missions in America in the early 1800s, church workers soon became aware that denominationalism was a significant feature of American religious life. As a result, Moravian leaders began to rethink their position. By the early 1800s, an effort was underway to begin establishing church buildings to serve Moravian missionary work in America, and by the Civil War a major thrust of the Moravian effort in America was directed toward the establishment of fixed churches.

Note 3 (p. 91): Christmas Was a Special Time in Early Ephraim — During the period between Ephraim's founding and the early 1900s, the Christmas season was of great importance to the community for both social and religious reasons. In good part this was because the village was isolated from the outside world, especially in the wintertime. The Christmas season brought members of the community together to count their blessings and celebrate the birth of Jesus. Children were made to feel a special part of the Christmas celebration, and Iverson made certain that they were carefully instructed in the significance of the Christ child. The tradition of involving children in Ephraim's Christmas celebrations continued for over a century. Even today adults who were children in the 1940s and 1950s speak with fondness of the plays, the singing, and the festivities associated with the Ephraim Moravian Church at Christmastime. Until the middle of the 1900s, the two focal points in the lives of young people of Ephraim, outside the family itself, were the church building and the schoolhouse. The Christmas season brought families, church, and school together—it was a time of warmth and goodwill, and the children reveled in the occasion.

Note 4 (p. 91): The Age of Andrew's Children — Although Iverson says in his recollections (21) that Anna Munda was nine years old when she contracted whooping cough in early 1863, she was really only eight. She was born on November 5, 1854. There are several other instances where Iverson mentions his children's ages and lists them as a year too old. His method of calculating their age may have been simply to subtract the year of birth from the current date, ignoring the month in which they were born. Dates of births and deaths are shown in Figs. 4 and 5.

CHAPTER 7

Note 1 (p. 99): About Homeopathic Medicine (34,56) — Both Iverson and H.P. Jacobs were adherents of homeopathic medicine, and both men were important to the community in their efforts to treat illness and infirmity. Homeopathy or homeopathic medicine is based on theories advanced by a German physician (Samuel Hahnemann, 1755-1843) in the early 1800s. The main theory of homeopathic medicine is that small doses of a substance or drug that produces symptoms of the sickness in a healthy person can be used to cure an individual who is ill with that disease. A secondary theory, now out of favor, was that all diseases are the result of some kind of suppressed itch. This sounds strange until one realizes that even conventional physicians of the period had a few peculiar ideas about the origins of disease states—for instance, it was widely believed that some diseases, such as malaria, were caused by bad air (in Italian, the name literally means "bad air").

Various kinds of herb extracts and potions are part of the homeopathic physician's arsenal. For example, an infant with chronic skin rash might by washed in "bran-water" in an attempt to relieve or cure the condition (36). Homeopathic medicine gained many followers in the 1800s, partly because physicians of the day could do very little about most diseases, and families of the afflicted were willing to try anything. Another attractive aspect of homeopathy is that treatment stresses the doctor–patient relationship. Although Iverson was well-read, he was not formally trained in homeopathy until much later. It probably appealed to him because the doctor–patient relationship is similar to the kind of intimate relationship that can develop between minister and parishioner during spiritual counseling. His interest in homeopathy also stemmed from his great interest in helping people and the fact that one could easily practice this kind of "medicine" after reading books related to the subject, without formal study and licensing. Although homeopathy is not widely practiced in Western cultures, in India it has gained the status of an accepted, traditional form of medicine. In the United States, homeopathy is often practiced as part of the alternative medicine movement that treats mind and body as one, and today there is renewed interest in this approach to healing.

Note 2 (p. 107): Recalling the Death of Anna Munda — The death of Anna Munda was one of the most emotionally wrenching experiences of Iverson's life, and recounting it was tremendously difficult for him. The impact of the event is made clear by the length of the account—it occupies 10 pages in his recollections, while other mentions of his children usually consist of a sentence or two.

Iverson (21) remembered Anna Munda's death and the events surrounding it in remarkable detail, even though he was writing 30 years later. He was able to bring to mind long passages of what Anna Munda said, and he vividly retained the memory of his conflicting emotions as he watched his daughter die. He recalled dates, times, sequences of events, details of conversations, and names of hymns, but it was necessary for him to carry these memories with him for a long time before he was able to write about them. When he did write (21), around the age of 75, he noted the following: "It has been my desire hundreds of times to write the history of our blessed child, Anna Munda. I have been persuaded by dear friends who knew this remarkable and gifted child who was with us nine years, but it seemed impossible for me to do so. Now at least [sic] I have been able to do it ...."

The whole topic of Anna Munda's death was so emotionally charged that there remained portions he could not bear to describe, such as his last farewell to his daughter: "The final sad parting I will not—I cannot—describe. I am drawing the curtain over the final scene." But despite his near total recall of the last three days of Anna Munda's life, his anxiety over officiating at her burial was so intense that he could remember very little about it. "I cannot recall in detail this very touching, solemn burial."

One of Iverson's fears in recounting this event was that he would not be believed. He felt compelled to state: "it is the naked truth without any exaggeration ..." and "I want to testify as the naked truth that no pen can completely describe or draw a picture of ...." Regardless of the accuracy of his memory, the intensity of his feelings is clear and his extraordinary account "done with my somewhat shaking hand" is a moving tribute to his greatly beloved daughter.

Except for this emotional description of the death of the second Anna Munda, Iverson does not spend much time in his recollections talking about his children (21). Since he was writing a church history, not a family history, this is not surprising. The title he gave his recollections indicates the focus of his narrative. In contrast, his letters to Bethlehem contain many references to his wife and children, and they make it clear that he cared very much about his family.

Note 3 (p. 107): Andrew and Laura Iverson's Children (Fig. 5) — With the exception of Anna Munda, Iverson recorded very little substantive information about his six children, and details of their births, lives, and deaths are difficult to find. The following information about them was pieced together from the occasional references in his recollections (21), as well as from tombstones, cemetery records, obituaries, records of the Ephraim Moravian Church, and from interviews with descendants. The six children are listed below.

ANNA MUNDA LAURENZE (December 31, 1849–August 2, 1850): Andrew and Laura's first child was born in Milwaukee. She died, apparently of cholera, only seven months later. Her death on a steamship going from Milwaukee to Green Bay is poignantly recorded in Iverson's recollections (21), as is her burial in an Indian cemetery in Green Bay.

ALFRED MARTIN LEONHARD HILDEBERT (July 4, 1852–October 18, 1902): Alfred was born in Fort Howard after Iverson and his congregation had broken with Otto Tank. He married Regina Solway, with whom he lived on a farm on Bay Shore Drive in Sturgeon Bay. Alfred's five children were: Lawrence, Cora, John, Laura, and Martina. Alfred died of tuberculosis and is buried in the family plot in Bay View Cemetery, Sturgeon Bay.

ANNA MUNDA ELEONORA (November 5, 1854–April 2, 1863): Anna Munda was born at New Denmark/Cooperstown where Andrew and Laura were spending the winter. Her life is joyously celebrated in Iverson's recollections (21), and her death is movingly recorded as well. She is buried in the Ephraim Moravian Cemetery. The lettering on the headstone of her grave is still faintly legible and a photograph of it appears in *Pioneer Cemeteries, Door County Wisconsin*, by Kahlert (25).

JOHN HUSS (July 16, 1857–February 22, 1902): John was born in Ephraim. Although his birth is not mentioned in Iverson's recollections (21), his baptism is recorded in the Church Register kept by Iverson, where he is listed as Johan Huss (38). He never married. His death occurred in the Park Avenue Hotel fire in New York City, where he rescued several people before succumbing to smoke and flames. He is buried in the family plot in Bay View Cemetery, Sturgeon Bay.

LAURITZ JOSEPH ANDREAS (February 20, 1861–August 26, 1864):

Joseph was born in Ephraim. The only known mention of his birth is in the records of the Ephraim Moravian Church (38), where his birth and baptism are recorded in his father's own handwriting. He died from complications stemming from measles and is buried in Leland, Illinois.

ANNA MUNDA ELEONORA (April 26, 1863–February 22, 1864): Named for her sister who died 24 days before she was born, this third child to bear the name of Anna Munda is buried in the Ephraim Moravian Cemetery. She shares a headstone with her sister (25).

CHAPTER 8

Note 1 (p. 109): Reverend F. Hagen Was Dispatched from Bethlehem to Investigate Discord and Accusations — There is no doubt that Iverson was having problems in Ephraim in 1862. The exact nature of the difficulties and how far-reaching they were may never be known, but it is clear that he was losing the confidence of his congregation. And although he does not mention it specifically in his recollections, there is ample evidence that he was physically ill and deeply depressed.

Iverson's problems were probably precipitated by his strange relationship with Elizabeth Morbek, which began in 1862. Apparently Elizabeth's much older husband, Tobias, had his suspicions about the relationship, and according to Naess (31), on August 27, 1862, the trustees of the Moravian Church (Nils Lindquist, Tobias Morbek, and his brother, Zacharias) met in Iverson's absence to discuss the situation. It appeared to them that Iverson was physically and mentally unwell and should be relieved of his responsibilities to the congregation. His own physician advised him to avoid writing and intellectual work of any kind. In September of 1862 Iverson wrote to a colleague in Bethlehem and explained his problems as follows (31): "It is a gradual sinking of strength and wasting of muscles, without any cough or expectoration. Digestion normal, yet hardly any appetite." "The right side is in some way suffering, the brain is dull and great nervousness. Preaching and writing, as well as all oppressing mental exercises afflict me most. Handworking is beneficial."

The following month, Zacharias and Tobias Morbek, unknown to Iverson, wrote a letter to H.A. Shultz in Bethlehem accusing Iverson of misconduct (31). They apparently included no specific details in their letter, but they did request that an emissary from the Church be sent to Ephraim to investigate. Thus Reverend F. Hagen was sent to Ephraim in November. Iverson (21) describes this visit in his recollections, but he remembers Hagen visiting in 1863. Based on records in Bethlehem, the visit actually took place in November of 1862 (31).

According to Naess (31), Hagen made his report to the governing board in Bethlehem at their December 28 meeting. The minutes of that meeting contain the following statement: "Brother Iverson's health seems better than it was. Being of a very nervous and excitable disposition, he is subject to occasional depression, which, together with discouraging experiences recently made, has caused the wish to arise in him for a change. It is likely that he will labor with renewed vigor and success in some other field." The word "field" here is taken to mean another church setting, not another occupation. It is apparent that Hagen failed to understand the seriousness of the charges made by Zacharias and Tobias Morbek, probably because they failed to articulate exactly what they believed Iverson had done. Hagen and the church leaders in Bethlehem seemed to view this as a resolvable difficulty between Iverson and several members of his congregation.

With Tobias Morbek's illness and death on December 2, 1862, Iverson was once again obliged to interact with the Morbek family. His ministrations on Tobias's behalf are recalled movingly in his recollections, and he makes no mention of any animosity between them. Zacharias Morbek and others, however, continued their efforts to replace Iverson. In August 1863, Morbek and 11 other married men of the congregation sent another letter to Hagen in Bethlehem petitioning for Iverson's replacement (31). Among other things, the letter said "the prospect of having a Moravian congregation prosper here or even continue with Brother Iverson as a minister is in our opinion gloomy and is becoming more so every day." Although no specific charges were leveled at Iverson, they said that if they had to they would "write about it as plain as we can." Among the signers of the letter were Ole Larsen, Henry Johnson, H.P. Jacobs, Abraham Oneson, and Gabriel Wathne (9).

Iverson was made aware of the letter sent to Hagen and, in fact, was shown a copy by someone in Ephraim. He must have been devastated when he learned that some of his oldest friends had turned against him. He wrote to Hagen on September 7, 1863, and tried to rationalize the situation by pointing out that H.P. Jacobs was a chronic troublemaker, that some had signed because they misunderstood the petition, and that in another case a person had signed in behalf of someone who was absent (31). Basically Iverson's letter was an epistle of denial, but one telling line in the letter makes it clear that members of the congregation were attempting to replace him for a specific act or acts, rather than for inadequacies in the pulpit. The line is "And now, can anyone prove that I have done it? Not one, never, never!" (21).

It is possible Iverson was referring to gossip suggesting a connection between his relationship with Elizabeth Morbek and the subsequent death of her husband, Tobias. Holand (18) refers to this as "King David's notorious misdemeanor," where the coveting of another man's wife could result in the husband's death (the Biblical story of David and Bathsheba). Holand believed that the rumor about Iverson was "utterly groundless" and was started when "Some of his sympathetic words, spoken at a sickbed, were misconstrued by a bevy of gossiping biddies."

No one is around today who can tell us exactly what caused Iverson's congregation to turn on him. We asked this question of the one living person in the community who might be in a position to provide an answer. She said she could not, because when she was young her elders always began speaking Norwegian in her presence when Iverson was discussed. Unless first-hand written evidence turns up some day, we can only guess about the basis for the accusations made against him in Ephraim. There is no doubt, however, that through his ministry and through his practice of homeopathic medicine, he sought to establish a close relationship with people who came to him for counsel. It is also likely that Iverson sometimes physically touched people who sought his help, which could have put him at risk for criticism from settlers, most of whom held fast to conservative and even puritanical values. He enjoyed the angelic faces of the children of his congregation, and he probably enjoyed looking at and being around attractive women. Whether there was more to it than that in Ephraim is speculation.

Note 2 (p. 110): Iverson's Mood Swings — Iverson's recollections, written when he was well along in years, provide many glimpses of his mood swings, as well as information about his various physical problems. And his letters to Bethlehem are even more revealing about the various afflictions that troubled him—particularly during the period of 1862 to 1864 (31), when his life was in turmoil and he was under tremendous emotional stress (see Note 1 above). Many other letters written during his years in the ministry reflect periods of ill health and/or depression.

In his recollections Iverson reveals not only periods of tremendous energy when he was constantly on the move, but also periods of depression and nervousness to the point of being incapacitated. In addition, he describes several euphoric episodes: his trip to Bethlehem to be ordained (p.18), the mission visit to New Denmark/Cooperstown in the spring of 1860 (p. 83), Christmas eve of 1861 (p. 92), and Ephraim's second revival meeting (p. 95).

The pattern of ups and downs revealed in Iverson's writings suggests that he was somewhat manic-depressive in his behavior, probably of the type with shallow swings in mood most of the time. Naess (31) reached similar conclusions, and he indicates that Iverson "resembles the stereotyped artist—childlike and changeable almost to the point of the manic-depressive." This is not to say that he was a mentally unstable person. Rather it is a reasonable explanation for his behavioral swings that ranged from periods of great energy when he seemed to be restlessly moving from place to place or indefatigable during a revival, to periods of depression when he felt physically ill. History is replete with great achievers who shared the double-edged sword of mood swings, and there is a strong correlation between the "artist's temperament" and manic-depression (10,22). Mood swings and depression appear to have a genetic component, but interviews with Iverson's descendants indicate little evidence of this trait in other members of the family. Artistic talent, on the other hand, shows up frequently.

CHAPTER 9

Note 1 (p.121): Recapitulation of Events Leading to Iverson's Departure from Ephraim –

- Summer of 1862 – Iverson ministers to Sister Morbek over a period of weeks.
- August 27, 1862 – In Iverson's absence, trustees of the congregation meet to discuss Iverson's health and whether he should continue to serve the church.
- September 2, 1862 – Zacharias and Tobias Morbek write to H.A. Schultz in Bethlehem and make veiled accusations about Iverson; they request that someone be sent to investigate.
- November 4-12, 1862 – Reverend F. Hagen, a representative of the Church, spends over a week in Ephraim evaluating the situation.
- December 2, 1862 – Iverson writes to Bethlehem and asks to be transferred because of his mental and physical state.
- August 30, 1863 – Zacharias Morbek and 11 other male members of the congregation send a signed letter to Bethlehem asking that Iverson be replaced. This letter suggests that if Bethlehem cannot provide a replacement, the Moravian congregation might join with the Lutherans to establish a Lutheran Church in the community.
- September 7, 1863 – Iverson writes Hagen in Bethlehem questioning

the validity of the letter sent on August 30 and defends his position in the matter.

- September 29, 1863 — Administrators in Bethlehem (the Provincial Elders' Conference/Board) decide that the Ephraim congregation's objections are too vague to warrant further investigation. However, since the congregation has lost confidence in Iverson, it concludes that he should be replaced.
- February 1864 — Iverson writes his friend H.A. Schultz in Bethlehem saying that he feels his congregation in Ephraim wants him to stay. This was only wishful thinking, and Iverson gradually realizes that he will have to leave Ephraim.
- Early July 1864 — Iverson leaves Ephraim.

Note 2 (p. 122): Speculation as to Why Iverson Never Returned to Ephraim, Even to Visit — At first thought it may seem strange that Iverson apparently never returned to the community that meant so much to him. In later years when he lived in Sturgeon Bay, the village he founded was only an hour or so away along a well-traveled road, and it would have been easy for him to visit Ephraim. Certainly Iverson enjoyed many happy moments and personal triumphs as he labored, physically and mentally, to establish his Moravian settlement. On the other hand, his memories of the 11 years spent in Ephraim were infused with a tremendous amount of pain and loss. Perhaps a return visit to his beloved village would have been too much for him to bear, and that the "trail of tears" still haunted him. Perhaps he wished to remember Ephraim and Eagle Harbor as being as serene and colorful as they are in the watercolors he painted (Figs. C1 and C2).

CHAPTER 10

Note 1 (p. 139): Circumstances Surrounding Iverson's Being Deposed by the Church — There were two Moravian churches in Green Bay in the late 1800s—one on the east side that mainly served the German community and another on the west (Fort Howard) side that Iverson established to serve the Scandinavian community (Fig. 23). The best evidence indicates that the minister of the east side church employed a 17-year-old housekeeper named Mary Nelson, who was a member of Iverson's church. In early January of 1883 the minister's wife was helping Mary with a load of washing that included items of Mary's clothing worn while cleaning house. As the wife checked pockets for objects or paper before placing clothing in the wash water, she discovered a note

FIGURE 23 -- The West Side (Fort Howard) Moravian Church established by Iverson in 1869. He was pastor of this church when he was deposed from the ministry on January 25, 1883. Postcard photo.

to Mary written by Iverson, the contents of which made it clear that an intimate relationship existed between the two. The pastor's wife informed her husband of her shocking discovery.

The confrontation that followed verified a sexual relationship between Iverson and Mary. Church leaders in Bethlehem were quickly advised of the circumstances, as noted in minutes of the governing board on January 13, 1883, where it is stated that "Rev. A.M. Iverson of Fort Howard is living in a state of adultery with a member of his congregation, seventeen years old (31) ...." On January 19, Bishop E. de Schweinitz departed hastily from Bethlehem to interview Iverson personally, and he later reported the following (31): "On meeting the guilty parties, both Bro. Iverson and the girl, Mary Nelson, confessed that they had lived in adultery since the month of November; A.M. Iverson was advised forthwith to leave Fort Howard and his deposition from the Ministry was published in the Church papers, in accordance with a resolution of the Synod." Iverson was officially deposed from the ministry on January 25, 1883, with the public notification signed by Bishop de Schweinitz.

The scandalous news quickly made headlines in Milwaukee and Door County. Iverson, the immigrant evangelist known throughout the area for his piety and good works, was to suffer another tragedy, that of his public denunciation and humiliation. Among other things, headlines of a news article in the Milwaukee *Sentinel* called him "A Reverend Rogue" (Fig. 24). Shortly thereafter, the following article appeared in the Door County Advocate (Sturgeon Bay) on March 1, 1883. The article was entitled "A Church Scandal."

> "For a week or so past a rumor has circulated in this village concerning a scandal which has developed in the Moravian church in Fort Howard, but we were unable to locate the report until the Milwaukee *Sentinel* of Sunday gave publicity to the matter as follows.
>
> "A large-sized scandal has developed in Fort Howard, the principal being Rev. A.M. Iverson, for a number of years pastor of the Scandinavian Moravian Church at that place. A short time since a buxom young maiden of his congregation proved to be in an interesting condition, she being pressed by friends, told the whole story, naming the pastor as the author of her shame. The surprise cannot be expressed. He is an elderly man with a grown up family, and one who for years had been looked upon as a model of purity and godliness. He enjoyed the confidence of his congregation in the largest degree. He was absent when the development occurred, and when he returned he found a council called to consider his fate, with the ranking bishop of that denomination on the ground. Being confronted with the charge, he was overwhelmed with both fear and shame, and in the most trembling manner acknowledged the truth. He has been formerly [sic] tried and deposed from the ministry, and he forthwith left for Chicago, where he is at present engaged in the study of medicine.
>
> "The publication of the foregoing will no doubt astonish many people in the county, among whom Mr. Iverson is well-known, having formerly resided here. He enjoyed the confidence and esteem of his parishioners, and his fall from grace is therefore felt all the more severely.

"Let Iverson's downfall be a warning to all others occupying similar positions, and not permit themselves to be led into temptation."

A REVEREND ROGUE.

A Green Bay Pastor Playing the Part of a Gay Lothario

He Skips the Country for Parts Unknown.

BETRAYED BY HER PASTOR.

[Special Dispatch to The Sunday Sentinel.]

GREEN BAY, Feb. 24.—A large-sized scandal has developed in Fort Howard, the principal being Rev. A. M. Iverson, for a number of years pastor of the Scandinavian Moravian Church of that

FIGURE 24 — Headlines from a newspaper article about Iverson's career-ending indiscretion (Milwaukee Sentinel, February 25, 1883), from which the Door County Advocate obtained information for the above story.

Iverson's dismissal from the ministry when he was 60 years old was a crushing blow to him. How can his behavior be explained? Was it the stress of seeing his congregation dwindle away? Was it the erosion of his evangelistic self-esteem as he failed to win converts and his listeners began to lose interest in his message? Was it his mood swings? Loneliness? Or was he beginning to wear down and face his own mortality? Perhaps all these factors played a role in his actions, along with a lingering anguish over the loss of so many loved ones over the years. There is no doubt that he communicated his pain and unhappiness to the Church in Bethlehem, and that he requested a transfer during his last years at Fort Howard (21,31), but the comment in his recollections (21) that "they didn't act in time" is weak justification for his behavior.

After being deposed from the Church, Iverson moved to Chicago. There he spent his time studying homeopathic medicine as he tried to put back together what remained of his life. He tried and failed to convince his family that he was physically unable to consummate the intimacies of which he was accused, and he began to proclaim in public that he had not committed the sins for which he was dismissed from the Church (31). When Church authorities in Bethlehem heard of Iverson's efforts to rationalize the circumstances, he was advised to cease and desist or the Church would take further action. Iverson was also reminded that he and Mary Nelson had made a full confession to Church authorities.

After a year or so, Iverson thought about returning to Fort Howard to practice homeopathic medicine, but his wife let it be known that he could not live with her. Finally he decided to move to Sturgeon Bay and live with his son, Alfred, who had a farm just north of town. Alfred allowed his father to set up a medical office in a small room attached to the farmhouse, and Iverson practiced homeopathic medicine there (apparently no licensing was required). Over the years, he established a modest following, including many Indians who considered him a medicine man with considerable power.

Although forbidden to preach by the Church, Iverson remained a devout Moravian for the rest of his life. Even as a very old man (Fig. 25), every Sunday he walked two and a half miles to the Moravian Church he helped establish in Sturgeon Bay. By all accounts, he loved and enjoyed his five grandchildren, and he was at peace and serene in his waning years. The writing of his recollections (21) when he was in his 70s undoubtedly contributed to his peace of mind. He was encouraged to write about the past by Reverend John Greenfield, who remained on friendly terms with Iverson. Greenfield (the anglicized version of Groenfeldt), son of J.J. Groenfeldt, was the fourth pastor of the Ephraim Moravian Church. While not condoning Iverson's behavior, Greenfield realized that Iverson could make a valuable contribution to the history of the area by documenting his years as a frontier preacher. Iverson died in 1907 at the age of 84, having outlived all of his six children, as well as his wife, Laura.

(In addition to the references cited above, information was obtained from interviews with Reverend John Groenfeldt, Jr., as well as from Cedric Iverson and Lawrence Iverson, great-grandsons of Andrew Iverson)

Note 2 (p. 139): Iverson Family Members Buried in Sturgeon Bay — Those buried in the same plot and with the same gravestone at the Bay View cemetery in Sturgeon Bay include:

A.M. Iverson, Dec. 27, 1823 - Jan. 16, 1907
Laura Iverson, Mar. 24, 1824 - July 21, 1893
Alfred M. Iverson, July 4, 1852 - Oct. 18, 1902
John Hus Iverson, July 16, 1857 - Feb. 22, 1902
Regina Solway Iverson, Wife of Alfred, 1854 - 1922
Laura Iverson Hanson, Wife of Capt. Al, 1878 - 1962 (daughter of Alfred and Regina)

Figure 26 shows the Iverson family grave marker in Sturgeon Bay. The marker is located in Bay View Cemetery, beneath a huge maple tree, a short distance down the road from the farm where Iverson spent his last years.

FIGURES 25 AND 26 — Fig. 25 (left) shows Iverson as an old man; his eyes still had their intense look (photo source: Sturgeon Bay Moravian Church). Fig. 26 (right) shows Cedric Iverson, Andrew's great-grandson, beside the family gravestone in Bay View Cemetery in Sturgeon Bay.

A FINAL NOTE

What do we make of Andrew Iverson? Was he a saint or a sinner? How should history judge him? What is the significance of his contributions to the early development of Door County?

As to whether he was saint or sinner, it is fair to say that he was both, as is the case for nearly everyone. The difference, of course, is that he was a man of the cloth representing the higher principles of Biblical goodness and perfection. He was a disciple of Jesus and an interpreter of the word of God as espoused by the Moravian Church. But it is worth remembering that Jesus believed us all to be sinners, and that forgiveness and redemption are key tenets of Protestant doctrine. Iverson suffered for his sins. In fact, his life was filled with suffering.

A number of individuals have spoken of Iverson's achievements and his importance to the history of the region. In an interview in 1993, Reverend John Groenfeldt, Jr., summarized his thoughts about Iverson as follows: "Iverson had a great sensitivity to the needs of the immigrant people and devoted much of his life to serving the immigrants from Northern Europe." Graf (11) wrote that "Iverson gave the Moravian Church a solid foundation in the area upon which later ministers could come to build." Naess (31) felt that Iverson had reason to be pleased with his achievements and that he had "created something of lasting value." Naess also noted the contribution made by Iverson's recollections (21), stating that they show "the special mixture of pride and humility that characterizes great autobiographical literature ... making some of its sections memorable reading."

The only writer who personally interacted with Iverson was Hjalmar Holand (15), who was convinced that Iverson's achievements were under-appreciated. He was "not only [Ephraim's] founder, he was also its nurse and educator. He made Ephraim what it is. Like a mother watching over her little baby so Iverson worked for Ephraim with unceasing diligence and love." Holand (15) thought of Iverson as the spiritual guide and friend to all those living in the village. "He shared their physical labors with them, he untangled their business difficulties, he watched by their bedsides and eased their pain with homemade remedies, [and] he prayed for them and with them at all opportunities. May Ephraim always be true to the memory of its founder!"

Has Ephraim been true to the memory of its founder? It apparently has, for many writers have observed that Ephraim, thanks to its Moravian heritage and the faith of its founders, remains a village that holds cultural and moral values in high regard. Hoyler (19) observes that "This accounts for the fact that Ephraim never had a saloon or public dance-hall." Ephraim is an unusual community, boasting not only great scenic beauty but a set of values that was created by its founders and remains part of the fabric of the community even today. In 1934 residents of the village voted on a referendum to answer the following question: "Shall licenses be granted for the sale of beer and intoxicating liquors within the limits of the village of Ephraim?" There were 78 "no" votes to 54 "yes" votes, indicating that only 31% of the voting community believed that Ephraim should sell alcoholic beverages. In 1992 a similar referendum was held. Almost 60 years after the first referendum the outcome was much the same, for only 35% of the voters felt that alcoholic beverages should be available in Ephraim.

There is no doubt that Iverson made great contributions to the spiritual life of the settlers of northeastern Wisconsin. He was a gifted evangelist who touched the lives of many people, not only in Ephraim, but in many other communities as well, some as far away as Keokuk, Iowa. He was the driving force behind the establishment of Moravian churches in Ephraim, Sturgeon Bay, and Fort Howard. He preached to and counseled hundreds of immigrants who discovered that life on the frontier often held just as much hardship and required just as much back-breaking work as the land from which they had emigrated. Iverson made himself available to help immigrant settlers in any way he could, and he was as ready to minister to their illnesses as to their souls. He was there for baptisms, he was there to preach the gospel of hope, and he was there in death to hold their hands and pray for their salvation. Holand (18) recognized that Iverson could be obstinate, petty, and querulous, but when he was "working with the pioneers in the wilderness, he became eminently great."

Should Iverson be judged by the breadth and significance of his contributions or on the basis of his transgressions? The reader will have to decide.

ACKNOWLEDGEMENTS

We thank Cedric Iverson, Lawrence Iverson, and Patricia Iverson Baierl, great-grandchildren of Andrew and Laura Iverson, for providing us with the oral history of the Iverson family and for sharing with us records and other material handed down from Andrew. We also appreciate their candor in providing their views of Andrew's life.

We are greatly indebted to Harald S. Naess, retired Professor of Scandinavian Studies at the University of Wisconsin at Madison, who allowed us to use material from his unpublished manuscript dealing with Otto Tank and Iverson (31). Naess's manuscript, in part, is based on a careful review of the original Norwegian version of Iverson's "*A Brief Account...*" (21), as well as John Boler's translation. Naess also spent time examining papers relating to Iverson in the archives of the Moravian Church in Bethlehem, Pennsylvania. Naess, now living in Kristiansand, Norway, provided valuable insight to Andrew and his mission work in Wisconsin.

Reverend John Groenfeldt, Jr., generously provided information about Andrew and the Ephraim Moravian Church. Later, his wife Eva went out of her way to contribute information that was useful to us in writing this book. We appreciate their thoughtful assistance and we regret that John died shortly before our book was finished. Groenfeldt's father, John Greenfield, was the fourth pastor of the Ephraim Moravian Church, from 1895 to 1902, and knew Andrew personally. He was a key influence in persuading Iverson to write his recollections. The grandfather of John Groenfeldt, Jr., was J.J. Groenfeldt, the second pastor of the Ephraim Moravian Church (1864–1883), and his uncle, Samuel Groenfeldt, was pastor from 1914 to 1918.

Professor Charles F. Calkins, of the Department of Geography at the University of Wisconsin, Waukesha, has a great interest in the history of the area and was willing to share some of his research materials on Door County. We were pleased to have his support in this project.

Reverend Paul Graf, Pastor of the Sturgeon Bay Moravian Church, allowed us to copy and use a photograph of Iverson; he also provided us with access to his unpublished document dealing with the history of the Sister Bay Moravian Church, which includes information pertaining to Iverson. We also appreciate the assistance and insights of Dr. Gary Kinkel, recent Pastor of the Ephraim Moravian Church. He kindly provided access to certain church records and was available to provide information about the Moravian Church in general. He also allowed us to copy and use several of the church's photographs and paintings.

Sally Jacobson, Archivist-Administrator for the Ephraim Foundation, was always ready to help us find what we needed in the Foundation's archives. We appreciate her thoughtfulness—she is a valuable asset to the village of Ephraim. We express appreciation to the Ephraim Foundation for allowing us access to photographs and materials, and to Dorothy Halvorsen for taking the time to translate words and passages written in Norwegian. She is an important custodian of Scandinavian traditions.

The curators at Heritage Hill, in Green Bay, went out of their way to be helpful as we sought answers to questions about what was worn by settlers in the 1800s. Jeanne Novak and Dennis Jacobs provided a wealth of information about wearing apparel common to the period.

After we had a rough draft of our book in hand, Irvin Oneson, great-grandson of Abraham Oneson, one of Ephraim's original settlers, shared a great deal of historically significant material he had collected about the early history of Ephraim. Information gleaned from some of this material allowed us to make substantive additions to several chapters. He also kindly gave us permission to use information from an unpublished manuscript he wrote in 1985 (35).

Harold Grutzmacher, a scholarly neighbor in Ephraim and a purveyor of fine books, read over the manuscript and provided many valuable suggestions. Susan Peterson also read an early draft and made constructive comments. Professor Sally Frost-Mason, a friend and colleague from the University of Kansas, is an experienced proofreader and editor, and we appreciate her taking the time to carefully review a draft of our manuscript. Mary Burchill, of Lawrence, Kansas, is a fine librarian with experience in the art of indexing books. She provided a preliminary index which we then modified to meet our needs.

The historically accurate painting on the dust jacket is the work of Karsten Topelmann, who agreed to create the painting just for this book. However, he first asked if he could read the manuscript. We provided him with an early draft and a few suggestions, and after about three weeks we were allowed to see the finished artwork. We believe he captured with pigments something of what we attempted to capture with words. We appreciate, and are awed by, his contribution to this book. We also appreciate being allowed to use one of Charles Peterson's paintings depicting Iverson's spirit watching over his beloved house. Thanks to Peterson and to Gene and Carol McGrevin, owners of the painting, who made arrangements to obtain a high-quality photograph of the piece for use in this book.

Fortunately for us we discovered that local artist Jan Jablonski shares our interest in history and period clothing. With skill and flair she enthusiastically created ink sketches that depict settlers' clothing in the middle 1800s. Her drawings add a great deal to our book.

A special thanks to the Clifford and Clara Herlache Heritage Foundation, Inc., for generously providing a grant to help print this book. The commitment shown by this foundation to supporting the preservation of area history sets a wonderful example for the community.

Thanks also to Vernon Nelson, Archivist at The Moravian Church Archives in Bethlehem, Pennsylvania, for providing some last minute information that made its way into the book. He warned us in 1993 that "Iverson is a difficult topic." He was right.

Finally, we thank Russell Hayes for suggesting the title to the book.

INDEX